FOR HARDY BULBS

LEVEL

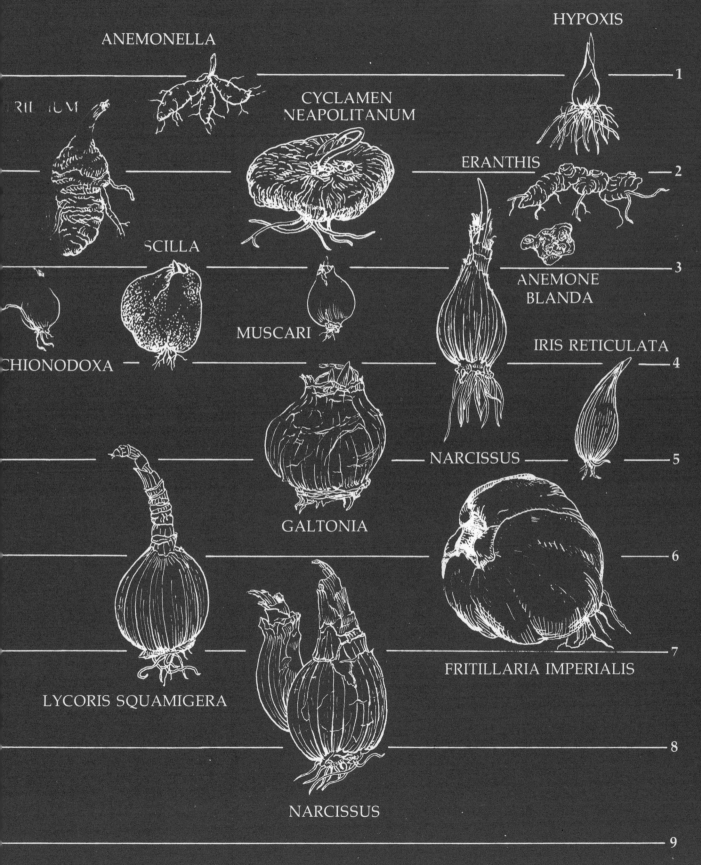

ANEMONELLA

HYPOXIS

— 1

TRILLIUM

CYCLAMEN
NEAPOLITANUM

ERANTHIS

— 2

SCILLA

— 3

ANEMONE
BLANDA

CHIONODOXA

MUSCARI

IRIS RETICULATA

— 4

NARCISSUS

— 5

GALTONIA

— 6

LYCORIS SQUAMIGERA

— 7

FRITILLARIA IMPERIALIS

— 8

NARCISSUS

— 9

BULBS
FOR THE
HOME GARDENER

BULBS

FOR THE

HOME GARDENER

by BEBE MILES

Illustrations by JUDY SINGER

*All photographs in this book
are by Bebe Miles
unless otherwise indicated*

GROSSET & DUNLAP

A Filmways Company

PUBLISHERS • NEW YORK

Published by Grosset & Dunlap, Inc., New York, 1976.
Published simultaneously in Canada.

An original work created and produced by
Vineyard Books, Inc.
159 East 64th Street
New York, New York 10021

ISBN: 0-448-12721-0

Printed in Hong Kong by Mandarin Publishers

CONTENTS

Anemone pulsatilla

FOREWORD

My love affair with bulbs began long before I knew much about what they were or how to grow them. When warm spring days brought the blue squills blooming down a hillside in my mother's garden, I imagined that it was a waterfall, fed by melting snow on some faraway mountain. Then there was that enchanted spot in the woods where spring-beauties and trout-lilies grew so thickly we had to step gingerly to avoid bruising them. And the man who worked the railroad-crossing bars down the road made a big impression on me with the neat, round bed of cannas he planted every summer next to the house he used for shelter.

Of course, I grew up to be too sophisticated to emulate the neighbor who spelled out words with crocus bulbs carefully planted in his lawn, but if I had the right kind of hill—well, I might still be tempted to plant out a whimsical message, for as a child I thought flowers that could spell were magical.

Bulbs are ideal for beginning gardeners of all ages. It may take experience to be able to tap out a straight line of seeds from a paper packet, but a child can grasp a crocus and put it in a hole. A firm bulb is nature's packaging device for producing a nearly instant garden. If the bulb is winter-hardy, all you have to do is dig a hole in autumn, drop the bulb in the bottom and replace the soil. You can be almost certain of discovering flowers there the next spring. Results with tender, summer-flowering bulbs can be even quicker.

The introductory pages of this book detail many ways to get the most from your bulbs—and from your efforts. Bulbs are an integral part of any good garden, indoors or outdoors, but they are only one facet of many. To make the most beautiful appearance possible, bulbs need the companionship of many other plants, some of which I suggest in the pages of this book.

While growing bulbs is one of the easiest parts of the delightful pastime we call gardening, it is also an ever-expanding pursuit. Even the largest property may eventually reach the point where another tree cannot be planted without sacrificing something else, but this problem seldom arises with bulbs. There is always some niche where you can tuck in another dozen.

Moreover, bulbs are so varied that even a long life does not allow time enough to know and grow them all. Having succeeded with some of the more common ones, you can become an adventuresome gardener as you broaden your bulb horizon beyond the known to some place at the end of the rainbow. There are always rare bulbs to work into an established garden, as well as new ideas for growing and showing off the old standbys.

Perhaps because bulbs are so easy to grow and so undemanding, they are sometimes dismissed as being of no great lasting importance. Living memorials, for example, are usually trees. Yet how often I have come across a solitary stray daffodil clump beside a road or on the edge of second-growth forest and realized that on this spot there was once a house with a garden which time or the bulldozer has all but obliterated. But the daffodils have survived to greet me and future generations.

The splash of squill in my mother's garden began as a small trickle, the overflow of seedlings from the original planting beneath a tree at the top of the hill. Long after she had died it had increased to a great torrent. You will read later about the vigor of the exciting new hybrid lilies as contrasted with the often sickly species that were the lot of an earlier generation. Nevertheless, I remember planting some *speciosum* lilies with my mother, and they were still blooming beautifully when I showed them to my own daughter some decades later. Any experienced gardener can quote other examples.

I don't expect worldly recognition for tucking a dozen daffodils into the earth, but who knows how much pleasure they may bring to someone? The world needs more gardeners—not just for the beauty we help to create, nor for whatever ecological good we may sow. But today as never before we need optimism, and that is the mark of every gardener. When I am laboring on my knees, tending a little section of earth by getting my hands dirty with no more thought of reward than the vision of a flower six months hence, I feel a wonderful sense of peace. And you don't have to possess a garden to feel this communion with nature; it can be just as real as you tend a potted plant indoors.

I have organized this book into two sections: one for the winter-hardy bulbs and one for those that are too tender to survive in the ground where temperatures drop below freezing. Within each section the bulbs are listed alphabetically by botanical name rather than by family affiliation or by some popular name, both systems sometimes used. If you know only the popular or common name for a bulb, you'll find it in the index, cross-referenced to the botanical name. As plants are rapidly becoming a major national sport, there is a noticeable trend toward using their true, scientific names. Using them yourself not only signifies your seriousness; it will also help you get exactly what you want as your plant interests broaden.

Even knowing intimately the beauty of the bulb flowers gathered in this book, I marvel at the skill with which artist Judy Singer has captured them with her brush. She has not exaggerated. The flowers are truly this lovely. When you plant them you will discover two other factors we could only hint at: the ethereal fragrance of many of these blossoms and the grace with which they move in the breeze.

My whole gardening experience has been an exercise in learning. I am grateful to so many people I could not begin to list them all. This book is a distillation of what they have taught me plus lessons inspired by handling the bulbs themselves. Special thanks for aid in the preparation of the manuscript go to my family and to James P. McCarvill of the Pennsylvania Horticultural Society; to Charles H. Mueller of New Hope, Pennsylvania, whose exhibition garden has been an inspiration to me; and to my co-workers in the Doylestown Nature Club and Bowman's Hill State Wildflower Preserve, Washington Crossing, Pennsylvania.

Finally, Judy and I dedicate this book with affection to our editor, Lucille Ogle, who more than anyone else made it all possible. *Bulbs for the Home Gardener* is a tribute to her skills in many fields.

BEBE MILES

Doylestown, Pennsylvania

INTRODUCTION TO BULB GARDENING

Of all the plants you can grow, few will bring more pleasure with less effort than the beauties offered as bulbs. Many gardens feature a few popular daffodils or gladiolus, but they are only a small part of the bulb story. All it takes is a little planning ahead of time to have your garden filled throughout the growing season with the tremendously varied and decorative bulb flowers.

After you have read and studied this book, the world of bulbs will begin to make sense to you. Catalogs of the bulb specialists will come alive, and you will be better able to relate to the garden writers who extol the virtues of bulb treasures each year in other books and magazines—not to mention classes taught at local horticultural societies and displays made at flower shows.

The economics of the bulb business are such that there are actually fewer varieties of bulbs offered today, even in some of the best catalogs than there were a few years ago. With profit margins slim, the suppliers are tending to concentrate on the most popular types. However, as more and more people are getting into gardening, it is to be hoped that soon the lists of bulbs will again be growing. If you are unable to locate bulbs of something described in this book, I suggest that you write the suppliers directly. Most are dedicated gardeners themselves who will be pleased to hear of your interests and eager to help you find a source of supply. Gardeners as consumers have to be assertive too, so speak up.

While some unusual kinds of bulbs or varieties of them may be elusive, the fact remains that hundreds if not thousands of glorious bulb flowers are readily available to brighten the garden in all seasons. Snowdrops and winter aconites are easy to locate; they flaunt their flowers even while snow is still on the ground, and dozens of others follow to brighten the first part of the growing year. If you have limited your spring to a

few Red Emperor tulips, some King Alfred daffodils and perhaps a crocus or two, start now to add to the variety of your spring garden. The selection of major spring bulbs has improved greatly within the past generation—and the little bulbs, once referred to as "minor," are growing in popularity, especially among gardeners who are cramped for space.

As summer warms the temperate world, dahlias, ismene and a host of lesser-known bulbs create still another wave of color. Many of these are not hardy outdoors where freezing occurs and may present some problems for the gardener who has limited time and storage space; but a few selections from among these imports that come from the more tropical parts of the world add important spots of interest to the summer garden.

When autumn takes over, the colchicums, sternbergias and fall crocus pop into bloom as a cheering farewell to summer before winter sets in. These bring joy to my heart even as my back is aching from fall planting and the chores of readying my garden for its annual rest.

Here overplanted with annual alyssum, sternbergia is a hardy bulb that extends the flowering season into October.

What would a spring garden be without bulbs?
Courtesy of MALAK, Ottawa, Canada.

Bulbs adapt well to thin, narrow beds. Note crown imperials behind tulips.

Finally, while frigid storms rage outside, cyclamen and amaryllis, clivia and fragrant eucharis blossom in winter windows. There is scarcely a week of the year when bulbs do not brighten my world, and just as surely, wherever you live, there is a bulb for flowers in every season.

Of equal importance, there is a bulb for every garden. If you live in the woods, spring trilliums and summer tuberous begonias inject color into the shade and make as lovely a spot as any sunny border. There are not as many bulbs for shadowed places as there are for sunnier spots, and you will have to be more careful at picking the right locations than the gardener who has all-day sun. Often, however, the garden where sun and shade patterns change from hour to hour through the day is easier to take care of. In hot weather such a garden is also more likely to be part of your leisure hours.

If your gardening is limited to a tiny plot, bulbs are even more valuable. Often you can overplant them with a ground cover or annual flowers to provide color in two different seasons. Bulbs in containers are still another part of the story. You can shift them around to give a favorite spot a splash of bloom. Even apartment dwellers with no more space than a balcony or windowsill can use bulbs this way.

The use of bulbs in public plantings seems to be growing as we expect more of our environment. Kinds such as spring daffodils and grape hyacinths or fall crocus need little care and can remain in place for several seasons without need for moving. Combined with easy-maintenance ground covers or summer annuals, they are ideal for narrow strips or islands of greenery and flowers that add to the beauty of our cities.

Summer-flowering bulbs are not quite so adaptable for exhibition gardens of this type, at least in the more northern states. They have to be planted fresh each spring, dug up at the approach of cold weather and stored safely for another season unless funds are available for the purchase of new ones each year.

Not far from my home in Bucks County, Pennsylvania, there is a tourist mecca called Peddler's Village. Although it is not much different from other such settlements in the range of shops and restaurants, it has great appeal because of the imaginative plantings at all seasons of the year. Even if you have no shopping to do, a stroll through its grounds can be a joy. Obviously, the person who comes to see the flowers may buy something on impulse.

The part of the country you garden in makes little difference as far as bulbs are concerned. There are some that withstand the harshest winters; others revel in the cozy warmth of southern climates. And the bulb suppliers cater to the whims of the gardener who wants tulips in Florida or caladiums in Michigan. You can buy precooled tulip bulbs from cooler climes to plant for bloom in the tropics and tropicals already started in pots to lengthen the season in northern gardens. Having unlocked some of nature's secrets, the bulb suppliers can give us such out-of-season treats as hyacinths ready to blossom for Christmas, freesias to plant outdoors in late spring and amaryllis prepared to bloom during many months of the year.

Bulbs in a commercial setting. Colorful spring tulip display (**ABOVE**) was followed with red, white and blue summer annuals (**BELOW**) in front of shop in Peddler's Village, Lahaska, Pennsylvania.

North American Indians relished camassia bulbs as food, but today's gardener finds them a fine decorative for late spring.

Native to Many Lands

As might be anticipated from such great versatility, bulbs are found as native plants in nearly every corner of the green world. Cannas and caladiums come from lush tropic areas, while daffodils and tulips grow wild on dry slopes of the lands bordering the Mediterranean. Dahlias were first cultivated in the Mexican gardens of the Aztec Indians, and camassia bulbs were eaten by North American Indians. South Africa is the home of a great number of interesting tender bulbs such as calla lily, chincherinchee and freesia.

Some kinds of bulbs are found wild in only a small area, but others have varied species scattered over many continents. The madonna lily, for example, has been a favorite for both garden decoration and medicinal use for literally thousands of years and probably originated in one of the lands of the Bible. There are other lilies native to northern Europe and to North America. Some of the most gorgeous lilies come from Japan; others were discovered only in this century in the remote mountains of China.

For some gardeners, perhaps, details of the history or discovery of a particular bulb are not nearly as important as those of its color, height and cultural requirements. The land where a bulb originates is a good clue, however, to its hardiness. If you live where frost penetrates the ground in winter, you can assume that a bulb that grows wild in the tropics or subtropics cannot winter over safely in the ground. If you live in a warm place such as Florida, bulbs like tulips and crocuses will need a cool treatment before you plant them. This is to duplicate their natural climatic conditions.

There are some bulbs that are offered only as species. These are exactly like what you would find if you were to visit the land of their origin and see them growing wild. Many of the more popular bulbs, on the other hand, have been intensely hybridized over many years. Today's gladiolus are far different from the wild species of Africa.

In many cases the hybrids are better garden subjects than the species. They have been selected and bred to give healthier plants and better flowers. Generally, there is a greater range of color, shape and height among the hybrids than there ever was in the wild. There is also a factor called hybrid vigor, which, simply explained, means that a plant of mixed parentage may be expected to be better for gardening than either of its parents because of the combination of inherited characteristics.

This does not mean that the species of even as highly bred a group as the tulips are not worth growing. More advanced gardeners find the species tulips challenging; for some garden situations they are handier choices.

Zephyranthes are native mostly to South America. They are often called rain-lilies because they pop into bloom after watering.

Take a Trip

You can learn a lot about gardening by reading widely and asking questions of those more experienced. Of course, you can find out more by actually digging and planting and seeing what happens through a few seasons, but there is another educational tool that is not utilizied by enough gardeners: Go see what someone else has been doing.

Every area has garden tours sponsored by horticultural groups of some sort, and many of us live not too far from exhibition gardens. Places that display spring bulbs are easier to find than those with summer and fall kinds. It is surprising what really great ideas you get when you see someone else's attempts. Uses and techniques it might take you years to learn on your own are suddenly there, all completed and ready to inspire you. Sometimes you will just take an idea home and copy it as closely as you can. Other times you adapt it for your own conditions or invent your own variation on the original.

I often wonder why more gardeners don't take advantage of this way to learn more effective ways to enjoy their hobby. A garden tour can be a pleasant way to spend a day. Unlike your own garden, where a walk always leads to something crying for attention, such a meander can be a restful interlude. Watch your newspapers in spring for suggestions of places worth visiting or check with other gardeners or the nearest horticultural society for addresses of plantings where bulbs are imaginatively used.

Many bulb suppliers maintain an exhibition garden. I often make at least one spring trip to see Charles Mueller's "Living Catalog," which is located near me in New Hope, Pennsylvania. Seeing the bulbs there in bloom beats thumbing through any list. Write one of the bigger bulb suppliers who operates within driving distance of your

Massed blue of wood-hyacinths (endymion) contrasts with azaleas and dogwoods at Winterthur, Du Pont estate in Delaware.

home and inquire of the facilities and the best dates to visit.

Or locate the nearest arboretum or botanical garden. If they themselves don't have anything available to see (which is highly unlikely), they will surely know of worthwhile places in your area. All-America trial gardens are another possibility; they are located all over the United States. Peddler's Village, at Lahaska, Pennsylvania, is one such place I visit, and it maintains lovely spring bulb display gardens as well as the trials.

Gardens farther afield can be just as inspiring, so when traveling always ask about good ones. In the East are such as Longwood Gardens, Kennett Square, Pennsylvania; Winterthur, Wilmington, Delaware; Colonial Williamsburg, Virginia; and Brookgreen Gardens, Georgetown, South Carolina. Or try Kingwood Center, Mansfield, Ohio or Golden Gate Park, San Francisco, California. In Europe is the greatest bulb garden of them all: the Keukenhof near Lisse, Holland. It has literally millions of spring bulbs, is at its best from late March to mid-May.

Flower shows can be educational, too. Unfortunately, some of the big ones have fallen by the wayside. Try, however, to catch such shows as the ones in Philadelphia, Boston or Chicago for an early preview of spring on a splendiferous scale. The small shows of local societies are often of even more interest although not so breathtaking. They will tend to concentrate on what grows best in your area, and they are easier to get to. Watch for announcements of shows by local branches of some of the societies listed on page 203.

Be sure to take a note pad and pen when embarking on any of these ventures to widen your garden horizons. Without such aids to memory, your head begins to whirl in confusion at such an abundance of riches. Most shows and formal exhibition gardens are good about correct labeling, so it is easy to take home the specific names.

A SHORT HISTORY OF BULBS

When you tuck a bulb gently into the soil of your garden in autumn, you have every right to feel a kinship with a long line of peaceable forebears. No one will ever know when the first bulb made the change from the fields to a cultivated garden, but artifacts show us that crocuses, lilies and other bulbs of the Mediterranean lands have been treasured for many thousands of years.

We in the Western world can sometimes seem to imply that nothing has arrived until we have recorded it in our chronicles. Take the dahlia, for example. The Spanish conquistadors discovered it in the Mexican gardens of the Aztec Indians in the sixteenth century and took it back to Europe. Since then, this brilliant summer flower has been selected and hybridized to the point that the American Dahlia Society has more than a dozen official classifications for show purposes. This may sound remarkable, but the Aztecs had selected forms and colors to such an extent that botanists are still not sure which are the true species.

All of which is not meant to disparage the work of the modern plant breeder. Nor does it detract from the accomplishments of plant explorers who brought many of the great bulb decoratives back to "civilization" from some of the remotest parts of the world. Liberty Hyde Bailey in his great *Cyclopedia of Horticulture* notes that tulips fell out of favor in the gardens of the wealthy English during the eighteenth century. In their stead the newly discovered flora of the United States became the rage. This desire for what is new leads to much wider dissemination of garden-worthy plants and in turn even to new varieties.

The story of the regal lily is a good case in point. It was discovered in 1903 by Ernest H. "Chinese" Wilson in a remote river valley of western China. The first bulbs were flowered in England in 1905. In 1910 Wilson went on a hair-raising journey to bring back 6,000 bulbs to America. They were transported on men's backs and by boat some 2,000 miles across China. Wilson himself had broken his leg during the gathering and accompanied the bulbs at first on a stretcher, then on crutches. The regal's adaptability to differing growing conditions and its ease of propagation by seed as well as its beauty made it an instant favorite. Because of the regal's innate stamina and disease-resistant qualities, in time it became one of the parents of some our finest hybrid lilies.

This beautiful lily has never been seen wild outside a radius of about 50 miles from where Wilson discovered it. He described its habitat thus: ". . . narrow, semi-arid valleys . . . surrounded by mountains composed of mud-shales and granites, whose peaks are clothed with snow eternal. . . . In summer the heat is terrific, in winter the cold is intense, and at all seasons these valleys are subject to sudden and violent windstorms against which neither man nor beast can make headway."

Our gardens would be much poorer in many ways if the regal lily had not been brought from its remote home. So in one sense there is justification in assigning importance to dating when a particular bulb entered the mainstream of horticulture. We just need to be careful not to forget that all species have a wild home and that they are likely to have been a joy to those who lived there for much longer than the dates we assign them would indicate.

What is surprising, in view of the great amount of hybridizing that has occurred over the past several hundred years since Western man had time for and an interest in gardening as a pleasurable pursuit, is that many of the same plants we grow today have been in gardens for a long time.

Some bulbs we can date easily by the year

Madonna-lily has been a religious symbol of purity throughout much of the Christian era. Reproduction of "The Adoration," relief in glazed terra-cotta, from the workshop of Andrea della Robbia (1435–1525), Italian (Florentine), fifteenth century. Bequest of Adele L. Lehman in memory of Arthur Lehman, 1965.

Courtesy Metropolitan Museum of Art, New York

in which they were introduced by the breeder. These may be either hybrids or selections chosen for an outstanding characteristic of some sort. Gardeners are still planting the venerable tulip Keizerskroon, which was first described in 1760. And the King Alfred daffodil, which represented a breakthrough in narcissus breeding, began its official career in 1899.

For other bulbs we can find written references that prove they have been in our gardens at least that long. The bright spring *Crocus susianus*, which we often call Cloth of Gold, is supposed to have been introduced to Europe in 1587. We have no idea how long it may have been a favorite in the Crimean lands where it is native, but for us it has a pedigree nearly four centuries old.

Obviously, bulbs would have been one of the easiest plants for the ancients to have moved about with them in their travels. The dormant period many bulbs undergo would make it possible to carry stock even under the most primitive conditions. Those that were important either as food or medicine would naturally have had preference. Thus, the onion in its various forms was distributed widely around the ancient world, but the story only begins with the edibles.

The madonna-lily is believed to have originated in western Asia. Yet it was used as a vegetable and to make a medicinal salve in ancient Egypt as well as in classical Greece and Rome. The latter two civilizations also used its flowers in religious observances associated with the most popular female goddesses. By the Middle Ages this lovely white lily was well established as a Christian symbol of purity. European monks grew it in their protected monastery gardens both to use as a decorative indoors and out and as an herb for cooking and medicinal purposes.

So, too, the saffron crocus spread from Asia Minor to most of the known classical world. Used as a drug, dye and a perfume, as well as in cooking, it may have been present in Egypt as early as 2650 B.C. Solomon mentions it in the Old Testament, and we know it was highly esteemed in both Greece and Rome as well as eastern Asia. By the Middle Ages the saffron crocus was widely grown in all of Europe. One of the most famous sites of the industry it once supported is an English town known as Saffron Walden. Personally, I have never noticed anything outstanding about the fragrance of the flowers. One wonders if some enterprising promoter perhaps established it as an early status symbol, for only the dried reddish stigmata of the flower are used. It takes an astonishing number to get even an ounce of saffron.

At any rate it is easier to document the early use of such bulbs because of their utilitarian nature. It is a mistake, however, to underestimate ancient man. If he did not have formal gardens, he still had the fields where he could obtain flowers. Watch any small child instinctively reach to pick a flower and you will realize it is a longing as old as mankind itself.

We know, for example, that crocus flowers adorn jewelry, vases and frescoes from prehistoric Crete. The Egyptians left bunches of dried narcissus in funerary wreaths, and the Romans raised them in greenhouses for the decoration of patrician homes and banquets. Descriptions of crocuses, daffodils and anemones occur constantly in early Greek literature.

Mankind's delight in seeing flowers reappear after the winter is no recent emotion. We can find happy allusions to the daffodil in Greek poetry that predates Homer, hear it mentioned again and again in Shakespeare and quote Wordsworth and Herrick. In our own century a whole generation wept with Amy Lowell over the irony of the reappearing daffodils and squills in "Patterns." My children adopted "Hocus-pocus, the crocus," with great glee from a well-loved book and still use it as a watchword.

Many of the most popular spring-flowering bulbs are the result of know-how and hard work on the part of growers in the Netherlands. Growing conditions there are perfect for producing mature bulbs for export. We should not, however, sell the rest

This 18th-century Pennsylvania Dutch chest, now part of the collection of the Metropolitan Museum of Art in New York, is highlighted by an unusual tulip design.

Courtesy Metropolitan Museum of Art, New York

of the world short. Some of the biggest breakthroughs in breeding daffodils took place in England and Ireland, and lately breeders in New Zealand and Australia have also been notably successful. Several splendid newer daffodils have also been introduced by United States breeders, especially in the Northwest. That area too is the most important home of the modern hybrid lilies.

It is interesting to contemplate how many thousands of years bulb flowers have been delighting mankind, but much of what we plant nowadays is also the product of modern genetic and horticultural techniques. The prepared hyacinth for early forcing dates back only to 1910, for example. The first "pink" daffodil was introduced in 1923, and the Red Emperor tulip took its first award in 1931, although its popularity did not sweep the world until after World War II.

While there had been some successful crosses during the 1800s, today's lilies are truly twentieth-century creations. Concentrated effort to produce hybrid lilies began around 1925, but some of the greatest introductions were not available until the 1950s and 1960s. Moreover, the story of the new advances in lily breeding is far from over. Each year sees new breakthroughs and refinements among various representatives of this most beautiful of bulb flowers. Strangely, the most venerated lily, the madonna, is the least changed so far.

There is always a temptation to order something advertised as "new" in the catalogs. Many times the modern hybrid does represent a truly wonderful breakthrough, and selected superior forms are also good garden decoratives. But some of the loveliest and least demanding bulbs are to be found among the various species. This is true both among the little bulbs and among such popular favorites as tulips.

In many ways the bulb story has neither a true beginning nor a foreseeable end. In ad-

19

After its discovery in China in 1903, the regal lily became one of the most popular lilies for home gardens. Courtesy W.Atlee Burpee Co.

dition, public fashions change. A few highly touted entries in a modern catalog are really new. Others are merely staging a comeback.

A quick review of that springtime favorite, the tulip, is a good illustration. A Cretan vase estimated to be 3,500 to 4,000 years old shows a small tulip, and bands of tulip designs are found on Assyrian artifacts, but these are isolated instances. The tulip does not seem to figure in early written history.

The wild tulips are native to Mediterranean lands, Asia Minor and the Caucasus. A few are assigned to Kashmir and central Asia. The first people to cultivate them were probably the Turks. The early sultans thought so much of these flowers that they organized tulip festivals and honored those who grew new varieties. Many of the old palaces in Istanbul were decorated with tulip figures, as were the mosques. Tulips occur frequently on tiles and embroidery from Turkey even today.

By the time the first tulips reached Europe in 1554, the Turks had been hybridizing for

20

an unknown period of time. They much preferred those types with pointed, reflexed petals. These forms are reflected today in the lily-flowered sorts that have become increasingly popular in the past few decades.

At any rate, those first seeds and bulbs were brought back to Vienna by the Austrian ambassador, Busbecq, who reported seeing them in gardens in Constantinople. Since the Persian and Turkish word for tulip is *lalé*, there is conjecture that Busbecq misunderstood his interpreter, for the source of his "tulipam" is the Turkish equivalent of "turban" (dulban). The new flowers, whatever their name, became a sensation in Europe and were rapidly disseminated over the continent. They reached England about 1578, where they became favorites of rich and poor alike.

Credit for introducing the tulip to England is usually given to Clusius, a professor of botany at Leyden, Holland. He had been propagating them extensively in his own country, not without problems, however. His prices were high, and the story goes that thieves finally ruined his garden. Among the engravings in books by Clusius and his contemporaries there are no tulips with rounded petals, but it was not long before the chunkier tulip with erect broad petals became the preferred type in the Western world. It is exemplified by the modern Darwin tulip.

Clusius died in 1609, and by then tulips were firmly established as a crop in the Netherlands. Breeding and selection were concentrated to get the rounded petals and to increase the color range (the Turkish tulips were mostly reds and yellows).

When King Alfred was introduced in 1899, it began a whole new era in daffodil hybridizing. (TOP)

Fiery red, the Red Emperor's correct name is Mme. Lefeber. Dating from 1931, it marks a milestone in tulip breeding. (MIDDLE)

Lilium *Harmony dates from 1950 and is one of the De Graaff Mid-Century Hybrids that spurred modern lily hybridizing.* (BOTTOM)

Tulipomania and the Lily Bubble

Then near disaster struck in the form of a wild speculation that is known historically as "tulipomania." The tulip itself must share some of the blame. Self-colored garden tulips will "break" into variegated striped, flamed and feathered colors when they are infected with a nonfatal virus known as mosaic. Offsets of a broken bulb will show the same odd markings and colors although seedlings are again self-colored.

Not knowing about mosaic, the Dutch growers thought they had scored a great breakthrough. Each tulip that bloomed for the first time after being inadvertantly infected with the virus was treated as a freak of nature. Prices began to climb, for everyone wanted one of the "new" tulips.

From 1634 to 1637 virtually the entire country gambled on futures in tulips. Bulbs were seldom actually exchanged. They remained in the hands of a dealer while being traded back and forth. Normal life was virtually suspended at the height of the craze. Everyone was investing in bulbs, hoping

The Croft Strain of Easter lilies precipitated an American lily speculation that rivaled Tulipomania. (BELOW, LEFT)

Bouquet tulips, first introduced early in the twentieth century, are now having a resurgence in popularity. (BELOW, RIGHT)

that one of the "bizarres" would appear in his backyard. The New York office of the Associated Bulb Growers of Holland quotes the following record of the price of one bulb: "A load of grain, 4 oxen, 12 sheep, 5 pigs, 2 tubs of butter, 1000 pounds of cheese, 4 barrels of beer, 2 hogsheads of wine, a suit of clothes and a silver drinking cup."

Government intervention finally ended it all. The courts of Holland were flooded with suits, and the story is told of one Leyden botany professor who lost his scientific objectivity to the point where he struck with his cane at every tulip he saw. Luckily for us, his countrymen did not drop the flower. The myriad forms of tulips that decorate our gardens are almost all the product of Dutch patience and know-how in growing and breeding, as are a great many other bulbs.

Incidentally, it hardly behooves us to look down our noses at the Dutchmen who became entangled in tulipomania a few hundred years ago. In *Lilies*, co-authored by Edward Hyams and Jan de Graaff, the greatest modern lily hybridizer, mention is made of the Croft lily bubble in America. This variety of the popular Easter lily was first grown in 1928 in Oregon. Not only was it a superior form, but it increased rapidly

from offsets. It became the favorite commercial variety. Then came World War II and the cutoff of exports from Japan. Of the 24,000,000 lily bulbs imported into the United States in 1937, for example, about 90 percent came from Japan. Most were used for forcing as cut flowers or potted plants. When this supply was cut off, growers on the West Coast began to concentrate on Easter lilies. Land prices in the area went from $25 to $1,000 per acre, and a single planting-size bulb of Croft's variety rose to $1. De Graaff points out that the bulb-raisers were more likely to have made money than the flower growers because a bulb of this lily increases 50-fold in one season. At any rate, the market was oversupplied, and the boom ended.

Returning to tulips, it is strange to see the headings in bulb catalogs. What is "new" is often just a recurring fashion. Double tulips, for instance, were illustrated in a book dated 1613. The same volume had a "green" tulip (a double at that); nowadays the types with green on the petals are much in demand by flower arrangers. Parrot tulips were first introduced in 1665. These curiously colored and shaped tulips have been in and out of vogue ever since. Today's catalogs feature a variation, too—the fringed or crystal tulip. Its petals are laciniated at the edges, but the total effect is neater than that of the parrots, many of which have their petals twisted into odd shapes. Some of these fringed tulips are fairly recent, but New Look, a white tinted with rose, was introduced in 1953.

At one time the lily-flowered tulips were actually rogued out of the Dutch growers' fields, but they too have been rediscovered and are recommended for their graceful garden effect. Around the turn of the twentieth century another type of tulip, the multiflowered hybrids often termed bouquet tulips, gained popularity. Dropped as unwanted novelties after a time, they have lately staged a comeback.

What this means to us is that far more types and colors of almost all large groups of bulb flowers are available for our gardens. Choose from among them those that fill your particular needs, not what is necessarily popular at the time. You can also enjoy a feeling of kinship with the gardeners of all other times. Even if the flowers are not always quite the same—usually they have been improved in some way—the appreciation of similar beauty is a lovely legacy.

Other tulipa hybridizers have concentrated on kaufmanniana *hybrids, such as* Heart's Delight. (BELOW, LEFT)

Dreamboat is just one of many outstanding Greigi Hybrid Tulips now entering bulb catalogs. (BELOW, RIGHT)

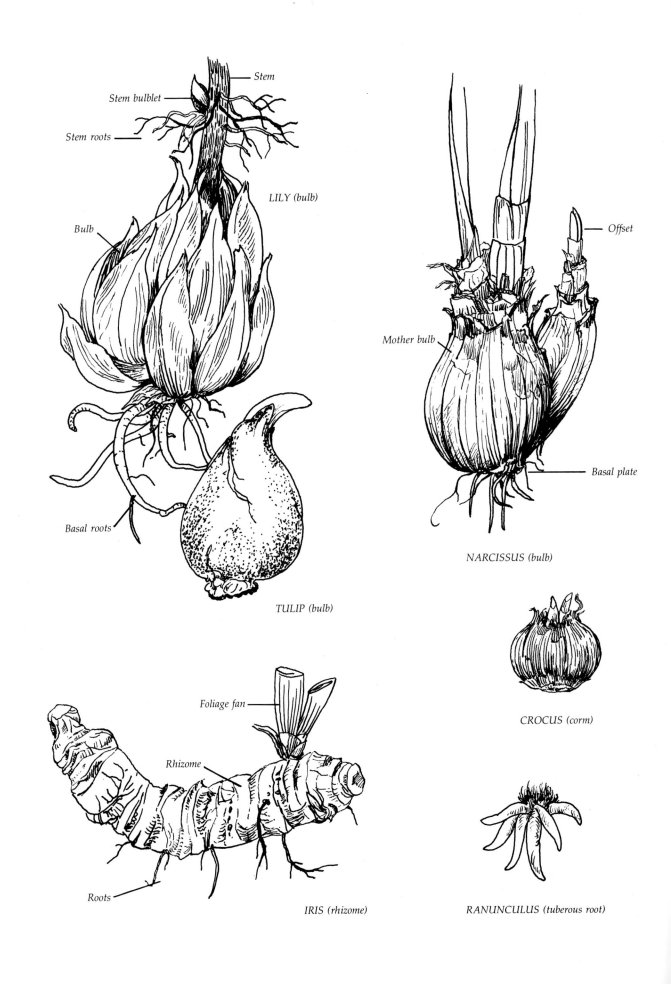

Stem

Stem bulblet

Stem roots

LILY (bulb)

Bulb

Basal roots

TULIP (bulb)

Offset

Mother bulb

Basal plate

NARCISSUS (bulb)

CROCUS (corm)

Foliage fan

Rhizome

Roots

IRIS (rhizome)

RANUNCULUS (tuberous root)

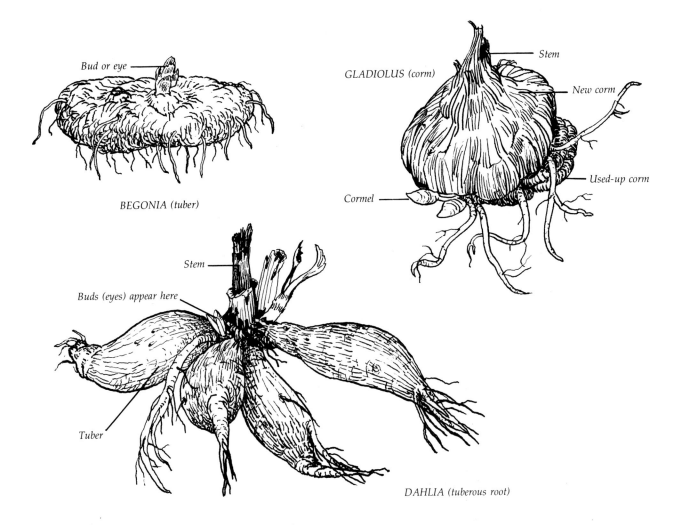

Bud or eye

BEGONIA (tuber)

GLADIOLUS (corm)

Stem

New corm

Used-up corm

Cormel

Stem

Buds (eyes) appear here

Tuber

DAHLIA (tuberous root)

TYPES OF BULBS

Strictly speaking, many of the plants cataloged as "bulbs" are not true bulbs. Some are really corms (gladiolus and crocus), tubers (begonia and cyclamen), tuberous roots (mertensia) or rhizomes (blackberry lily). Even true bulbs may contain scales (lilies) or be made up of concentric layers (daffodils).

Some idea of the differences in appearance between the various vegetative storehouses we call bulbs can be seen from the drawings on the these two pages. What is common to them all is that they possess a thickened rootstock of one kind or another that serves as a storage center for the nutrients the plant will need in its growing season. If you buy mature, healthy bulbs,

success the first season is almost guaranteed. What happens to the storehouse in subsequent seasons is your responsibility, but that first year the work has already been done for you by the grower.

Because most bulbs have a dormant period, they can be safely taken out of the ground, stored and finally shipped to the gardener. Mail delivery of many growing plants is not always successful, but you can order bulbs with every expectation that they will make the journey in good shape. With most bulbs you can delay a bit before you plant without harm. Lilies and those plants that grow from thickened rootstocks are the exception; they should be kept out of the ground as short a time as possible.

PLANTING DETAILS

What kind of bulb you have at hand is mainly important in propagating your stock. For details of this process consult pages 136–139. When planting, the important thing to remember is that where and how you place the bulb influences how much it increases, which in turn affects your design.

Rhizomatous and stoloniferous bulbs and creeping rootstocks tend to move outward from the original planting spot. For this reason they are usually not wise for the highly formalized garden plan. They are better used in an informal garden or on the edge of shrubbery or woodland where their movement does not matter much. Where severely restricted, they sometimes die out.

Bulbs such as daffodils, which increase with relative speed by offsets, in time will become too crowded. You can slow the process by planting them as deeply as possible for the type of soil you have. If your soil is light and sandy, always plant bulbs the maximum depth recommended. If the soil is clayey, plant them toward the minimum

depth recommended. The water table can dictate planting depths, too. If it is very high, deeply planted bulbs may rot. The size of the bulb also governs at what depth it is best planted. Bulblets should not go as deeply as mature parent bulbs. If you prepare the soil well underneath a bulb, it can always pull itself downward by the action of the roots. So it is better to err on the shallow side, especially in soils with a large percentage of clay or questionable drainage.

Corms increase on top of themselves, and the old corm shrivels away. After a few years a planting of crocus will work its way to the top of the soil, and the topmost corms should be replanted for best bloom. One easy way to do this with any cormous plant is to scratch with a hand cultivator at the surface after the foliage has ripened. All the corms in the first two inches of soil should be replanted. Such treatment every few years takes only a few moments. It also keeps the top corms from being frozen in the winter or too easily located by rodents.

When it is mature, a tulip splits into several bulbs. This is different from the daffodil, which produces smaller bulbs at the side of the parent. Many times a planting of tulips will be simply glorious the first year and then look quite scruffy the next. If you are patient, the new bulbs will enlarge in a few years, and your tulip planting will once again give lots of bloom. Many times the tulip bulbs move somewhat because new ones are produced on stolons. It is these habits that prompt the caretakers of exhibition gardens to dig up tulip plantings annually and plant new bulbs every fall. The home gardener does not have to go to this trouble unless there is a particular spot that requires absolutely uniform bloom height and size for special effect. Deeper planting of tulip bulbs seems somewhat to inhibit their breaking, but you should be philosophical and realize that the best show from hybrid tulips will always occur the first spring after planting.

Planting depths are measured from the top of the bulb. To ensure good root development, check that soil under bulb is soft and easily crumbled. Never leave pocket of air beneath bulb.

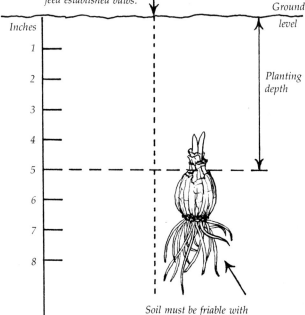

Bonemeal worked into soil in autumn will reach roots to feed established bulbs.

Ground level

Inches

Planting depth

Soil must be friable with no air pockets below bulb.

26

HOW DEEP?

The question of how deep to plant a bulb can worry new gardeners. Magazines and books with fancy drawings about how deep to plant bulbs should be read with some skepticism. Smaller bulbs should be planted less deep than larger ones of the same kind, as I have already noted. Old gardeners have a rule of thumb that works surprisingly well: Plant a bulb three times as deep as its diameter. In other words, a tulip bulb two inches thick is planted six inches deep. Of course, if you have a mammoth bulb, don't inter it permanently by placing it at an unreasonable depth. With bulblets, don't place them so close to the surface that they will be subject to frost damage.

Where winters bring zero degrees and colder weather and frost goes deeply into the ground, you may have to plant deeper than I do here in the Middle Atlantic states. In that case, check the section on drainage carefully on page 19, particularly if you live in a lowland area. You can moderate frost depth to some extent by using extra mulch atop bulb plantings. In the far North it may be better to plant small bulblets in a cold frame for the first winter if you are trying to get rapid increase of a special bulb favorite.

Much of the advice another gardener can give you is subject to some experimentation on your part. It also helps to ask questions of other gardeners in your area. They will know what works best for where you live. Planting depths are more important for hardy bulbs that endure a dormant period in the ground than for tender bulbs that begin to grow soon after planting and spend the winter safely stored in the house. Remember always that a hardy plant can rot in an area with a high water table if planted deeply, or freeze from frost if placed too shallowly.

Conditions differ even within the same garden. Almost any small bulb is going to do well two to three inches deep if the soil below it has been well cultivated first. With larger sizes of daffodils and tulips, you can plant them progressively deeper until you find the maximum applicable for your soil. Or you can keep to an average of five to seven inches deep. One more rule that is helpful is to make sure all the bulbs in one particular planting are at the same depth; otherwise they may not all bloom at the same time. For little bulbs the easiest way is to dig a large hole and plant them all in it at the same time. With larger bulbs, such as double-nosed daffodils, separate holes are usually dug for each. Learn to gauge the depth of your excavations with your trowel. Some tools even have inch marks engraved in the metal.

HOW TO PLANT

Generally you will get a better show for your money if you plant bulbs in groups of a single color and type. Most catalogs list mixtures of bulbs at slightly lower cost than an equal number of one particular kind. The difference in price, however, is a poor bargain in many cases. I remember with dismay a planting of "Peacock Tulips" that in my innocence I put in the most conspicuous spot in my front yard many years ago. Admittedly, the individual blooms in this mixture were scintillating beauties, but some of the colors did not harmonize at all, and only about half the flowers were in bloom at any one time. I would have had more effect for my money if I had ordered a slightly smaller number of Greigi Hybrids by name.

Clumps of bulbs are much more decorative than straight lines. Again you get the effect of more bloom this way. There is more grace, too, to a rounded grouping. Many large bulbs produce stiff stems, particularly hybrid tulips, daffodils and hyacinths. Placing them in single file emphasizes their stiffness. You are, after all, trying to create a garden, not a parade ground.

Another useful technique is to try to repeat a particular planting more than once in the same garden. Thus two groups of a dozen tulips each are stronger sometimes than a single big spread.

The Importance of Good Drainage

Bulbous plants may be adaptable to many different situations and climates, but there is a cardinal rule that no one many safely ignore: They absolutely have to have good drainage. You can count on the fingers of one hand those few that prosper in wet situations, and even these cannot be left to stand in water for long periods of time.

In the main, it is never wise to plant bulbs where water collects. If you think about it, this admonition makes sense even if you have never gardened before. A bulb comprises that portion of a plant that is a starchy storehouse full of food. Think what happens to a bag of potatoes that is stored too wet, and you can imagine the effect of too much wetness on dormant flower bulbs.

Gardens where other perennial flowers have been prospering are not likely to present any problems. Only a few special plants do well in poorly drained spots, so the health of the rest of the garden is a good barometer. However, if moss covers the ground where you are thinking of planting, the soil is almost surely not well drained.

If you are making a new garden, look over the site after a good rain to get some idea of its drainage. Dig it deeply all over before you plant. This will help in the formation of adequate roots and will encourage good drainage. If the land is naturally high and the soil sandy, drainage should be no problem. But if you have heavy clay or if you garden in a valley, you may have to think carefully about where you plant your bulbs. Clay soil may be lightened by digging in humus such as compost or peat moss. If the natural drainage is poor, however, the bulbs are likely to rot long before they flower.

One solution is to plant bulbs on a slope. In most cases this will ensure that they will not sit in puddles of water. Make sure that the ground beneath and around the bulb planting has been well cultivated first, too.

Otherwise, in heavy clay soil rain can collect in pockets where the bulbs have been planted in softer earth.

If no other solution can be found, make a raised bed. Use bricks, stones, wood planks or some other barrier to hold the soil. Depending on how high your water table is in wet times, the top layer of soil in the bed should be at least six to 12 inches above the level of the rest of the land. Err on the high side if you are not sure. There are some other suggestions about these problems in the section on the whole garden at the back of this book.

Paradoxically, some of the most splendid daffodil gardens I have ever seen were situated in bottom land. Infrequently some of these gardens even undergo flooding, but the water does not lie long. The fact that the daffodil roots have a good supply of moisture accounts for their prodigious health and increase. But the bulbs do not sit in water; it is the roots that tap the moisture. The same conditions account for the beautiful daffodil plantings often found around lakes and streams. In your own garden you can duplicate these conditions by seeing that there is adequate irrigation if it does not rain enough during those crucial weeks just after flowering. It is then that the bulb foliage is pumping food back into the underground storehouse.

A raised bed aids soil drainage.

Wall of rocks or railroad ties

Bulbs planted on raised ground

Grass

Hill made by piling dirt up behind wall

Terraces and walls ensure good drainage. (OPPOSITE)

Encourage Bulb Foliage

To produce good bloom from your bulbs for years, you have to guarantee the production of healthy foliage. If the bulb itself is a storehouse of food, it follows that the leaves are the manufacturing factory where the important process of photosynthesis takes place. To refresh your memory of basic botany, photosynthesis is simply the process by which green leaves are able, in the presence of sunlight, to manufacture carbohydrates, which the plant then stores for future use. The plant's leaves use carbon dioxide during the process, and one of the by-products of their work is the life-giving oxygen that animals need to breathe. It is certainly one of the most important miracles of natural chemistry, for without it there would be no life on earth.

When you pick too many leaves with the bulb flower or if you cut the foliage off while it is still green and growing, the storehouse cannot be restocked. Consequently, it will not be able to produce flowers of the same size and quantity as during that first year when the bulb grower provided you with a mature, energy-packed bulb. Without eventual restocking, the bulb will vanish— bloomed out, as it were.

Even though allowing the foliage to complete its natural growth cycle may not make for quite as neat a garden as you might wish, this is a necessity for daffodils, tulips, gladiolus—and all other bulbs. If you have naturalized bulbs, do not mow the grass where they are planted at least until after their foliage is turning yellow. Should spring be rainless, water your bulbs so that the leaves do not brown up too rapidly before they have had a chance to manufacture the food the bulbs will need the next year.

One solution is to plant giant tulips, daffodils and other spring bulbs with large leaves toward the middle of a bed. Later-blooming plants positioned in front of them will help to hide unsightly bulb foliage as it discolors. Daffodils are particularly slow in maturing their leaves. As their foliage begins to flop over, gently push it behind other plants.

Once bulb leaves have begun to turn brown and dry, they have completed their work for another year. This is the time to gather them up. You may notice that some stems leave large holes where they emerged from the soil. Gently cultivate with your trowel at these points until the holes are covered so that insects or rodents will not have an open invitation to disturb the dormant bulbs.

The maturing leaves of smaller hardy spring and fall bulbs do not present much of a problem. By the time their foliage is no longer sightly, it is nearly mature. Even many of the early shorter tulips can be considered in this category, and there is no reason why you cannot plant any of these in the foreground of the garden where the flowers will show most advantageously.

Whatever you do, avoid anything that might bruise or injure bulb foliage during the weeks when it is actively growing. One practice to avoid is the braiding of daffodil foliage as it begins to mature. I find this grotesque to look at, and, besides, who has time for such folly at the height of spring planting? Tied-up foliage cannot possibly work efficiently at catching the sun and absorbing the air and thus manufacturing the food the bulb needs.

Some summer-flowering bulb foliage will not brown off before frost. Take this into consideration when you plant such bulbs and try to use the foliage to your advantage. The ismene, for example, creates large fountains of wide, straplike leaves that are interesting as a green summer accent. Gladiolus and its near relatives have tall, swordlike leaves that give a good vertical line in the late-summer border. Colchicums in spring produce bold foliage that can add a luxuriant note at a time when most leaves are still new and small. When they are placed in front of shrubbery or to the back of the rock garden, I find these leaves interesting in spring and really don't mind their brief browning-off period.

If for some reason you have need of many cut bulb flowers, you will find it a good idea to grow some just for this purpose in an out-of-the-way spot such as along the vegetable plot. While it is fun to pick some flowers from the garden for indoors, denuding the garden of all bloom tends to defeat the purpose of having one. A section for cutting will allow you to have all the bouquets you want without spoiling the garden's design. You can even treat such a spot as an annual garden, picking all the foliage needed.

Go Easy on Fertilizer

Adequate watering in times of drought is much more important to the health of your bulbs than fertilizing. High-nitrogen fertilizers, such as are used on lawns, are not advised. With many hardy bulbs this makes them produce lush foliage at the expense of any flowers at all; with others it appears to make the bulbs more susceptible to disease. A great number of hardy spring bulbs are native to mountainous regions where the soil is poor. I use only bone meal for feeding my bulbs, applied in the spring after the shoots appear. There are special bulb fertilizers on the market that others prefer. You can garden quite nicely without any fertilizing at all, although bulb flower size may decrease eventually.

However, the tender bulbs that come from jungle habitats, such as cannas, benefit from fertilizer during the growing season. You can sprinkle some dehydrated cow manure around them, being careful not to let any touch the foliage, or you can use a water-soluble, all-purpose flower fertilizer, following directions on the container. I recommend this treatment especially for potted bulbs, but my practice is to use the fertilizer at slightly less than the recommended strength. When adding granular fertilizer before planting any bulb in the garden, make sure that there is soil between the fertilizer and the bottom of the bulb.

Combine kaufmanniana *and* fosteriana *tulip hybrids with daffodils for early spring.* (ABOVE) *Late double tulips and blue polemonium beneath a dogwood beautify late spring.* (MIDDLE)

Late summer: Bedding annuals fill in after spring bulbs and early perennials are finished blooming. Note that tall liatris in center is just budding. (BELOW)

Learn to Mulch

Generally, if your garden has decent soil in which other plants are growing well, the bulbs you add will also thrive. Most gardens benefit from the addition of compost or about an inch of organic mulch every year or so. This keeps the root runs of all plants cooler in summer and warmer in winter, conserves moisture, discourages weeds and gradually adds to the physical health of the soil as the mulch breaks down. Choose wood chips, shredded leaves or bark, chopped corncobs or whatever material is in good supply where you live.

Do not use peat moss for top mulching. It is excellent as a conditioner when mixed with the soil, but as a mulch it forms a hard crust and actually may rob the plants of moisture. The other mulches allow rain to penetrate, and their covering on the ground also protects flowers from being spattered with mud during hard rains.

If you have never practiced mulching before, you will be pleasantly surprised at how much easier it makes your gardening. It isn't just that it keeps the weeds down, although that is certainly one of the advantages. Mulching literally betters the consistency of the soil. Earthworms carry particles below the surface; and every time you cultivate or plant, some of the mulch is integrated with the soil. This increases its humus content, one of the greatest things you can do for soil.

Given a choice, and unlimited funds, I would choose shredded bark as the best mulch. It is neat-looking, breaks down easily and is found in nearly every garden and hardware outlet as well as many discount houses. I try to use shredded bark for those areas that are most noticeable. In the vegetable garden and behind the foreground of a big border I sometimes use piles of weeds as mulch, preferably those that have been pulled before going to seed. But if the mulch is fairly thick, even weed seeds will not have much success at sprouting.

The river stones popular nowadays for mulching are neat in appearance too, but they are too heavy for most bulb beds. The young shoots simply cannot emerge without damage. Fine gravel would probably not have this effect, but I have not tried it. Rock gardeners have long used pebbles to create well-drained screes, so it ought to work. Make sure, however, that any rock mulch does not affect the acidity of the soil. Any with high lime content would be a poor choice for mulching beds that contain azaleas or other acid-loving plants.

It really doesn't make much difference at what season you apply mulch. Everything else being equal, just after planting bulbs is as good a time as any. This applies whether in fall after the tulips go in or in spring after the dahlias are planted. The mulch will keep down the weeds until the bulbs take over, and it will also remind you that bulbs are in that space when you go about other gardening tasks.

Oftentimes there is other planting to be done after a mulch is in place. It is really no effort to brush the mulch away, put in plants and then sweep the mulch back around them. This is particularly true of the shredded tree-bark type that I favor. The chunkier mulches such as those made of pieces of bark last longer, but they are not as easy to work in. I find them better for surfacing the basin around trees or some other spot where there will not be much work going on. Unfortunately, the big chunks float in water, and sometimes on a slope this can make a mess after a storm. Some birds can defeat your try at neatness. Our brown thrashers, for example, continually toss the bark chunks from around the holly planting into the lawn as they probe among them for insects and other food.

Most gardeners keep the mulch from being directly against tree and shrub trunks. Whether such a precaution actually does discourage mice from gnawing at the trees in winter, I can't say, but I usually leave a few inches bare around mine.

Lightweight materials such as buckwheat

Shredded pine bark furnishes a tidy and attractive mulch for early bulbs.

or cocoa-bean hulls will be blown away by strong winds unless wet. Such materials are poor choices for windswept gardens. During the warmer months it is always a good practice to apply mulch after the ground is wet either from rain or sprinkling. This prevents the dry mulch from absorbing ground moisture on contact and helps set the mulch in place. During very hot weather it is sound practice to sprinkle the area with water before and after applying the mulch.

Occasionally I hear some expert say that mulches should be removed at season's end, but I cannot imagine why. This is a needless chore, and, besides, when left in place all winter, my mulches have never done any harm, and I am glad to have them break down gradually and thus improve my soil.

Other Cultural Details

Bulb flowers make wonderful bouquets. By all means use them that way, taking care not to remove too much foliage when picking. Often, however, the gardener does not wish to spoil the outdoor garden picture by picking too many flowers. If that be the case, at least be conscientious about removing the spent flowers before the seed pods form. Producing seed uses up much of a bulb's vitality. Except for those small bulbs that you are trying to increase into wide swaths of color (and among which flower size is unimportant), break off the flower heads of all your bulbs as soon as the petals fade.

Successful gardening consists of matching plants to the site available. If yours is a mostly shady garden, you will need to choose the bulbs that naturally want that sort of environment. Yes, you could grow beautiful daffodils for one season because the bulbs have been prepared for you by the grower. But the next year your daffodils will be going downhill. The one question I am asked most often is "Why don't my daffodils bloom well any more?" Many times the reason is simply that maturing trees cast ever-increasing amounts of shade where the daffodils once prospered; the bulb leaves are no longer able to make efficient use of photosynthesis. Of course, sometimes the answer is that the daffodils have proliferated to such an extent that the bulbs are just too crowded, but usually this is evident even to the novice by the greater amount of foliage.

Homemade planting marker can be made from discarded aluminum freezer package; ballpoint pen presses legend into metal.

Shade-loving bulbs such as tuberous begonias are not as amenable to the wrong conditions. Set in full, hot sun, they often falter the first year. Learn too the difference between constant shade (as on the north side of a building or under big evergreen trees) and filtered shade or the high shadow of tall deciduous trees where there is actually a considerable amount of light even if not direct sun. You have to get out into your garden to discover these things. Like everything else, gardening can be learned better by doing than reading.

Before ordering many bulbs, at least draw a rough diagram of how you will plant them. Consider height and foliage spread. Select colors for harmony or pleasant contrast. Keep in mind the rest of the garden's inhabitants too. Orange tulips beside a pink-flowered crab apple tree are not the wisest choice. There is more on the whole garden and these interrelationships in a special section at the back of this book.

Markers are often unnecessary in a small garden, but you may wish to use some lest you dig into a dormant bulb. All sorts of labels are on the market, but you can make an inconspicuous but adequate one by cutting an inch-wide strip from a discarded aluminum freezer container. Make it long enough so that you have several inches to stick into the earth and about two inches for writing. You can do this by pressing a blunt pencil or ballpoint pen into the aluminum. You can write merely TULIP or PINK TULIP or you can use its full name. After you plant the bulbs, insert the marker into the center of the clump and bend it down.

Many gardeners aren't particularly interested in exact labels. They just sink a wooden clothespin or a small drink stirrer or some similar marker where they have planted a clump of bulbs. This reminds them not to dig there for some other purpose while the bulbs are dormant. Often I overplant bulbs with a ground cover to accomplish the same thing.

34

Bulb Diseases and Pests

By and large, bulbs are much less prone to disease and insect pests than many other garden inhabitants. This is especially true of those that flower in early spring before warm weather brings out the hordes of summer that feast on nearly every leaf and blossom in sight. Once in a while you may notice aphid infestations on tulips. A quick spraying with any pesticide labeled for aphids may be called for, but often you can merely rub them off the bloom.

Bulbs that are fed too much, particularly with high-nitrogen mixtures, seem more susceptible to disease, as I have mentioned already. Be forewarned and save both time and money by keeping your hardy flowering bulbs on a low-nitrogen diet.

One way to save yourself lots of trouble is to be careful what you plant. Any bulb or root that is soft, very light in weight or moldy may harbor disease. It is better discarded than planted on the off chance it will grow, for it is quite likely to introduce some harmful virus. The growers are conscientious about inspecting bulbs, but an infected one can slip by.

There is a dangerous disease that can appear among tulips. It is called fire blight, and it prospers in damp spring weather. The most obvious signs are twisted and discolored foliage and flower petals. If you suspect its presence, immediately pull all the leaves right out of the bulb in the ground and burn or otherwise dispose permanently of the foliage. There is no other good treatment, and it is far better to sacrifice one colony of tulips than to let this disease run wild in your garden.

It is not a good idea to plant tulips again in the same ground where you suspect there was such an infection previously. Wait at least three years before you replant such a spot with tulips. Lilies are susceptible to some of the same diseases, so they should not go in ground where tulips have not done well. I used to think it a poor idea to mix tulips and lilies in the same garden, but modern American-grown lilies are much healthier than the stock we used to get from abroad. Also, today's smaller gardens do not allow as much leeway of placement, so you might as well enjoy them both.

It makes sense, too, to think that after some years of growing, a particular kind of bulb may exhaust the soil of the nutrients it needs. Therefore, if you have to transplant bulbs that have increased too much, it is wiser either to replant them in a new spot or to work over the original soil, adding humus and some complete fertilizer at the same time. A bulb that is struggling to get along on less than what it needs is much more likely to succumb to disease or pests than one growing vigorously.

Summer-flowering bulbs are not likely to give much trouble, but Japanese beetles will flock to cannas. You can spray against them, but a better solution is to buy some milky spore disease and introduce it to your property. It attacks the beetle grubs and gradually spreads outward over the years from where it was applied. In all but the coldest parts of the United States it is worth trying. Meanwhile, feed the cannas well; they will recover from the beetle invasion and be presentable in time for the fall blooming season.

Thrips are a problem on gladiolus and their relatives as well as on dahlias. Malathion, used strictly as directed, is a safe treatment. Keep weeds down around such plantings to discourage various bugs that not only do their own eating but also carry diseases.

Sanitation is vital to a healthy garden. Old stalks often contain eggs or pupae of insects. This is particularly true of stems that are hollow such as lilies or dahlias; gather and burn these in the fall.

Diversification is another good precaution. If all your bulbs belong to one family, disease could run rampant easily. Of the popular hardy bulbs, lilies, tulips, colchicums, hyacinths, muscari, trillium, scilla and chionodoxa all belong to the lily family. Make sure that your garden has some plantings of other families. Daffodils, snow-drops, snowflakes and sternbergia are some important hardy amaryllis family members. The iris family includes such favorites as crocus, tigridia, gladiolus and belamcanda. Mixing your plantings not only makes them more interesting but also lessens the chance of disease sweeping through the entire garden.

Most likely you will have more trouble with four-legged animals than pests. If you are next to a wooded area where deer are prevalent, you will not be able to grow tulips or lilies except near the house. Even tall wire baskets around the growing bulbs will not always work, for many of the loveliest lilies are six feet high in bloom. I have seen deer wait until a lily was just in bud and then come to eat it. Deer do not seem to touch daffodils, however, so you can enjoy them in such a situation.

Rabbits are a real menace. They will eat crocuses in flower right to ground level, dine daintily on tulip shoots and even nip off a stray daffodil leaf or stem. The narcotic property in the daffodil or narcissus, how-ever, puts them off, so you can usually let the daffodils fend for themselves.

Discarded evergreen branches may be used to discourage rabbits. I gather all the old Christmas trees I can locate in the neighborhood, clip off the branches and pile them where I can remember there are tasty plantings. As the shoots appear in early spring to show exactly where the bulbs are, I stick the evergreen branches into the ground in a circle about a foot high around special colonies of plants especially savored by rab-bits. This way I can enjoy the bloom of crocus and still protect it. Often, tulips that have advanced beyond six inches in height seem to be less attractive to rabbits. You

A hungry rabbit ate tulip leaves but discarded most of the flowers.

Evergreen branches around fall crocus will protect its foliage from rabbits during the winter.

could, of course, make wire baskets of hardware mesh or chicken wire to surround all such plantings, but it is a lot of trouble.

I have tried many other antirabbit devices: sprinkling pepper or dried blood meal, placing mothballs, burying soda bottles halfway in the ground. None has worked well or for long. My dogs have never done anything helpful to control rabbit populations either, except perhaps to make the animals a bit nervous; and though the neighborhood cats hunt my hedgerows, the rabbits are always with me.

Mice, chipmunks and squirrels concentrate on the bulbs rather than the foliage. Good general sanitation procedures are of some help. Lots of dead leaves and debris make it easier for mice and rats to get around in a garden. Where a wall or other feature gives them a snug home, it may be advisable to use poison bait, but remember that many baits are harmful to pets and birds as well as small children. Be careful where and how you use poison. The rodents can find bait under a board or a rock where it will not attract animals you wish to protect.

Where squirrels are pests, try to outwit them. After planting one of their favorite foods, such as crocus, step hard on that bit of ground so you don't call their attention to that bit of soft earth.

Baskets of hardware mesh that are stuck into the ground after the hole is dug will prevent rodents from tunneling into a planting, but the top is still vulnerable. If things are that serious, it might pay to get a hungry cat and cut down the population for a while. One clever gardener I know advocates using lots of stone chips when planting lily, crocus and tulip bulbs in areas where rodents are a real problem. She sprinkles the stones at the bottom of the planting hole and with the earth as she refills, then piles more chips on the top. This is a lot of trouble but possibly the only solution if you very much want a colony of something special.

As with other points like sun and shade and drainage, diseases and pests will help you choose what is best to plant. Gardening ought always to be a pleasurable experience, and if you can't outwit or fence out your pests, try kinds of plants they don't like.

CULTURE OF HARDY BULBS

By a gardener's definition hardy bulbs may winter safely in the ground where temperatures dip well below freezing and frost may go several inches into the soil. They are usually planted in the fall for bloom the following spring. However, some kinds that are only marginally hardy in your climate are often better planted in the spring if available. This way they get a good start before undergoing a winter. I have had best results with hardy begonias (*B. evansiana*) this way, for example. And by this approach you will get at least one season of bloom out of your purchase even if your winters are too severe for it.

Most of the bulbs that are termed hardy need no such pampering. They are best ordered for fall planting since they have a naturally dormant period in the summer during which they can be shipped with least likelihood of their drying out or sprouting ahead of time. Most of them may be left undisturbed for many seasons of bloom.

Because most bulbs increase well by offsets, the time will come when there are simply too many bulbs occupying the same piece of ground; they will not be able to obtain enough nutrients to make a good show of themselves. The signal to dig them for transplanting occurs when flower size or quantity drops. If you have lots of leaves but few flowers in a mature clump of bulbs, you can be almost certain they need separating.

Unless you have a special reason to want quick increase, save yourself work by planting them as deeply as you dare in your type of soil, a point I explain in the earlier general section on planting. If you space them far enough apart, you ought to be able to count on daffodils taking care of themselves without effort on your part for at least four seasons after initial planting. With such technique your daffodil planting will look a bit skimpy the first year, but the saving of work in subsequent years is really worth it. There is little pleasure in a garden where one constantly has to be digging up things.

Smaller bulbs like grape hyacinths, crocuses and scillas can be left alone much longer. Many of these increase by seed as well as offset bulbs and will spread into great sweeps of color under shrubbery or in the foreground of the garden. This makes for delightful garden pictures with no effort at all on your part, except that you have to remember not to do deep cultivation where they are established during their dormant period.

If you decide that a clump of hardy bulbs needs dividing, wait until the foliage begins to yellow off in late spring, then dig carefully so as not to injure the bulbs. For large daffodils, a spading fork is a good tool to use. Place it beyond where there is foliage and insert into the earth all around. Then pry up the loosened bulb mass. Separate the bulbs carefully, making sure each bulb has some of the basal plate left on it. With a very crowded mass of bulbs, it is often better to wait a few days until the outsides of them dry a little before separating.

Once you have the bulbs broken apart, spread them to dry on a screen in a cool, shaded spot, such as a garage, for about a week, then replant. All things considered, it is probably better not to put them back in exactly the same soil as before. If garden design demands they go back into the same spot, try to replace some of the soil there with new earth and add some bone meal and extra humus. If this is done while the bulbs are drying, the soil will settle and be ready when you come to plant.

If it is necessary to store hardy bulbs for any period, choose a cool spot with good air circulation and do not pile them deeply. Keep them from drying out and also from undue moisture that might encourage rot. The Dutch bulb growers are adept at such techniques. They even send an inspector on the ships in which the bulbs are carried. He regulates vents in the hold to ensure that the bulbs are kept at optimum conditions for their health. A good bulb supplier is equally

Massed hyacinths at Peddler's Village, Lahaska, Pennsylvania, show how effective grouping by single variety is when planting bulbs.

careful about the storage of bulbs until they are sold.

With your own bulb increase, the wisest course is to get them back in the ground as soon as possible after the skins dry. It does seem to cut down on spoilage if they are first given a few days to dry, but a whole summer in a hot garage will take the vitality out of the best bulbs.

By the same token, plant your fall bulb orders as soon as you can after they arrive. Open the bags for inspection and keep them in a cool, airy, dry spot for up to a few days—but don't delay planting for long. Tulips, perhaps, can go in later, but they too are better in the ground than drying out in the house, particularly after the heat goes on in the fall. (The humidity in a centrally heated house is too low.)

There is another reason for quick planting besides storage problems. With all hardy bulbs, but especially daffodils and the many small types, a good root system has to form before cold weather arrives if you are to have satisfactory bloom the next spring. In most parts of the northern hemisphere this means getting them in before the end of October at the latest. If you do not believe this, try digging up some dormant daffodils in late summer. You will find they are already putting out new roots.

Once in a while conditions are such that you cannot wait until the optimum time to move bulbs. It is possible to dig a clump while the foliage is still green, replant them immediately somewhere else or heel them in somewhere temporarily. They will need to be watered faithfully the same as any transplanted growing plant; and you may well find that you will lose a season of bloom after such treatment. It is also possible to dig bulbs while they are dormant and no foliage shows to give you an indication of their exact location. I do not recommend it, however, owing to the likelihood of slicing through the bulbs on the first cut.

Because early planting has so many advantages, it pays to get your fall bulb orders in as soon as possible in the summer (most catalogs are ready by late July). If you order immediately, your order will not be delayed, but don't expect immediate delivery. Orders cannot be processed until shipments arrive from overseas, but at least yours will be among the first to go out. The subsequent earlier planting will be better for the bulbs and much more pleasant for you because you can plant while autumn days are still warm, and few chores are more delightful than planting bulbs on a warm fall day. The pleasant, optimistic mood of such a job evaporates if you wait until the wind is chill and the ground wet and cold to kneel on. Since supplies of many bulbs are limited, the early order is much less likely to include substitutions.

Sometimes things happen in the best-run gardens to throw you off your schedule. If this happens to you, plant your bulbs as soon afterward as you can. They will be better off going into the ground during a mid-winter thaw than staying in the house. Flowering after such late planting is often delayed, and the stems are nearly always shorter than normal, but this is preferable to throwing the bulbs away.

Some years bulb orders arrive far later than is desirable. This is particularly true of certain lilies that do not go dormant for shipping until late in the fall. If you live where frost enters the ground early, you can make things easier for yourself with some prior preparations. Turn the soil over to the correct depth where the bulbs are to go, then cover the area with old burlap, a tarpaulin or a piece of strong plastic. On top of this pile a foot or so of tamped-down leaves, straw, excelsior or something similar. Anchor this with boards against the wind. Then when the bulbs arrive, you can remove the mulch and usually find the earth still unfrozen. Failing such precautions, the only thing you can do is pry up the first few frozen inches of

soil with a pick or mattock, a fairly difficult way to plant bulbs. There is no guarantee that your late efforts will prosper.

When preparing the soil for any bulb planting, but especially for hardy subjects that will occupy the same spot for many seasons, always dig deeper than the bulbs are to be planted. Making sure the soil beneath a bulb is soft encourages good root development and promotes drainage from the crucial point right underneath the bulb. Should the bulb need to be deeper than you planted it, the soft base of earth will enable it actually to draw itself down farther into the soil by root action. This is one reason why I oppose the use of a tool called a dibble or of a tube bulb planter. Both are often touted for bulb planting, but neither is recommended by those who garden well. They are advertised as time-savers because you need only sink them into the ground; the dibble compresses the soil to make a hole, while the tube removes a divot of dirt. Neither action can possibly ensure soft, cultivated soil at the bottom of the hole. The only advisable use of either tool is in plots where the entire bed was deeply dug previously and is still friable and soft.

When planting, a small quantity of compost, peat moss or other humus can be mixed with the soil too. Fertilizer can be added then also, but sprinkle it at the bottom of the hole and cover with some soil to separate the bulb from the fertilizer beneath. These preparations may sound like extra bother, and certainly many gardeners do not follow all these directions; but you plant these hardy subjects only infrequently, and the only time you can improve the soil below the bulb (where some of the most important growing action takes place) is before planting. Bone meal above the bulb on the surface of the soil may take a long time to get down to the roots that use it. Cultivation above the bulbs can do more harm than good if shoots are damaged.

Unless rain comes within a few days after fall planting, it is advisable to give new bulb plantings a good sprinkling with a hose.

Summer annuals and bedding plants take over spot pictured in photograph on page 39.

This encourages the bulb to break dormancy and begin root development. It also helps settle the earth snugly around the bulb. Not only is this good for the bulb's general welfare; it also makes it harder for squirrels and other pests to locate the spots where you have just planted delectable new corms and bulbs.

Your bulbs will look much more at home in the garden if you plant them in clumps of a single kind rather than spotting them here and there. If you have two different kinds that bloom at the same time, you can interplant them with delightful results at blossomtime if they are nearly equal in height. Or you can place a smaller companion in front, as with blue chionodoxa and taller early daffodils. It takes some experience to fashion a garden where two hardy bulbs flower together in the same spot at the same time. Position has a great deal to do with it. A specific bulb may bloom two weeks earlier in a warm spot than in a frost pocket, so you

may have to experiment a few times with various kinds together. There is a section at the back of this book on companion planting that will be of aid for this kind of garden picture planning.

Having bloom that overlaps, however, is easy. Just choose a sequence of bulbs from early to late bloomers, and your garden will provide changing scenes all spring. Most of the hardy bulbs are through their display by June, but there are a few, described in the alphabetical section, that will extend the season into the months that follow. And of course you can overplant with annual flowers for later bloom, too.

Oddly enough, while positioning and the vagaries of a particular spring may affect when the first bulbs bloom, the later ones seem to equalize and flower at nearly the same time every year. If you want to do some serious experimenting with your garden, the next section has some helpful suggestions.

41

One of the first tulips to open is T. pulchella violacea, *a bright species from Asia Minor.*

Stretching Bloom Times

One of the most satisfying pastimes of the dedicated bulb fancier is to see how far bloom time can be stretched. This game has several ramifications.

At first one usually concentrates on making spring come as early as possible, but eventually it becomes a challenge to see how far into winter outdoor bulb flowering can be pushed, too. Then one seeks to extend the bloom season of a particular genus. Before long the real enthusiast is enmeshed in trying to prove that bulbs that ought not to be hardy can safely make it through the winter in his or her garden.

Some of the success of such techniques is predetermined by where you live. The climate of my home just north of Philadelphia is moderate by comparison with much of the rest of the United States. Our last frost usually comes at the end of April and our first

just before Halloween. Under these limits I have had some bulbs in flower outside during every month of the year, but, admittedly, not every year. Seasons vary, but the sequence is the same. Even if you live under much more severe climatic conditions than mine, you can push the boundaries of bloom both ways in comparison with your own neighbors.

Let's consider spring first, since its arrival does so much good for those of us in northern climes. Two factors interact in this game: Choose species that are naturally early bloomers and plant them in the most favorable spot. The exact species are often discovered by reading the small print in the catalogs. Snowdrops (*Galanthus*) are notoriously early flowering to start with, but the variety *G. elwesi* is earlier than any of the others and often so described. More years than not it shows buds in January *where I have it planted*. (The italics are important. On any property there are a variety of microclimates. In some the snow melts first, the frost is never as deep and the chilling winter winds never penetrate as much. These are the mild spots in which to put the earliest blooming things so as to advance their flowering, often by as much as several weeks.)

In the United States such microclimates are almost always south-facing. Houses, stone walls or boulders trap extra heat from the sun and afford wind protection; even a thick evergreen tree or shrub will create a small, warmer microclimate on its south side. Because cold air moves downward, it is warmer toward the top of a slope than at its bottom, and of course drainage is better too at the top, so the soil dries faster and warms up sooner. Position your early bulbs in a spot where all these factors are favorable, and no one will be able to beat you to the first bloom.

There are other bulbs that will bloom early if planted in one of these warm pockets. *Eranthus hyemalis* (winter aconite) usually is the second thing to flower for me. *Crocus imperati* has been the earliest to bloom of any spring-flowering crocus I have tried, but in the right situation the following are close runners-up: *ancyrensis, vernus* Vanguard, *susianus, chrysanthus* Zwanenberg Bronze. With catalog in hand to suggest some of these harbingers, do some experimenting on your own.

Among daffodils, the first good splash is most likely with hybrids from the *cyclamineus* group; February Gold is dependable. Among the hybrid tulips, one of the Kaufmannianas should be your choice. Several small species of both daffodils and tulips are even earlier, but it takes a lot of bulbs of these diminutive wildlings to get bold color.

At the other end of the year, the latest-blooming bulbs, such as autumn crocus and hardy cyclamen, should go into one of your microclimate winter resorts, too. This often prevents their blossoms being cut short by a sudden early freeze. Actually the technique

is more crucial for these late bloomers than for the early ones of spring which will always flower eventually because spring does come, even to the coldest places. Some of the autumn crocus are programmed to blossom so late in the season, however, that they cannot be grown in the far North. I boast that I have had *Crocus medius* in bloom after Thanksgiving and *C. sativus* at Christmas (once), but for me it is hard to keep *C. ochroleucus*, one of the very latest to flower. I blame this on the fact that it begins growing so late that the leaves are hardly up when hard frost arrives. My next patch of it is due to be set in the same niche where those first snowdrops have prospered.

The hardy cyclamen of both spring and fall should get this kind of treatment in all but the gentlest of climates, not so much to stretch their season as to ensure their survival. Many northern gardeners find that sternbergia requires the same attention. Like the autumn crocus, hardy cyclamen and sternbergia do their serious leaf development during the winter months, so they need a spot with a maximum of winter sun, a minimum of snow cover and least ground freezing—all criteria of a winter resort for plants.

Being successful with these just-mentioned bulbs is the first step in stretching your bulb year; next try plants that are not ordinarily considered hardy in your climate. They all need placement in one of the spots where your winter is somewhat milder. Experimentation is the only way to find out what you can do in your own little corner of the world. What is unusual in North Dakota differs greatly from what we consider unusual here in the Middle Atlantic states.

This phase of your season stretching is the least important to your garden, even though it may be the most fascinating. The bulk of the selections for any garden anywhere should always be plants that you know have a good chance of surviving. Otherwise, one really nasty winter could wipe out most of your decoratives. Nevertheless, these treasures that need pampering have great appeal, especially as your gardening grows more sophisticated.

Some experimenting is always interesting. Prices of many bulbs are not so high that you cannot afford to buy a few just on speculation. Plant and enjoy them one season if you can, then see what happens another year. Old gardeners who have lived a long time in one spot are a good source of advice, but don't be discouraged if they tell you something is impossible. You may be cleverer than they.

Here are two examples to illustrate my point about experimentation. Poppy anemones are not thought of as reliable much north of Washington, D. C., but my neighbor here has them in quantity. They are planted close to the house in a high, well-drained spot sheltered from the worst wind by the house itself on one side and a tight fence on the other. The site gets some afternoon shade, which suits the anemones after it grows warm, but the spot does not get the full brunt of winter.

In my more open garden another protective technique has so far worked, although I am well aware that a severe winter could wipe out the plants involved. By adding a heavy mulch of evergreen clippings and leaves, held down against the wind by some heavy branches, I have successfully wintered over two calla-lilies (*Zantedescia*). They are from the Crowborough Strain, supposedly hardier than others. Both were planted in pots the first spring and wintered over inside at a sunny window that first year to give them a good start at producing roots. The second spring I gently knocked them from the pots and planted them in the ground without disturbing the roots. Some mulch was placed as soon as fall frost had blackened the foliage and several inches more again after Christmas when our temperatures begin to drop. Imagine my delight when they first flowered that next May!

Mulching does two things. First, it lessens the alternate thawing and freezing so prevalent in a climate such as mine where snow cover is a sometime thing. This prevents root upheaval. A heavier mulch, applied before the frost has gone far into the ground, can prevent its penetrating as deeply. There is always the danger that rodents will take up winter quarters in such a spot. When they do, they usually dine on the roots or bulbs involved. But it is worth trying if you want to broaden your range of gardening possibilities.

Perhaps your problem or interest is to extend winter rather than summer. This could be because you live far enough south that many northern genera falter in the heat. You can still enjoy tulips in Florida if you will first give the bulbs a cold treatment. Precooled bulbs may be obtained from some sources, or you can do this yourself by placing the bulbs in your refrigerator (not the freezing unit) for about six weeks before planting. Make sure the bulbs do not get wet while being chilled.

With bulbs that require cool growing conditions, the southern gardener can help a little by planting them in more shade than ordinarily called for. Extra humus in the soil, adequate watering and a good mulch to keep the soil cooler help some too. Pebble mulches seem to keep the ground cooler and moister than any other kind.

Suppose that your weather is fairly divided between hot and cold, but you want to prolong the daffodil and tulip season because you hate to see spring end. First choose daffodils such as those from the *tazetta* and *jonquilla* divisions and tulips from the Darwin, bouquet and late double groups. These are naturally later-blooming. Then plant them in exposed situations—an open bed on the north side of the house, for example. Make sure it has adequate sun for the all-important foliage maturing, however. Some shade in late afternoon from a bush or tree helps prolong bloom too, but you will have to do some careful checking at various times of day because these bulbs are not shade-lovers. A frost pocket if well drained is ideal for such purposes. You can locate these spots in early fall by noticing

Colchicum Water Lily, a double hybrid, brings color to the autumn garden.

where marigolds first show frost damage on their foliage or by watching where the first frost rime shows on the ground longest in the morning.

As a gardener you may have simpler desires than I have been describing. Maybe you want merely to have daffodils and tulips for as long as possible in the spring. The easiest way to satisfy this want is to choose different classes of both bulbs. If you order some that are naturally early-flowering and some that have built-in later-flowering genes, you can plant them in the same garden and prolong your flowering season some months with no other action.

For many summer-flowering bulbs, you can stretch the season by starting them early inside in pots. Caladiums and tuberous begonias are good examples. With others, such as gladiolus, you can stagger blooming by when you plant them. Some glads can go in the ground as early as it is warmed up and then at two-week intervals for a month or more, depending on your first fall frost. Catalogs of gladiolus specialists note the number of growing days needed before flowering. By choosing varieties with different maturity times, you can have bloom over a longer period, too.

If all this sounds more complicated than you want your gardening to be, there is an even easier way to stretch the season for your bulb flowers. Simply plant a few new things each year. Read beyond the first pages of the bulb catalog, which are usually devoted to tulips, daffodils and hyacinths. Look under miscellaneous bulbs to make some new friends. As I write this the calendar is well into the third week of June. Most of the bulbs of spring are long gone, and annuals are taking over their places. But there is still color from the golden *Allium moly* and its rosy relative, *A. ostrowskianum*. Both are as undemanding as any bulb you could plant, giving you a colorful reward for pennies and a few minutes of planting.

In woods daffodil bulbs are planted in clumps of a single variety to make best showing.

Naturalizing with Bulbs

Some strange notions exist on how to naturalize bulbs. One suggests that you throw a handful of crocus corms over your shoulder on the lawn and then plant them wherever they happen to fall—presupposing that you can find them all. It may well be that in its native habitat the crocus is found on grassy slopes, but you can be sure that it is neither the lush greensward of a lawn nor a spot mowed constantly from spring to fall.

Here in temperate Pennsylvania we begin cutting lawns in late April when the crocus foliage is still growing. Keeping a section unkempt until the crocus leaves mature does nothing for the appearance of a small property. And in competition with lawn grasses, the crocus corms cannot reach their true potential. Rather, plant your crocuses in the foreground of the garden where they can increase and prosper. In a few years even a dozen corms will multiply to provide

46

a splashy note of color where it can be most appreciated.

Throwing the bulbs in that casual manner is touted as a way to get an informal-looking planting. All you need remember is not to put them in a straight line. An interesting effect can be achieved just as easily by concentrating the bulbs in one grouping and then planting a few here and there off to the edges. In time natural increase will fill in the whole area, but those few on the periphery will make the design more irregular.

Until you have seen how crocus can increase and flower under these kinder conditions, you have not used them to their peak possibility. Almost any bulb can be similarly used. It will take fewer individual bulbs of some larger-flowered varieties to create the appearance of a flowing colony than with the smaller bulbs, but the technique is the same.

Fall crocuses need overplanting to set their flowers off to best advantage, but the spring types (and all other bulbs that blossom with accompanying foliage) are better left to grow alone if you are trying to get maximum increase to make opulent-looking groups. You can put a shallow-rooting annual atop them if the garden design requires it, but in many cases a good mulch is sufficient.

Being taller and more robust, the larger classes of daffodils can adapt to being planted in grassy areas if there is no mowing done until at least the end of June, so that the foliage can complete its entire cycle of growth before being cut off. Such areas should never be fertilized with high-nitrogen mixtures or treated with herbicides for weeds.

When planting initially in such a site, place the individual bulbs of big daffodils at least a foot apart to allow for natural increase and years of bloom before division is a necessity. You will find that the resulting picture has much more substance if you buy labeled naturalizing mixtures. Plant all of one kind in a colony by itself. White groups here and there heighten the effect. Those daffodils with white perianths and reddish cups are especially effective for this kind of accent.

Done on a large scale, such plantings do create pretty effects in April, but they need to be confined to spots where the uncut grass can be ignored. Much lovelier scenes are possible in areas where there are high deciduous trees with plenty of leaf drop. There the daffodil foliage does most of its ripening before the trees cast too much shade. The natural leaf mulch prevents weeds and grass from competing with the daffodils, and increase is usually much better. Flower size is maintained for more years, too.

Even a small copse of only a few trees can be decorated this way, with bulb planting kept to the eastern, southern and western fringes of the trees. Ferns and real shade-loving plants can go on the northern side of the copse.

If you are starting with small trees, keep the lower branches trimmed out so that sunshine can enter. What you need to remember is that the daffodils are not woodland dwellers; they need a good dose of sun to mature the foliage if they are to bloom well in succeeding years. Early fall planting, which is recommended for daffodils, makes it easier to site the bulbs. The tree leaves will still be there to indicate where areas of too deep shade exist.

Real woodland bulbs belong in the shadier spots. Jack-in-the-pulpits, wood-hyacinths, trilliums, European fritillarias, Solomon-seal and its relative, smilacina, are better choices for such areas.

In truth, if you were naturalizing daffodils, crocuses and tulips botanically, you would be more likely to pick a rocky outcrop on a slope where the soil is poor and the drainage sharp. Such a spot would more closely approximate what these bulbs would find in their native lands, although the many man-made hybrids have been selected partly to do well in kinder situations. With boulders at their back, many such flowers are shown to perfection. Interspersing with ground-hugging junipers and mulching with pebbles would make such a garden nearly maintenance-free as well as neat in appearance. It would not need to be on a large scale to be effective. Most of the little bulbs are made to order for rock gardening, incidentally.

Water is a lovely accent in a natural scene, but great care has to be exercised when adding bulbs to such a spot. A swift-rushing stream that stays within its banks or a small pond whose water supply can be controlled is no problem. Confine your bulb plantings to the higher ground, and the water will merely reflect and double the beauty you create.

Wet lowland ponds or streams that often overflow and leave puddles for days are not places for most bulbs, however. Certainly not for the daffodils and tulips of the Mediterranean, which revel in hot baking during the summer and rot if they spend the winter in standing water. An occasional flooding that quickly disappears may actually benefit the area, but boggy land is not for most bulbs. You can put them in a low spot only if drainage is quick.

There are a few bulbs that do manage to grow well in areas where the soil is moist though not wet. Claytonia, camassia, Jack-

Colonies of contrasting spring crocus can be naturalized in even the smallest garden.

in-the-pulpit, some erythroniums and mertensia are good choices. Some summer-flowering tropicals also like such a home if there is sufficient sun. Canna, caladium, zantedeschia and hymenocallis are some to try. They will not, of course, winter over in the North outside.

What all this is meant to suggest is that naturalizing does not mean putting bulbs into any circumscribed habitat. It may be a woodland or a sun-baked spot and still qualify. And it does not need to be a large area. An estate such as Winterthur near Wilmington, Delaware, stretches for many acres. You can duplicate one of its corners on your own property by placing some azaleas beneath a few trees, mulching well and then introducing some bulbs here and there on the sunnier fringes.

If your budget is small, spread your expenditures and your planting over the years. A dozen of one type of daffodil, 25 endymion, several dozen of different crocus, 50 scillas—none of these represents a large expense. And each year the plantings will be increasing by themselves. A good mulch of wood chips in such a spot pays for itself many times over. Everything from trees and azaleas to the bulbs themselves grows better, and your time will not be devoted to constant weeding.

I stress the mulching and the combination of trees and shrubs with the bulbs because for the ordinary property you get much more for your time, money and effort if you make garden areas that are connected, rather than a series of small, round beds or even long, thin borders. That such a spot eventually becomes what appears to be a naturalized setting is merely a bonus. Eliminating the trimming alone around a lot of little beds is reason enough to garden this way. Try such a garden in the corner of a small property, and you will be delighted with the results. So will your neighbors. These areas need very little extra care.

And for most of us such a planting is much more satisfactory than the meadow of the poets ablaze with golden daffodils for a few

Mertensia is traditionally a favorite for damp, deciduous woods.

weeks but unkempt for many months. Only the largest estate can afford so much space for such a short display.

If you have a large woods already, the naturalized garden where trees and plants live together is much easier. The backbone of the garden exists already. Introduce some shrubs, particularly evergreen types, to create more interest. It may be necessary to thin some of the trees if the growth is too thick. Those that are left will grow the better because they are not crowded.

If you desire, pathways can be cleared for easier enjoyment. Make them wide enough for at least two abreast. Old logs are good for outlining the path, wood chips ideal for the actual walkway. With plenty of leaves, the chips may not even be necessary. Clear out the brush along the paths.

Now you can begin to plant your bulbs. Site them so that they get some sun and so that you can see them from nearby seating areas, windows or a turn in the path. It makes little sense to hide them.

Remember that in practice a "naturalized garden" is an all-encompassing term. Almost any garden in which plants meet the site's demands and which blends in harmony with the surrounding area might truthfully be termed "natural."

49

THE HARDY BULBS

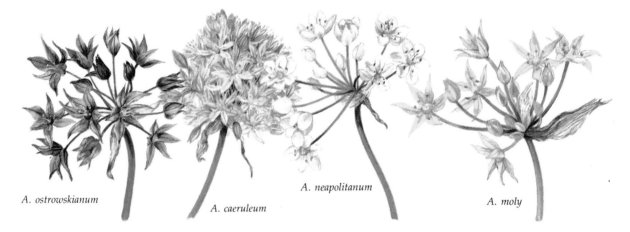

A. ostrowskianum

A. caeruleum

A. neapolitanum

A. moly

Allium

ORNAMENTAL ONION

No good cook would want to operate without onions in the larder, and the knowledgeable gardener feels the same way. Chives (*Allium schoenoprasum*), with their short, fluffy, pinkish-lavender blossoms, actually are pretty enough to be planted in the border as well as in the vegetable garden. From a practical viewpoint, however, cutting the aromatic leaves to add to salads, soups and omelets discourages good flowering and makes the plants look ragged periodically.

However, there are many other alliums highly recommended for decorative purposes. The foliage of all has an onion smell when bruised, but this is no drawback to the eye. Almost all like full sun and will thrive in any well-drained soil. The umbels of bloom,

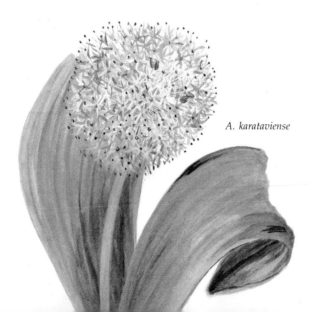

A. karataviense

whether fresh-cut or dried, are favorites of flower arrangers. Various species of *Allium* are native to almost every part of the northern hemisphere.

Most useful for the gardener are those species that stay under 12 inches tall. These are lovely in a rock garden or in the forefront of a spring garden. Most species have fairly long, narrow foliage, but *A. karataviense* puts forth two oval leaves that are broader than an inch at the center. They nearly hug the earth; the large umbel of silvery-lavender flowers seldom exceeds six inches. The North American *A. tricoccum* has wide spring leaves also, but they fade away before the small cluster of white flowers appears in summer. Known as wood leek or ramps, it wants half shade and looks best in flower arising from a light ground cover such as May phlox or wild ginger (*Asarum canadense*).

Among other American species, *A. cernuum* bears nodding lilac flowers one foot high in summer, and *A. stellatum* bears upright rose umbels in autumn.

A. ostroskianum wants full sun, and its bright pink umbels are eight to 12 inches high above rather insignificant foliage.

Among the taller-growing alliums, *A. caeruleum (A. azureum)* is a favorite because its small summer blossoms are pure cornflower blue. It may grow as tall as 26 inches. The foliage is grassy but not particularly sightly. For that reason it is a good idea to place it behind some other plant. It is wise also to mark well your clumps of thin-leaved alliums lest you weed them out, thinking they are grass or the pesky wild garlic, a common weed found in many cultivated gardens.

Some other easily located alliums are *A. rosenbachianum*, with large purple-violet umbels three feet tall; *A. schuberti*, with rose-red flowers one to two feet; and *A. aflatunense*, with round purple-lilac umbels crowning stems to two and one half feet tall. *A. neapolitanum* and *A. cowani* both bear white flowers but are not as hardy as the others. *A. giganteum* may reach four feet, with large violet balls that are highly prized for bouquets. It is best planted at the back of the border since the plant is ungainly.

Some alliums, such as *A. tuberosum*, spread too quickly for the small garden, but most of those offered in bulb catalogs are well worth trying, especially those that blossom in summer when bulb flowers are in relatively short supply.

For the half-shady garden no allium is better than the yellow-flowered *A. moly*. Its foot-high flat umbels come in late spring and are a clear, bright gold. It does well in sunny spots, too, but its ability to flower and increase under less light endear it to the shady gardener. Make sure it gets about half a day of good light so it will prosper. The best planting I ever had was situated on the eastern edge of a garden of dogwood trees. With their limbs trimmed high to let the sun in, this allium got a healthy dose of light all morning, and its gold lent a sparkling note to a garden that otherwise held somewhat subdued colors. Known as lily leek, *A. moly* was given all sorts of miraculous properties in ancient times; it is still hard to beat as a brightener for an overcast day.

While most alliums will increase by offset bulbs, they are also quite easy to propagate by seed. I had long coveted the native American *A. stellatum* of the Midwest. Like many other American bulbs, it has not been given entry in the lists of the Dutch bulb growers, and wildflower specialists have ignored it, too. Finally, I was able to locate

A. giganteum

seeds. To my delight nearly every one germinated, and I shall soon have a fine stand of it. Blooming as it does so late in the season, it is a real treasure, but it is a spreader. Put it in a spot where it can do no harm.

Rock-garden catalogs contain some lovely short-stemmed alliums. From western North America are *A. drummondi* (lilac), *A. geyeri* (rose) and *A. acuminatum* (pale pink). Asiatic species include *A. farreri* (red purple), *A. senescens* (pink) and *A. sikkimense* (deep violet). None of these charmers exceeds 12 inches; many are shorter.

PLANT: two to five inches deep, two to four inches apart, in ordinary, well-drained soil; half to full sun.

A. schoenoprasum

A. blanda

Anemone

HARDY WINDFLOWER

Known as windflowers wherever they are native in the northern hemisphere, these relatives of the buttercup family number some fine perennials among their botanical listings, but here I am concerned mainly with those that have tubers and thus qualify as bulbs. Several half-hardy representatives are described in the tender-bulb section. Those to be considered here are winter hardy and can be planted safely in the fall and left in place for years of bloom.

A. blanda is called the Grecian windflower and was introduced into commerce in 1898, after being discovered in Asia Minor. *A. al-pennina,* which is native to the mountains of southern Europe, has been known horticulturally since 1575. Both have color forms in blue, white and pink, but recent hybridizing has concentrated more on the *blanda* varieties. Larger named forms in white, pink, magenta and blue are sold.

Both groups make mounds of dainty foliage in early spring, with daisylike flowers a few inches in diameter and from three to 12 inches high. The centers of all color forms are full of golden stamens, adding to the daisy effect. Inclement weather or dusk causes the flowers to close, so they are well able to protect themselves from even a late snowstorm. A colony stays in bloom for many weeks.

Where late spring and summer are hot, plant them in half shade so that the foliage will continue growing as long as possible. They do best in a humusy soil and should not want for water while the leaves are green. Since the foliage is delicate and almost fernlike, the plants are still attractive after bloom is over. Blue or white forms of chionodoxa and squill flower at the same time and make a beautiful companion planting either in separate groups or interspersed with one another. As with many bulbous subjects, these anemones look much more opulent if planted in colonies of a single color. Those placed in a sheltered spot will blossom weeks before those in a colder location, so it is possible to have them in bloom over a long period by planting in different exposures.

Among the blue forms, there is not a great deal of difference; all can be depended on to give a nice spread of lavender blue in the forefront of the garden. Several newer color selections in other hues are worth mentioning. White Splendour has larger flowers than the others and lends a cheerful tone to the spring garden because it looks for all the world like a miniature white daisy—a welcome note so early in the season. Radar has flowers much nearer red than the other pink forms, plus a white eye surrounding the yellow stamens in the center. Any variety with pink flowers is novel, however, since this color is hard to find among the early blossoms of spring. Plant it near a path where you can readily appreciate it.

Be careful what you plant with or alongside these anemones. It is important to keep the foliage growing as long as possible to ensure bloom another year, and they are so small that there is danger that some more burgeoning perennial will overshadow them. Where the anemones do not have to compete with other plants, they often will seed themselves freely. For that reason I try always to keep a good humusy mulch around them. This obviates extensive weeding and gives the tiny developing new anemones a chance. With this technique it is possible to create a thrifty colony in a few short years. Such an establishment is particularly pretty in front of shrubbery.

In climates where intense cold and deep frost are not winter factors, the poppy anemones (page 151) can also be handled as hardy plants. They are much more spectacular than these smaller cousins.

The strange-looking tubers of anemones should not remain out of the ground a minute longer than necessary, so plant immediately after your order arrives. Because of the time lapse between digging and shipping, it is wise to soak the tubers in a saucer of water overnight to plump them out before planting. Incorporate some peat moss into the soil where they will grow, too. Some rootlets should be evident to show which side is down, but, if in doubt, plant them on their sides.
PLANT: two to three inches deep, four inches apart, in humusy soil; half shade.

A. pulsatilla and *A. patens* are both known as pasqueflowers and have taproots rather than tubers. Both have purple and white forms and fluffy seed capsules. The lacy foliage stays green all summer, which adds a special distinction to their use. Since the flowers are quite spectacular but only a few inches high, they belong on the edge of the garden where they will not be overlooked. Try them in front of early yellow daffodils for a charming contrast.
PLANT: either in early spring or fall, with the crown about one inch deep in a fairly dry, sunny spot.

Anemonella
RUE ANEMONE

Native to the eastern United States, *Anemonella thalictroides* is perfect for the front of even the smallest shady garden. It needs good light or partial sunshine to do its best. In spring it produces a myriad of small white flowers above dainty leaves six to eight inches tall.

The diminutive tubers may be obtained from wildflower specialists. Rue anemone spreads by seeds, too, and it does not take long to make a generous stand. Bloom extends over a long period in the spring, and the leaves remain in decorative condition for much of the summer. It is a superb choice for the border of any garden where there is some afternoon shade and moist soil rich in humus content.

Rare double and rose forms are also available from wildflower specialists and worth every penny of their cost. Often you will notice that some plants of a large stand have semidouble petal structure, but the true doubles do not occur with much frequency. Those that are sold as doubles must be propagated vegetatively. Increase of the double forms is very slow because there is usually no seed formed. It would be wise to protect a planting of the rarer forms both from rabbits that might eat the foliage and from rodents that eat the tubers.
PLANT: one to two inches deep, two inches apart, in humusy soil; half shade.

53

Anemonella thalictroides

Arisaema

JACK-IN-THE-PULPIT

Here is one bulb that revels in a damp site. Every American child should have a chance to hear Jack "talk." This is caused by gently rubbing the bottom of the flower between two fingers. The hood acts as a sounding board for the complaints of the tubular spadix inside.

A. triphyllum is the typical plant of the eastern North American woodlands, but there are several other species. All have more or less similar leaves divided into three leaflets. Colors of the hooded flowers are various combinations of green, white and purple. The swamp Jack (*A. pusillum*) is seldom taller than one foot and grows in wet, mucky sites, while the others need a damp, humusy soil. In rich soil and part sun they may reach two feet. Clusters of bright red berries are borne in the fall. The green dragon (*A. dracontium*) requires less moisture and has an even stranger flower, with a long green tube extending some inches beyond the green bract. It produces a compound leaf and has orange berries.

Some call these plants Indian turnip, but the tubers contain a potent acrid property that is irritating. Never handle them with bare skin. Food faddists list these as a possible wild edible. Before use, they require preboiling to get rid of the same property that makes handling them so uncomfortable. I can still remember an adventure with them as a child. My hands felt as if impregnated with glass wool for several days. Since our wildlings need all the protection they can get, I think it is foolish for anyone to gather them for the purpose of eating anyway.

Common Jacks will prosper in areas that are quite moist. You can find they do not flower in the garden. Usually this is owing to lack of enough water during the summer. For good growth they need a deep, woodsy soil and a spot where the water table is fairly high or where you can give them extra water. PLANT: five to six inches deep, eight to 12 inches apart, in rich humusy soil; part shade.

Begonia evansiana

Begonia
HARDY BEGONIA

Native to Java, China and Japan, *Begonia evansiana* is worth trying at least as far north as New York City. It produces plants two feet high, with leaves that resemble those of tuberous begonias. Sprays of small pink flowers, much like those of the fibrous begonia, appear in late summer. A rare white form also exists. It is a splendid choice for the shady garden where earlier-blooming plants made a spring show.

Mark the planting site, because the hardy begonia is often late in emerging. It needs some wind protection. The small bulbs are offered in spring catalogs, but the tiny stem bulbils that form in fall can be planted immediately.

An eastern location that gets morning sun is the best choice for successful growing, and this begonia will spread into large patches. Because the large leaves are veined with red, a planting is decorative even when not in flower. Bloom here is in September. Where frost comes early, treat it as a potted plant.
PLANT: in spring one to two inches deep, six inches apart, in humusy soil; half shade; or pot in the North.

Belamcanda
BLACKBERRY-LILY

Prized for its loose sprays of spotted orange blooms in midsummer, *Belamcanda chinensis*, an iris relative, is popular also for dried arrangements because its seed pods split open when ripe and resemble blackberries. Though a native of China, it is found growing wild as an escape in the eastern United States.

Like the iris, blackberry-lily grows from rhizomes that multiply and spread, so allow for this in the initial spacing. The fanlike foliage is at least 12 inches high, and the flower stems may be two to three feet tall. A rarer yellow form, as well as hybrids in yellow and orange tones, are available now from mail-order nurseries.

Blackberry-lily may be planted either in the spring or fall. It is a splendid foil in front of the tall scapes of galtonia that bloom at the same time.

The flowers of this plant do not last long when picked, so it is more sensible to let it go to seed. Such action does not seem to harm the plant itself. Keep a careful watch in late summer and pick the sprays just as the pods begin to open. Dry upright in a container until all pods are open, then use as a striking jet-black note in dried bouquets.
PLANT: about one inch deep, in rich, well-drained soil; full sun.

Belamcanda chinensis

Bletilla striata

Bletilla
HARDY ORCHID

Bletilla striata, sometimes listed as *Bletia hyacinthina*, is a half-hardy orchid with a tuberlike pseudobulb and small pinky-lavender flowers in late spring. They are ten to 20 inches high and resemble cattleyas. The plant needs moisture while growing but cannot stand constant wetness. Best planted in the spring. It will spread into nice clumps where frost does not go deeply into the ground.

In a protected spot bletilla is hardy at Philadelphia; in colder areas treat as a house plant. In warm latitudes give semishade; on its northern limits it needs more sun. Filtered afternoon shade is best. A rare white form exists.

PLANT: four inches deep, six inches apart, in well-drained, humusy soil; sun to shade.

Numerous other terrestrial orchids are also fairly hardy. *Pleione limprechti* from Tibet is pink and white, four to eight inches high, needs a sandy loam and semishade; it is a doubtful choice for very cold climates. Many beautiful North American orchids are perfectly hardy but have special requirements not likely to be met in the ordinary garden. The easiest to cultivate is the yellow lady-slipper (*Cypripedium calceolus*).

Brodiaea
CALIFORNIA-HYACINTH

These natives of the western United States are interestingly varied. The flowers, which are borne in umbels, may be bell-shaped or starry in a wide range of colors and heights. The grassy foliage often disappears before flowering begins. For this reason, plant in groups and leave undisturbed; a sparse ground-cover companion is recommended.

Brodiaeas do much better in the Pacific states and the South but are a valuable addition to rock gardens if their special needs can be met. Many catalogs list them only in mixture, but wildflower specialists in the West offer various species separately. Seed of many species is more often available than bulbs; sometimes the bulbs are offered only by color.

In northern climates the brodiaeas are better treated as half-hardy bulbs. You can pot them either for summer bloom outdoors or for indoor flowering. In the latter case, treat much as for freesias. It is regrettable that American growers have not done more work with this lovely native.

PLANT: four inches deep, four inches apart, in dry, well-drained, gritty soil; full sun.

Brodiaea laxa

56

Calochortus

MARIPOSA-LILY

Actually the mariposas are only one of nearly 60 different calochortus native to western North America. Globe-tulip, fairy-lantern, butterfly-lily, cat's-ears, sego-lily and star-tulip are some of the popular names of the various species. *Mariposa* is Spanish for butterfly and refers to intricate markings of eyes and veins on the insides of the flowers, like that on some butterflies. Some species have interesting hairs inside the cups. Colors are varied, and bulbs are usually offered in mixtures.

There may be from one to many flowers in spring or summer. The slender stems may reach two feet and need other plants around them for support. Not easy to grow outside their natural area, they can be quite breathtaking in quantity. Give them a perfectly drained site with gritty soil and as little water as possible in summer. Alternate freezing and thawing are injurious. Shoots emerge very early, so a mulch is helpful. Full sun is advised for most temperate climates. They need water during early growth but then demand dry baking during the dormant period. Not an easy plant but very beautiful.

PLANT: three inches deep, three inches apart, in gritty, well-drained soil; full sun.

Claytonia caroliniana

Claytonia

SPRING-BEAUTY

In low wet spots in the eastern United States there are still great patches of this pretty little spring-blooming native. Downwind of such a colony, you will find the perfume quite noticeable. Two species are offered by many wildflower specialists: *C. virginica* has very thin leaves, while those of *C. caroliniana* are broader. Flowers of both are similar and bloom over a long period. There is much variation in the pinkness. While the plant prefers dampness in the wild, it adapts well to gardens. Buy the tubers rather than trying to collect them. Plants are about six inches high.

At Bowman's Hill State Wildflower Preserve we have both species planted quite close to each other. It seems likely they have been cross-pollinating, for there are seedlings appearing with leaves intermediate between the two. Were someone to subject these seedlings to selection, it is quite possible our gardens would be graced with a fine hybrid with better color and growth habit than either of the parents. Unfortunately, many native American plants have not been given this attention to date.

PLANT: two to four inches deep, two inches apart, in humusy soil; semishade.

Calochortus kennedy

Camassia cusicki

Camassia

INDIAN-LILY

Camas is another popular name for these North American natives. Western Indian tribes relished them as food, calling them quamash. All species are fine ornamentals for the cultivated garden.

This is one bulb that prospers in moister sites, although not in spots where water actually sits. It will take some shade but blooms best where there is at least a half day of sun.

For the gardener, height is an important consideration; the camassias require discussion in two groups. Because it has not been hybridized or carefully selected, the clan exhibits considerable variation in both color and height, even within the species.

Generally, the eastern *C. scilloides* and the western *C. quamash (esculenta)* produce airy spikes of blossoms 12 to 18 inches high. The eastern one is a lighter blue than the western, which is often an electric color. Both reproduce rapidly into clumps and are excellent for naturalizing in rich meadows. The foliage is insignificant and the plants go dormant quite quickly after bloom, so they are easy to work into any garden situation. Separate the bulbs every few years for best bloom. They also spread by seeding themselves.

Around my birdbath I have a planting of the western species, which is often called bear grass in its native haunts. Because the bath is hosed out almost daily during the summer, I wondered whether the camassia could survive in such a spot. Obviously, the bulk of the extra water falls on the bulbs during the time when they are dormant, but it does not seem to bother them in the least. They have increased to the point of choking out themselves. I can recommend this as one bulb that can take a lot of moisture without damage.

Two western species are much taller, often producing flower spikes three to four feet high. They rise above fairly large basal leaves. *C. cusicki* is a lavender blue and C.

Camassia quamash

Chionodoxa
GLORY-OF-THE-SNOW

This early-spring flower's common name is the English translation from the Greek—a well-deserved appellation, for they often brighten a late snowfall. Chionodoxas are native to mountainous regions of Crete and Asia Minor and very hardy. Most selections offered are in shades of blue, and some have a white eye. There are also a pure white form and several pink ones, of which Pink Giant is particularly good. It and the blue *C. grandiflora* are larger in every sense than other species, which seldom exceed five inches in height. Flowers face outward; increase by seeds and offsets is good. Foliage is unobtrusive.

Like all these small bulbs, the chionodoxas are much more effective if used in colonies of a single species or variety. In the case of this genus it is not only a question of pure color as it is with many others. There seems to be some variation in time of flowering between the various chionodoxas. Thus a planting of mixed chionodoxas may bloom over a longer period, but the effect is likely to be spotty.

Glory-of-the-snow is an excellent choice for planting in front of the earliest daffodils such as February Gold and other *cyclamineus* hybrids.

PLANT: three inches deep, two inches apart, in colonies of one color; sun.

leichtlini usually a lighter blue. White forms of both exist, and they have greenish tinges that are most striking in arrangements. There is also a rare semidouble white.

All forms benefit from extra watering during bloom and light fertilizing during the growing period. If bloom falls off, it is a sure sign that they need dividing and replanting. It may also be a signal that tree shade is encroaching on them. Since they bloom in May, the foliage is much more likely to suffer from lack of enough sun than earlier-blooming bulbs that are likely to be going dormant by the time the trees are in full leaf. Filtered afternoon shade helps prolong the blossoming period, however, so it is worth a little extra trouble to position them for optimum growth. The color of the blue forms is also likely to be much better when they are grown in partial shade.

If your larger forms of camassia do not begin to increase into vigorous clumps after a few years, the soil may not be rich enough. Give them extra water and liquid manure applied on the ground around them every week during the period of leaf development after flowering. They are much more effective in clumps rather than planted singly.

PLANT: four to five inches deep and at least ten inches apart for larger bulbs, less for smaller sizes, in moist, deep, humusy soil; full sun to half shade.

Forms of *Chionodoxa*

Colchicum Waterlily
in annual alyssum

Colchicum

Some catalogs list these fall-flowering plants as meadow saffron or as autumn crocus, but both names are misnomers and to be avoided. There are autumn-flowering true crocuses, and the dye, saffron, is collected from one of them. Colchicums form a wholly different genus that belongs to the lily family, while the crocus is part of the iris family. They are native to Europe and Asia Minor.

Colchicum flowers, particularly those of the hybrids, provide a fine splash of color in the garden during September and October. This is the time when summer flowers are faltering, so a hardy plant that comes into its own in the waning days of the season is a real treasure.

Unfortunately, most colchicums have two habits that make them difficult to work into the garden picture without some prior thought. First, they bloom without the presence of any leaves whatsoever, and the long flower tubes of many of the more spectacular hybrids look ungainly protruding from the bare earth. Second, the leaves, which appear in early spring and may be several inches wide, eventually grow as long as 12 inches for some types. Since they are floppy and do not dry off until late June, these leaves have to be reckoned with in the spring garden. The solution to the first problem is to use an appropriate ground cover as an underplanting for the flowers. If the companion plant is a substantial one, such as pachysandra, the second problem is solved also because the colchicum leaves can be tucked among the pachysandra as they begin to yellow. If a smaller ground cover is used, care should be taken as to actual placement of the grouping. Rather than planting the colchicums in the foreground of the garden, put them, perhaps, in the second row, behind a plant that blooms in spring but does not have a height of more than a few inches in fall. Arabis, clove pinks (*Dianthus plumarius*), saponaria and chrysogonum are a few plants that have medium height at spring flowering but are more mat-like by fall. If the colchicums are planted toward the back of such plants and the latter are then encouraged to grow over the colchicum planting, you can have the best of two worlds; the colchicum foliage will not be too untidy in spring and the fall flowers will have a green underplanting to set off their loveliness. Common thyme, *Phlox divaricata*, very dwarf forms of perennial candytuft (*Iberis*) and *Vinca minor* are other ground covers that make good companions for colchicums. Dwarf varieties of annual white sweet-alyssum are also excellent; their tiny flowers make a dainty foil for the colchicum blossoms. The alyssum will seed itself for years to come and will grow despite the spring bulb leaves of the colchicums, coming into its own later on.

Colchicums adapt very well to semi-naturalizing at the front of the shrub border or under high deciduous trees. There the spring colchicum leaves will get sun, but the fall flowers can benefit from filtered shade. If you live where autumn is still hot, try to give your colchicums afternoon shadow to prolong the blooms. These plants are also fine for the upper sections of a slope garden or a rock garden.

Once established, colchicums yield bunches of flowers from each corm over a period of time. The corms are available in late summer, so order as soon as possible and plant immediately on arrival. Advertisements suggesting that the naked bulbs be placed on a saucer to bloom in the house

Colchicum's spring foliage

are misleading; such flowers are poor and ugly. The corm belongs in the earth; from there it will provide color for years. The corms are also the source of the drug colchicine; they are too poisonous to be left haphazardly in a plate.

Of them all, I love best the tiny double *C. autumnale plenum* and the giant double hybrid Waterlily. Because they produce many graceful blossoms on stems of differing lengths, these tend to face themselves down to the earth and are quite presentable without a ground cover. Such a companion planting, however, helps protect the flowers from being spattered or beaten down in heavy rain.

The purply-pink *C. byzantinum* and the rosy-carmine *C. speciosum* have larger flowers than either the lavender or the white single forms of *C. autumnale*, but the latter are delightful for naturalizing and seldom exceed six inches in height.

Some colchicums have tessellated petals (that is, checkered with two colors), usually combinations of white and purple. *C. agrippinum* and *C. sibthorpi* are the most often

C. autumnale

61

offered. Lilac Wonder and The Giant are hybrids with striking flowers.

To generalize, the tessellated colchicums are not as hardy as other types and bloom later, too, so that their flowering may be cut short by frost in more northern gardens. If you are in doubt, start with the other types first to see whether your climate is to their liking. If you can grow the early autumn crocus, you can certainly succeed with some of the colchicums. Most years in my garden, for example, the hybrid colchicum Waterlily shows color before there is any sign of a fall crocus.

I cannot say enough in praise of Waterlily. As the September days begin to shorten and the nights grow nippy, my heart falters just a bit at the thought that winter is not too far away. And then one cool morning I will walk up the path from the drive and notice that the first tips of the Waterlily buds have broken through the earth. The flowers are a pinky lavender, just the shade to gladden my sense of color, which sometimes is a bit overwhelmed by the strident tones of fall foliage. Underplanted with lots of sweet-alyssum, a mature planting of Waterlily is

magnificent. A single bulb may produce six flowers at once. Moreover, this hybrid is a vigorous multiplier. It does not take long to increase a few bulbs into a really breathtaking planting. About every five years or so it is best to dig them up and separate the clumps as described in the text following. This makes for maximum flower production. If you finally run out of places to put your increase, there is no more lovely gift you can give a gardening friend.

Neat gardeners do not take to colchicums too warmly because of that blowsy spring foliage, but Waterlily is the best of the lot. Being double, it is sterile and so does not produce seed. Thus, it does not have as bushy a leaf structure as some of the others. It is really no problem to live with the fountains of Waterlily foliage in the spring. They are a bright green and provide a verdant accent for a long time before beginning to droop and turn yellow. I have them in several spots along that walk I take many times a day. When they finally begin to dry off, it is easy enough to gather up the old leaves.

Colchicum autumnale amidst vinca foliage

Sometimes an early frost will cut short the display of flowers, but often new ones will appear afterward in Indian summer.

Oddly enough, the foliage of the colchicums seems to be very hardy. It is apparent early in the year. Since the leaves do all their growing in the spring, colchicum is definitely a better choice for fall flowers in more northern climates than either sternbergia or the fall crocus. Both sternbergia and fall crocus need good winter sunshine to produce enough foliage to restore the bulbs for another year's flowering. Persistent snow cover makes it hard for the winter leaves to do their work. So the colchicums may be more adaptable for such a climate. Try planting them a little deeper in a well-drained spot if you doubt their chances for survival. The deeper planting will also inhibit too early emergence of the foliage.

All colchicums look best when they are planted in groups of a single species. Most reproduce freely, so do not put them too closely together initially. When flowering falls off after a few years, owing to their being crowded, dig them carefully in early July after the foliage is browning but before it dries up too much to locate the corms. Separate them carefully and spread out to dry for a week in a cool, ventilated place, then replant immediately. If they are not planted early enough, the first year's bloom may be sparse, but they will make up for it in the following years.

Rodents do not seem to touch either the bulbs or the leaves, so colchicums are a good choice for those who have trouble with hungry pests. They are also particularly good to brighten up a semiwoodland garden where the bulk of bloom is always in the spring.

It is interesting to note that the drug colchicine has been used in the treatment of gout since ancient times and is utilized by breeders to change the chromosome count in plants.

PLANT: two to three inches deep, six to eight inches apart, in almost any well-drained soil; full sun to partial shade.

Convallaria
LILY-OF-THE-VALLEY

Everyone loves the fragrance of this springtime favorite. Species are native to Europe, Asia and North America. Pink-flowered forms are known, but the white bells are showier. The creeping rootstocks are usually planted in the spring, and a dose of dehydrated cow manure every winter helps flowering.

This is an excellent ground cover for under trees and shrubs where it receives filtered shade. If planted in full sun, lily-of-the-valley does not do nearly as well, and the leaves look dreadful by midsummer. What it wants is high shade and rich soil. Under those conditions it will bloom prodigiously and grow so thickly that few weeds can compete. Eventually the roots will be too thick. You can thin at almost any time of the growing year, but immediately after flowering is my choice. Water well afterward until the rootlets take hold again. (You can tell by how the leaves stand up in the heat.) The red fall berries are poisonous. PLANT: one and one half inches deep, four inches apart, in rich, humusy soil; shade.

Convallaria majalis

63

C. chrysanthus
Cream Beauty

C. susianus

C. chrysanthus
Blue Pearl

C. Pickwick

Crocus

WINTER- AND SPRING-FLOWERING

No flower is more beloved than the spring crocus. Depending on which varieties you plant and how warm the spot in which you put them, they bring color to the garden for several months. Almost all crocuses can be used for forcing in the house, too. They are natives of the lands of the Mediterranean and Asia Minor.

Space permits describing only a few of the hundreds of species and their hybrids cataloged by the Dutch growers. You cannot go wrong by planting any crocus. You can, however, cheat yourself of a wonderful display if you sentence your crocus to the lawn only. There they must compete with the grasses for nutrients, and often their leaves are mowed before they have finished the task of adequately restocking the corm with food for another year.

Instead, plant crocus in the foreground of the garden; it matters not what kind of home you give them. They are equally delightful in a postage-stamp garden or enlivening a huge perennial border. As long as the site is well drained and gets springtime sun, crocuses will flourish and increase. After a few years the corms increase prodigiously in these kind surroundings. Instead of having to dig them up, as is the case with larger bulbs, you can harvest your crocus bonus much more easily. Simply scratch gently at the surface of a mature planting in late spring, after the grassy foliage has begun to dry up but while it is still in position as a marker. The extra corms that have formed on top of the others will be readily at hand. Remove and replant, and the original stand will be good for some years more. Each year the blossom crop will be greater.

Some crocuses are described as bunch-flowering; they do literally produce many blossoms from each corm. Many may be cataloged as winter or snow crocus. The latter often are a full month or more earlier in bloom than are the larger Dutch hybrids.

64

Spring-flowering crocuses come in a wide range of colors. There are fine whites and creams, a host of yellows and oranges and every hue of violet, lavender and purple. There also are some striking bicolors. All are more effective if planted in groups of a single color rather than mixed.

The earliest crocus often opens a few flowers during winter thaws. Some good ones are *C. ancyrensis*, a bright yellow, and the lilac or lavender *C. imperati*, *C. sieberi* and *C. tomasinianus*. Cloth of Gold (*C. susianus*) has been in European gardens since at least 1587.

Many early crocuses belong to the *chrysanthus* group. Blue Giant, Blue Pearl, Cream Beauty and Goldilocks are just a few of the good ones. There are some bicolors in this group that are really outstanding. Zwanenburg Bronze combines dark yellow and bronze, Lady Killer white and purple. Advance is yellow inside and light purple and white outside.

Pickwick, pictured here, is just one of many large-flowered later crocus hybrids. There are others in every hue. It is also possible to buy crocuses in bulk, simply by color, for mass planting. Where you want a large swath of color, this is the cheapest way to buy them. Insist that they come in bags of a single color. Then plant them in large patches of one kind with a few straying into the next section. Such techniques make for a really eye-boggling effect when done in quantity.

In the rock garden crocuses seem very much at home. If you plant your groupings in patches that run vertically rather than horizontally, you can fashion what appear to be waterfalls of color on a slope. Place more bulbs at the top and taper to a thin dribble at the end. I suppose the literalist would prefer such plantings of crocus with blue tones, but the "waterfall" of golden flowers is just as effective.

PLANT: two to three inches deep, four to six inches apart, in well-drained soil; at least partial sun.

C. ancyrensis

C. tomasinianus

C. biflorus

C. chrysanthus
Zwanenburg Bronze

Crocus

AUTUMN-FLOWERING

At the other end of the growing year is another group of crocus. Within it are autumn-flowering members of the tribe. They are just as delightful as the earlier types, but the range of color is much more limited. There are no yellows in commerce and only a few whites. Unfortunately, these crocuses are not as hardy. In climates where winter comes early, probably only forms of *C. speciosus* can be recommended, and they should be planted in a warm, sunny spot.

Here in Philadelphia early fall often is still very hot, so I place my earliest-blooming autumn crocuses where they will get filtered tree shade in the afternoon to prolong the life of the blooms; the later crocuses are given warmer sites. All are in spots where they will get as much winter sunshine as possible. This last point is important because the foliage of autumn crocus develops during the winter. If your corms are to flower many seasons, the leaves must be encouraged to grow. Choose a spot where drifts of snow are not likely to stay.

The early bloomers tend to flower before there is any foliage visible, so the use of a

ground cover is indicated, as it is with the colchicums. These crocuses also have very long flower tubes, and the ground cover helps support the flowers. Armeria, *Dianthus plumarius*, common thyme and arabis are my favorite plants for this purpose. Fall crocus corms are available in late summer and should be planted as soon as received.

C. speciosus albus is a fine early white species. The numerous selections of *C. speciosus* are in shades of blue violet, more or less veined, with orange stigmata in the centers. *C. pulchellus* is similar. Another early one is *C. karduchorum*, a cup-shaped soft lavender. Both of these have white anthers. *C. zonatus (kotschyanus)* comes in shades of lavender with a yellow throat.

Any one of this group is a good choice to start with if you are not sure whether your climate is adaptable to the schedule of the fall crocus. Being early, they have the best chance. There is little to choose about the display of the various *speciosus* varieties, but there is some difference in time of flowering. If winter comes quickly in your neck of the

Crocus speciosus and its white variety amidst dianthus foliage

66

woods, this can be an important factor. The type and its white variety have always been the earliest for me, with *C. globosus* and *C. pulchellus* following in a few days. When you can find them, these bulbs are not expensive, so pop in a dozen of *C. speciosus* and see what happens in your garden. Then you can go on from there.

Those that bloom later definitely benefit from having a warm, protected spot as their home. This not only helps the flowers survive the colder weather, but it encourages the production of good winter foliage—a necessity if the crocuses are to prosper in future seasons. The leaves grow all winter, then dry up in the spring. If you have snow cover most of the winter, you can succeed with these crocuses only if you can put them in a place that is protected from the snow by an overhang or some other kind of obstacle. A windswept spot might work too, but it might also be too frigid for the leaves to survive. Here in Philadelphia snow comes and goes, so we do not have to worry as much, but I still make sure these winter crocuses are where they get direct winter sunshine.

Actually rabbits can be a greater problem with autumn crocus. They wreak havoc in springtime species too, but the results are much more serious with the autumn kinds. For one thing there is less to eat during the winter months, and so rabbits seldom miss anything tasty and green. If your autumn crocus plantings do not seem to last long, try protecting them from rabbits either with a small basket of chicken wire anchored against the wind or with a fence of evergreen branches that still contain good needles. Stick the branches firmly into the ground and make sure that you place them closely enough so they interweave. In a spot protected from the wind, just arrange the branches around the crocus. These techniques allow sunshine to reach the crocus but seem to foil rabbits.

C. sativus is the source of saffron, which is made from the large orange stigmata, gathered and dried. It was much prized in

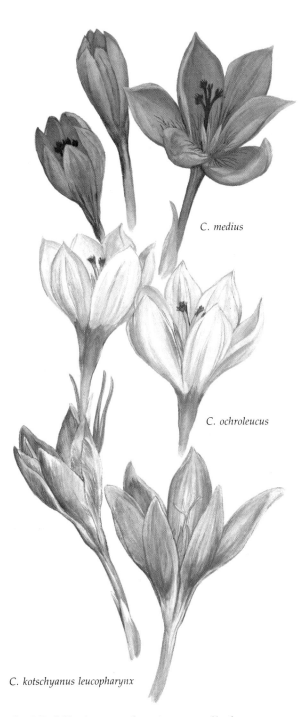

C. medius

C. ochroleucus

C. kotschyanus leucopharynx

the Middle Ages, when it was called vegetable gold. The flowers are variable in color but on the purple side.

C. medius, a fine purple, and *C. ochroleucus*, a tiny white, are among the later-blooming ones. *C. asturicus*, often cataloged as *C. atropurpureus*, is another good dark purple.

PLANT: two to three inches deep, four to six inches apart, in well-drained soil where they get maximum winter sunshine.

Cyclamen

HARDY FORMS

If you love the butterfly flowers of the florists' cyclamen, you will be fascinated by this tiny relative, called sowsbread in Europe. Except in old plantings where sheer numbers create color, this is one of those treasures that you must get on your knees to appreciate. The flowers are not even an inch across and are borne on slender stems only a few inches high. But they are similar in every other detail to the cold-tender beauties most of us keep in the house during the winter.

There are two main groups of hardy cyclamen. The easiest flowers in late summer and early autumn, the other in late winter and early spring. Where frost goes deeply into the ground or where there is constant snow cover, it is doubtful either can survive, but only experimentation will prove what the chances are in your climate. Try first *C. europaeum*, which seems to be the hardiest. Its rosy pink flowers are produced over a long period beginning often in July. Also fairly hardy, *C. neapolitanum* starts later and extends well after the first hard frost. *C. cilicicum* is considered less hardy.

Of the spring-flowering types the easiest to find is *C. repandum*, which is often called the ivy-leaved cyclamen. Its flowers vary from crimson and rose to white. (Most of the other hardy cyclamen also have white forms, but they are much rarer than those on the pink side.)

Another group of spring cyclamen are varieties of *C. orbiculatum*. You may find them cataloged as *C. coum*, *C. hiemale* and *C. atkinsi*. The latter is often considered a hybrid by experts.

All the hardy cyclamen I have grown have produced the lovely green and silver-mottled foliage in later summer and fall. It lasts all winter—a good reason to site these where there is shelter from the snow. Some autumn kinds flower before there are any leaves, but they soon appear to set off the last blossoms of the season. In early summer the leaves disappear for a short dormant period. Since cyclamen need a limey (alkaline) soil, I mulch my plants with marble chips. This keeps me from mistakenly digging there during the dormant period and should provide a leach of lime water to the tubers beneath. The addition of a light layer of rich compost during the summer when the leaves have disappeared is also a good idea.

Cyclamen may spread by seed where the site is to their liking. You will notice that the bud stems as they arise from the soil are often curled. The stems straighten during flowering, but then as the seed pod develops, the stem coils itself into a spiral that brings the seed close to the ground—an ingenious way to ensure survival. The tubers never divide. Rather, they grow larger, often quite quickly. From very old gardens there are tales of a single tuber weighing nearly a pound and many inches across. Such tubers may yield literally hundreds of blooms in a season. This is one reason to site your cyclamen carefully so they need not ever be disturbed. They need shade in hot weather, so they are a lovely choice for under deciduous trees. Be careful when planting; the slightly indented side with tiny rootlets is the top.

PLANT: one to two inches deep, six inches apart, in humusy soil with lime; part shade.

Cyclamen europaeum

68

Endymion

WOOD-HYACINTH

Most catalogs still list these May-flowering bluebells as *Scilla campanulata*, but the botanists have shifted them because of differences in the bulbs. Under whatever name you find them, they are a wonderful addition to a shady garden. In truth, they do very well in full sun, but since they bloom beautifully and increase well in open shade, they have become a favorite for that part of the garden where many other bulbous plants do not do as well.

There are two main types. *E. nutans* or *nonscriptus* is the famous English bluebell. The Spanish bluebell (*E. hispanicus*) is a somewhat more robust plant, and most of the named selections offered in catalogs are from its line. These often reach a height of 12 inches in full bloom. The Dutch bulb growers have produced several dozen named clones, but only a few are offered in America. Try to buy them by color choice and plant a single shade in groups. They are quite breathtaking when planted in great drifts among high trees, where the sun can filter through part of the day. Colonies of the blue forms are particularly lovely as an accompaniment to a planting of azaleas. In sunnier sites they are delightful in front of Darwin tulips.

Increase of wood-hyacinths is very rapid, but leave the bulbs alone until they form solid patches. Then transplant as soon as the foliage dies down in late spring. Forms with flowers in pink, blue, violet or white are available.

This is another bulb where a mixture is not nearly as effective as a planting of a single color. In many catalogs it does not make a bit of difference in price whether you order by color or the mixture, so you have nothing to lose by so doing. You will be pleased with the difference this small attention to detail makes in your garden.

I am fond of adding a patch of white endymion to either a planting of the red and yellow eastern North American columbine (*Aquilegia canadensis*) or to one of primroses. They bloom together, and the white bells of the endymion seem to make the bright colors of the other plants all the more vibrant. Endymion is also pretty in front of unfolding ferns. Where you are using these bulbs in a mass planting, do not place them any closer than a foot initially to save yourself extra work later.

PLANT: three inches deep, six inches apart, in well-drained soil; semishade.

Eranthis

WINTER-ACONITE

Natives of Greece and Asia Minor, these diminutive plants are treasured in gardens all over the world for the cheery note they bring to the dull days of late winter. In protected warm spots they often open their first flowers in February, keeping the snowdrops company. The golden-yellow flowers resemble buttercups, with a green ruff of bracts beneath to set them off. In bloom they are only a few inches high, but the finely cut foliage eventually reaches a height of ten inches.

Woodsy soil and partial shade are to their liking after the deciduous trees leaf out. Unfortunately the odd tubers are often too dry when they arrive. An overnight soaking in a saucer of water will restore their plumpness; then plant immediately. If you are not sure which side is up, plant them on their sides.

E. hyemalis is the most common form and best for naturalizing. *E. cilicica* blooms slightly later and has a bit taller stems. Their hybrid, *E. tubergeni*, is larger than either of the parents. Because it is sterile, the flowers last a long time, but for the same reason this form does not increase by seed. A hybrid selection, often called Guinea Gold, has par-

ticularly dark yellow flowers and foliage tinted with bronze. The hybrids are good choices for a small niche where space is limited, but the others, when left to their own devices, spread into lovely drifts. The leaves disappear by summer.

To help your aconites increase into a fine colony, give them a good mulch of leaf mold or small bark chips. This keeps down weeds and allows the seed to get a good hold. It takes about three years for a seedling to flower. It is also advisable to position eranthis so they do not need to compete with tree roots. This helps the leaves stay green longer, thus encouraging prolific flowering another season.

Early crocuses are charming with them, but confine yourself to white or lavender forms. I once planted a yellow crocus with some aconites, and the two shades were not pleasing to the eye. Do not put either crocus or snowdrops too close to the aconites, however. The eranthis foliage may reach a very wide spread at maturity, and this can smother the other bulb leaves.

PLANT: two inches deep, two inches apart, in humusy soil; semishade.

Eranthis hyemalis

Erythronium White Beauty

E. revolutum

E. tuolumnense

E. americanum

Erythronium
TROUT-LILY

Dogtooth-violet, adder's-tongue and fawn-lily are some of the many other common names for these lovely spring flowers. Excepting one species, all are native to North America. The exception is *E. dens-canis* of Eurasia, which is offered in color selections from white and pink through rose and many shades of violet. They adapt easily to gardens, but the species from western states are generally showier, and those from the lower altitudes are almost as easy as their overseas relatives. The American species need a slightly moister site in semishade; the *dens-canis* types seem to do well in almost any garden situation. Some species have marbled instead of plain leaves, some several flowers per stem.

Wildflower specialists offer many different American species, but a number are listed fairly often in regular bulb catalogs, too. Good ones to try: *E. tuolumnense*, from California, has bright yellow flowers on 12-inch stems, as does its hybrid, Pagoda; *E. White Beauty*, a natural hybrid from Oregon; *E. revolutum* and its hybrid, Pink Beauty; *E. hendersoni*, with lilac flowers; *E. californicum*, a creamy white; *E. grandiflorum*, a yellow from the Northwest; *E. albidum*, white and yellow, from the eastern states.

E. americanum, the most common species of the eastern states, is on the yellow side and a shy bloomer; it needs a much damper site but invariably produces more of its mottled leaves than flowers. Try placing a stone under the corms of this one to force bloom instead of bulb increase. This inhibits its habit of sending out runners underground to form new bulbs. In the wild the best blooming plants of this form are found often at the base of trees where big roots probably stop the wandering stolons.

Most of the western species do not have the stoloniferous habit and so tend to flower better. Give them a partially shaded site and deep humusy soil. Many produce more than one bloom per stem. Those that are considered to be of *E. revolutum* parentage will take much moister sites than the other western species, but they seem to adapt quite well. PLANT: two to four inches deep, four inches apart, in humusy soil; semishade.

71

Fritillaria

SMALLER SPECIES

Some very different flowers are grouped under this heading. The most widely planted are forms of *F. meleagris*, a European native that is variously called guinea-hen flower, dice-box, snake's-head or checkered-lily. Although there are several whitish selections, it is usually offered in shades of purple, more or less checkered. All produce one or two nodding bell-shaped flowers in April on slim stems 12 to 18 inches high. They do best in partial shade where the soil contains adequate humus and never becomes too dry. The purple forms show up best against a light background, such as a large stone or tree trunk. Few of the small Asian fritillarias are offered in the United States except for *F. camschatcensis*, which is also native to Alaska. It has nearly black flowers in May.

Several other Asians have lately entered American catalogs, but I have not yet tried them. *F. bithynica (citrina)* is described as being six inches high with one to three bells of citron overlaid with silver and the inside marked green. *F. crassifolia* reaches 15 inches, with a sturdy stem on which are large purple bells overlaid with jade green, which certainly ought to be interesting. Coming as it does from mountainous regions of Asia

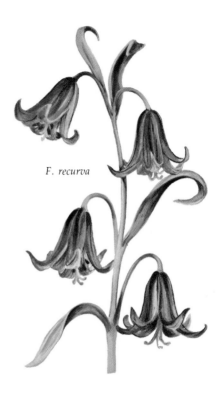

F. recurva

Minor, it should prove hardy. *F. persica adiyaman* is shown with large spikes of purple bells a good two feet tall. It is advertised as very hardy, but I am told it starts into growth early like the crown imperial. I suggest it too should have a location protected from morning sun.

PLANT: three inches deep, three inches apart, in humusy soil; partial shade.

Western North America is the home of many small fritillarias, some of which can be obtained from western wildflower specialists, as bulbs or as seeds. Not all are hardy or easy to grow. The best known is *F. pudica*, with nodding yellow bells; it does well in sunny rock gardens and is about eight inches tall. *F. pluriflora* has pinky-purple bells and is the adobe-lily of California. *F. recurva*, also from California, is called mission bells and may bear its scarlet-red bells 24 inches high. It needs a well-drained site with rich soil and is more likely to prosper in part shade. Mulch to prevent heaving of the soil in winter. These and other native fritillarias are challenging. More research needs to be done on their special needs outside of their native habitats.

PLANT: three inches deep, three inches

F. meleagris

apart, in friable clayey soil with not too much humus; sun to partial shade; a real attempt should be made to keep the bulbs as dry as possible during summer dormancy.

Fritillaria
CROWN IMPERIAL

Native to Iran and to the Himalayas, the crown imperials have been cultivated in European gardens since at least as early as 1665. This stately plant, a lily relative, makes a stunning accent in the spring garden, often three feet high, with large bells on top of a sturdy stem. Various horticultural forms may have flowers in shades of yellow, orange or red. All have large basal leaves, plus a surprising tuft of foliage on top of the flowers.

Oddly enough, the blossoms have a skunky odor, and so do the big bulbs that are scaled like a true lily. Folklore has it that a garden where crown imperials are planted will never be bothered by rodents. On poorly drained sites the bulbs often rot. Many gardeners plant the bulbs slightly tilted to prevent water from collecting in the scales.

Foliage appears very early. In cold climates try to position them where the first rays of the morning sun do not hit them to prevent frost injury. The foliage dies down fairly quickly after flowering; the plant likes a bit of lime. White trumpet daffodils are good companions.

PLANT: five to seven inches deep, eight inches apart, in rich, well-drained soil; full sun.

F. imperialis

Single and double forms of *Galanthus nivalis*

Galanthus

SNOWDROP

It is a thrilling experience to see snowdrops bravely opening their flowers in a midwinter thaw. Earliest of all is *G. elwesi*. Give it a warm, sunny spot where the snow melts first, and you may well have a welcome bloom even in January. Subsequent storms do not discourage the snowdrops. They emerge unscathed from their icy coats. *G. nivalis* is a slightly smaller and shorter species that does well in both sun and semishade. Its form with double flowers naturalizes well, too. Foliage is never messy and disappears quite quickly after bloom is over, so you can put drifts of snowdrops almost anywhere.

Often they are seen in spots that are shady after the leaves of the trees develop. This is all right, because the snowdrop is nearly finished for the season by then, but do not be misled into thinking that these are woodland plants.

PLANT: three inches deep, two inches apart, in any well-drained soil; sun.

Gladiolus

HARDIEST FORMS

Some varieties of this well-known summer flower will survive winters in the ground at least as far north as Philadelphia. Only a few are offered, mostly in shades of pink, rose or white, and they are usually either *G. byzantinus* or *G. segetum* or their hybrids. They are native to Europe rather than to South Africa, the home of the progenitors of most of the spectacular tender gladiolus hybrids. *G. tristis*, plus *nanus* and *colvillei* varieties, are also possible choices for this treatment. They are planted in fall and flower in June, the spikes are seldom taller than 18 inches and the flowers are small and widely spaced along the stem, delightful for bouquets. Replant every few years in the fall, because the new corms work their way to the surface.

Where winters are not too severe many other gladiolus will endure winter in the ground in sheltered spots. They are planted initially in the spring. A good much helps winter survival.

PLANT: three inches deep, six inches apart, in rich but well-drained soil; full sun.

Gladiolus byzantinus

Galtonia

SUMMER-HYACINTH

Only one species of this striking summer decorative is commonly available. *G. candicans* is known as berg-lily in its native South Africa. Sturdy stems, which may exceed four feet, support spikes of pendulous white bells. The long, glaucous leaves are borne mostly toward the bottom of the stem.

In colder sections these bulbs are planted in the spring and treated as a tender bulb. If this is indicated by your climate, dig bulbs after frost, cut off tops and store at 40° to 50°F. in peat or vermiculite to prevent drying out.

Here, near Philadelphia, they have proved winter-hardy over many years, but increase is slow. Take care that they do not want for water during the growing period, but make sure the site is well drained. A wood-chip mulch is helpful.

Used as a background accent, galtonia lends a fine, strong, vertical line to the summer garden. It is often grown behind the blackberry-lily, which makes a good companion to face the somewhat ungainly galtonia. They bloom at about the same time—late July and early August. The shoots emerge quite late in spring.

One of the nice things about this bulb is that the spikes never seem to need staking. If you consider the size of the bells, this is rather surprising until you notice how sturdy the stems are. Unfortunately, however, this strength gives them a less than dainty look. Thus they are best planted where other plants in front hide their lack of grace. Summer phlox and dwarf cannas in all the pink and red shades are quite effective companions. Tall cannas can be used alongside the galtonia at the back of the border. In the United States the bulbs are most usually offered in the spring, so they can be planted at the same time as the cannas.

PLANT: three to four inches deep, six to 12 inches apart, in garden loam; mulch well; full sun.

Galtonia candicans

75

Hyacinthus

HYACINTH

Not all hyacinths produce the sweet perfume so closely associated with their name, but those that do are treasures to be planted beside the path or porch for an early-spring delight. The others are still a pleasure for eyes weary of winter's gray tones. Wherever you put them, do not line them up like soldiers on review. Instead, plant them in groups. No less than six bulbs of one kind in a casual circle or clump make a really good show in the early garden.

As you can see in the illustration, hyacinths come in many different colors. Choose those that fit best into your garden scheme. Everything else being equal, those with the best perfume are to be preferred. Some noteworthy for their scent are L'Inno-

cence, City of Haarlem, Pink Pearl, Ostara, King of the Blues, Tubergen Scarlet and the doubles, Ben Nevis and Chestnut Flower. Their ancestors came from France, Greece and Asia Minor.

In severe climates hyacinths benefit from some winter mulch. They should also be positioned with protection to prevent damage of the trusses from the worst winter winds. For garden use, second-size bulbs are a better choice than the more expensive top size. The trusses of the latter are so heavy that they do not weather well. For mass bedding, hyacinths are sold even more cheaply by color only. All are best planted in early fall.

Our modern hyacinths are a far cry from the species *H. orientalis*, which is considered to be their parent. Intense breeding and selection over generations has gone into the ones we know. One of their most important features is that they bring a really good splash of pink into the early-spring garden. There are a few small bulbs in pink, but the hyacinth is the first major source of this appealing color. Some of the hyacinths described as scarlet or crimson are a bit difficult to work into the whole garden scheme, but they make a bright spot among shrubs or with white daffodils.

Blue or white hyacinths are pleasing foils for all of the yellow daffodils and also for many of the early species hybrid tulips, so many of which are vivid mixtures of red and yellow.

PLANT: five to six inches deep, six inches apart, in well-drained loam; sun.

Hyacinths are excellent for forcing, and catalogs usually indicate which are most suitable. Sometimes specially treated bulbs by color are offered for this purpose. There are also some miniature hyacinths, often listed as early French Roman by color, that are delightful for forcing. They have graceful spikes of loosely set flowers rather than heavy trusses.

Special hyacinth glasses for forcing are extremely easy to use, but buy top-size bulbs for this technique. Pour clean, cool water into the glass until it reaches just the base of the bulb; add a small piece of charcoal, then place in a cool, dark spot for rooting. Hyacinths also can be forced in pebbles and water, the same as paper-white narcissus. However you plant them, a good root system and about four inches of top growth are necessary before forcing can begin. Allow at least eight weeks for rooting and cooling (see page 132). Those bulbs that were forced in a soil mixture can go into the garden later, but discard those in water.

Two tiny relatives are sometimes listed as hyacinths, as *Hyacinthella* or as *Muscari*, depending on the catalog.

H. azureus provides vivid, long-lasting blue spikes of tiny bells a few inches high in earliest spring and is native to Asia Minor. *H. amethystinus*, from Spain, is slightly taller, with loose heads of light-blue bells in late May. Its flowers last best here if given a touch of afternoon shade. Neither plant has notable scent. White forms of both exist.

PLANT: three inches deep, four to five inches apart, in well-drained soil; sun.

H. azureus

H. amethystinus

Hymenocallis
occidentalis

Hymenocallis
SPIDER-LILY

Most of the bulbs in this book are fairly easy to obtain from many different suppliers; here is the exception. Like many other American wildflowers, *Hymenocallis occidentalis* has been neglected in favor of exotic bulbs from overseas. You may not be able to find any source, but if you begin to agitate for it, the plantsmen will get your message and start propagating it. Sometimes called basket flower, it is closely related to the popular tender Peruvian daffodils or ismene that grace so many summer gardens. Since it is found in the wild as far north as Indiana and is winter-hardy at least to Philadelphia, the bulb would be a fine carefree choice for many gardeners. The fragrant white flowers are borne in an umbel in late summer. In the South it takes to moist spots, but farther north it needs a sheltered site that can have extra water during the summer but is not too wet in winter.

A few dealers do stock the plant, but bulbs are fairly expensive. One solution is to treat it like the tender *H. calathina* until you have built up some extra bulbs to experiment with in your climate.
PLANT: four to six inches deep, eight inches apart, in sandy soil; full sun.

Hypoxis
GOLD STAR-GRASS

Native to a large part of the eastern United States, this charming American deserves much wider planting. If seed heads are snipped off regularly, *Hypoxis hirsuta* yields sunny clusters of small yellow flowers a few inches high from May to November. This bulb has the longest bloom period of any plant in my garden. When I consider how much trouble and money we are willing to expend for a few days of bloom from many other plants, I have to shake my head in amazement at the way hypoxis is overlooked.

Foliage of this faithful servant is grassy and never obtrusive. It is perfectly at home either in a rock garden or in the forefront of a border, where it should be encouraged to seed itself into a thrifty patch. Watering during summer drought prolongs blossoming; otherwise it demands little except humusy soil. I know of no insect or rodent enemies.

Bulbs are usually available from wildflower specialists in the spring. I have even transplanted it in bloom, taking a good hunk of sod. Hypoxis also does well in the higher elevations of a terrarium.
PLANT: one to two inches deep, five inches apart, in humusy soil on acid side; part shade.

Hypoxis hirsuta

Ipheion uniflora

Ipheion
SPRING STAR FLOWER

These poor flowers from South America have had their name changed so often by the botanists that they may be hard to locate in the catalogs, although most list them under *Triteleia*. *Ipheion* is currently the correct botanical name, but the genus has also been called *Brodiaea, Milla, Bouvardia* and *Leucocoryne*. By whatever name, this bulb makes a pleasant late-spring decoration for the front of the garden. Foliage is grassy and floppy so that it is seldom more than a few inches high. When bruised, the leaves have the smell of onion; the flowers themselves are sweet-scented and are borne just above the leaves.

Two species are offered. *I. uniflora* is the easiest to find, but a few sources offer *I. violacea*. Flowers of both are a pale blue-violet; *uniflora* has a white eye. There is only one flower on a stem, but each bulb produces several, so it is well adapted for drift planting. In the South *ipheion* spreads quickly; in colder climates increase is slower. Since it often produces winter foliage, a protected spot is a wise choice. To flower well it should have nearly full sun.

Like crocus, the early squills, snowdrops and chionodoxa, this is a fine bulb for mass planting among shrubs where it can be left to increase into great drifts.

Another popular use is in front of late tulips. Since the foliage is unobtrusive, it can go right at the edge of the garden without extra thought. After flowering, it simply fades away without ever causing any bother about its maturing leaves.

Except for a newer form cataloged as Wisley Blue, ipheion bulbs are reasonably priced, no doubt because they increase so well under favorable conditions. For that reason I would recommend its trial to gardeners everywhere. Here, just north of Philadelphia, it has proved completely hardy in any sunny spot in which I have tried it, and it is also reported winter-hardy in the Hudson Valley. We will never learn the northern limits of these lesser-known bulbs until adventuresome gardeners try them. So, for those of you to the north, give ipheion a whirl in a protected nook, but plant it early. Where snow cover is an all-winter occurrence, you will have to find a special spot where the leaves can get some sunshine.

PLANT: three inches deep, three inches apart, in any well-drained soil; sun.

79

Iris

Most irises grow from rhizomes, but two important garden groups have true bulbs. The first is sometimes called rock-garden iris and is very early-flowering. The second group is cataloged variously as Dutch, English or Spanish iris and blooms in May and June on much taller stems.

Of the early ones there are several distinct types. Most important are various forms of *I. reticulata*. These are so hardy they will bloom right through ice and snow on stems about six inches high, but in the far north mulch well. This type is a fine dark purple with yellow markings on the falls. There are several hybrids with flowers in various shades of purple: J. S. Dijt, Wentworth, Violet Beauty and Purple Gem. Others are closer to blue: Cantab, Clairette, Joyce. The species *I. histrioides* and *I. bakeriana* also have blue flowers.

At bloom time the leaves are only a few inches high, but they develop in a short time to several feet in length. They are thin and wiry and soon go dormant, so the foliage does not preclude foreground planting. They should all have a protected warm site facing south where they bake thoroughly in summer. Under these conditions, increase can be rapid. They are native to the Caucasus and Armenia.

I. danfordiae, from Asia Minor, is a bright yellow on four-inch stems and a lovely companion for the others. It often blooms well only the first year but is worth buying every year. It has the unfortunate habit of splitting into tiny bulblets after blooming. If left undisturbed, these may eventually grow on until once again of flowering size, but this requires several years. I have to protect my flowers here from what I think are hungry birds. Often I find torn petals of *I. danfordiae* if I forget to place a few evergreen branches to protect it.

I. vartani, a slate white from Palestine, blooms so early that it is often frozen solid in northern climates. Even in a protected spot it did not survive for a second year in my garden, but it is interesting where it will grow. Mine were in the same spot where forms of *I. reticulata* have done well, so I think the trouble is simply that it is too anxious to flower.

Books by English gardeners often suggest lifting these early iris bulbs after flowering and leaf production are over. This may be necessary in a cool, damp climate, but it is hardly required where the summers are hot. I have had several different forms of *I. reticulata* on two separate properties. All have increased and bloomed prodigiously without any care whatever after planting.
PLANT: four inches deep, four inches apart, in well-drained soil; full sun.

Florists often force the later-flowering irises for use in bouquets, but they are per-

Iris danfordiae

I. reticulata Cantab

I. reticulata

Representative Dutch iris

moist soil; the others require good drainage. Often a planting of these irises will persist and increase slowly in the garden. The plants do not require much space, so it is an easy thing to add a clump to a border where they give color after the tulips fade. They do best without extra fertilizer. Foliage is never obtrusive.

PLANT: three to four inches deep, six inches apart; sun.

Ixiolirion
LILY-OF-THE-ALTAI

Fine for cutting, this bulb from the Caspian Sea area produces loose clusters of small blue flowers on slender stems from 12 to 18 inches high. Catalogs list *I. pallasi* and *I. ledebouri*. Bloom is in May and June. Bulbs sprout very early in spring and so may be damaged by frost in cold climates. Plant in a protected spot.

I have not been able to keep this bulb in my garden for more than a few seasons. Perhaps it is better reserved for more southern climates. To make any kind of showing it should be planted in some quantity and may need support to look its best.

PLANT: three inches deep, four inches apart, in well-drained soil; full sun.

fectly good for garden use too. Plant them in groups of a single color to get the best display. The so-called Dutch irises are the earliest, hardiest and tallest, often reaching two feet. Spanish irises bloom about two weeks later, followed by the English types. All come in a wide range of colors. Those of all three in the trade are hybrids. Their common ancestors came from Mediterranean lands, both in Europe and Africa.

If fall foliage is produced, mulch after the first frost. Not recommended for very cold climates. Those listed as English need a rich,

Ixiolirion pallasi

Leucocrinum montanum

Leucocrinum

SAND-LILY

Some other nicknames for *Leucocrinum montanum*, a western American, are California soaproot, star-lily, desert-lily and wild-tuberose. Anything that can survive in South Dakota has to be hardy, but easterners are forewarned to give its rhizomes a site with perfect drainage. A rock garden on a slope would be a good choice, for it produces grassy foliage only a few inches high. The fragrant white funnel flowers have slender tubes as long as four inches and appear quite early in spring. A mature plant bears many in succession. Since the leaves die down not long after bloom is over, mark its spot well.

Unfortunately, this is another native that is difficult to find in commerce. Western nurseries are your best bet, and autumn planting is preferred.
PLANT: three inches deep, six inches apart, in sandy, well-drained soil; full sun.

Leucojum

SNOWFLAKE

Close relatives of the snowdrops (both are native to central Europe), the snowflakes have several points of difference. The flowers are bell-like, there are often more than one, and they are borne on much longer stems. They also bloom later in the spring and are delightful with tulips. They will take a little shade. The dwarfer *L. vernum* (spring snowflake) is the first to flower, usually in March. *L. aestivum* (summer snowflake) actually blooms in April and May and often reaches 18 inches. Its variety Gravetye is a larger, improved form. To make any show at all, snowflakes should be planted in clumps of at least a dozen.

There is a very rare form that blooms in the fall (*L. autumnale*); it requires a warm, sunny spot. Since this snowflake is native to Portugal, Spain and Morocco, it is understandable that it is much less hardy than the first two. There are other rare snowflakes, but none is regularly available.

L. aestivum is often found growing along stream banks where there is considerable moisture in the soil. In the South it even thrives in near swamp conditions.
PLANT: three to four inches deep, four inches apart, in humusy soil; semishade.

Leucojum aestivum

Liatris

BLAZING-STAR

Gayfeather and button snakeroot are other nicknames for liatris, a well-distributed North American. It is usually seen in shades of lavender, but good white ones come true from seed. There are various species native to both the eastern and western halves of the United States. All need a well-drained site in full sun. Plants are sometimes offered, but seed is widely available. Plants usually begin to flower two or three years after sowing.

Depending on the species, liatris sends up wands two to four feet tall in summer and early fall. Some are slender spikes tightly packed with the flowers, which have long, twisted petals. Others branch. Bloom begins at the top and works down each stem.

A few liatris grow from a thickened rootstock, but many form a bumpy corm that slowly grows bigger. Small corms may also form beside it. These may be removed and transplanted in early spring.

In too rich soil or shade liatris grows floppy. While it requires good drainage and will survive in very dry areas, it blooms best when given some water in periods of drought. Any species or hybrid is highly recommended, but Kobold and Silver Tips are especially good cultivars.

Apparently the liatris cross-pollinates easily. I have a white strain that varies greatly from plant to plant. Some bloom in August, others in late September. Some produce long, thin wands of flowers, others great branched trusses. The tallest ones require staking to remain upright.

If you can find the true species, *L. spicata*, it will take much more moisture than the others. It bears neat wands of flowers. There are also some fairly dwarf species, but they are seldom offered commercially. From seed you can depend on flowers by the third year, and in time a mature corm will produce a great quantity of flowering stems.

PLANT: one inch deep, 12 inches apart, in lean soil; full sun.

Liatris

83

L. candidum

Lilium

LILY

Yesterday's gardeners would not recognize today's lilies. In a single generation there has been a complete revolution in the lily world, and much of it has been the work of one man, Jan de Graaff of Oregon. Other American and Canadian hybridizers, as well as some from Australia, share the laurels. In addition to imaginative hybridizing, new techniques have developed for propagating and growing disease-free stock and for storing and shipping bulbs. Today we have lit-

erally hundreds of new hybrid lilies at our command, most of them at reasonable prices. The hybrid vigor bred into them means they will do well for many years under ordinary garden situations. A few lilies have not yet been hybridized, among them the lovely meadow lily (*L. canadense*) and the Turk's cap (*L. superbum*) of the eastern United States. The madonna lily (*L. candidum*), which is depicted in artifacts that predate written history, has also been shy about being hybridized, although *L. testaceum* (*L. excelsum*), a soft apricot, is a natural hybrid many years old. Some species lilies still offer characteristics not yet duplicated by comparable hybrids, mostly in daintiness or earliness of bloom.

With few other exceptions, I recommend concentrating on lily hybrids simply because they are so much easier to grow. Lilies are native to many differing parts of the globe, and meeting the needs of the species is not always easy, while the hybrids do not present as many difficulties.

CULTURAL DETAILS

Always remember this one vital requirement of lilies: They cannot exist without good drainage. Since many of the big hybrids are best planted many inches deep, this means that if your water table is high or the soil likely to puddle, you will find it difficult to have long-lived lilies unless you put them in raised beds.

A little light or filtered afternoon shade often preserves petal color and lets the flowers last longer too, but no lily does well in deep shade. Many like their root runs cool, but the leaves need sun shining on them. A deep mulch or low-growing plants in front of the lily patch is the answer. Since many hybrid lilies grow four to six feet high, they are excellent for pepping up a shrub border in summer and for positioning at the back of the garden or in the center of round beds. They are stunningly beautiful against a background of evergreens.

It may strike you as a bit odd initially, but one way to deal successfully with tall hybrid lilies in the average garden is to think of them more as shrubs than flowers. As with so many other bulbs, they look best if planted in groups of a single type. Just three bulbs of some of the vigorous hybrids create a great splash of color, for many bear tiers of individual blooms, each as much as seven inches across. The result is a truly significant landscape plant. If you visualize those bunches of huge flowers as being six feet tall, you can see that the comparison with a shrub is not as strange as it seems at first thought.

L. canadense

Enchantment

Corsage

Many small gardens simply cannot include such a massive planting without its looking out of scale among the other perennials. On the other hand, between shrubs or in bays among them, the lilies look quite at home. Nearly everyone has a few shrubs here and there, so you should have no trouble finding a spot for some of the tall hybrid lilies. Those that bloom in the height of summer are particularly good companions for spring-flowering bushes; the green of the shrubs helps set off the lily blooms.

Many lily species have definite preferences for either an alkaline or acid soil, but most hybrids do well in ordinary loam with a good humus content. Plant them in groups of three or more for best effect but not too close together to allow for increase. Leave in

Prosperity

place as many years as bloom is satisfactory, and move the bulbs only in late fall after the foliage has browned off. Mark plantings well to avoid disturbing.

Lily bulbs do not go completely dormant like many other bulbs, so they should be left out of the ground as short a time as possible. With modern storage, good bulbs can still be obtained in the spring, but autumn planting is advised in all but the coldest climates. Prepare the soil well and deeply, and mulch against frost if your order is late. Plant immediately after bulbs arrive and water well once to settle.

TYPES OF LILIES

Which hybrids you order depends on several factors. Colors to harmonize with your outdoors are surely important, but so is season of bloom. Many of the most spectacular hybrids flower in July and August. Height also is limiting; only a few hybrids stay under three feet. It is harder to find early and shorter hybrids.

So far, several different systems have been offered for an orderly classification of lilies. None has been universally adopted. Your best bet is to read over your catalog and choose those that fit your needs, as outlined earlier. Most of the classifications depend on the ancestry of the lilies involved, which is not too helpful to most gardeners. It does, however, tend to separate them by time of bloom, which is important to the gardener.

Types of bloom formation are varied. Some hybrids bear their flowers in an upright bunch, others in open candelabras. Blossoms may be outfacing or pendant; shapes may be nearly flat and open, recurved to various degrees, trumpet-, star- or bowl-shaped.

One other point is worth stressing. Many growers have gotten into lily breeding. Each wants to sell the progeny, and some named lilies do not differ greatly from others. In time there will be a weeding out, and only the best will survive, but for now there is a bewildering host of new lilies.

CLONES, STRAINS AND HYBRIDS

You should know that there are three types of lilies in commerce besides the wild species. Of the species you have to take whatever is available, but among the hybrids you should understand the meanings of *clone*, *strain* and *hybrid*. It makes a difference both to the appearance of your garden and to your pocketbook.

When you see lilies described as a type of *hybrid* (Olympic Hybrids, for example), you can expect considerable variation among them in height, color and even sometimes in flower shape. They are the result of crosses between two specific lilies as parents. Seed from the cross is raised in quantity, and these lilies are virtually disease-free. They are a good buy for the gardener who wants merely some colorful lilies.

Further selecting takes place by the hybridizers to produce a *strain*. Usually this is by color and shape of the flower. Thus among the Olympic Hybrids there are bulbs advertised as Pink Perfection Strain, Green Magic Strain, Copper King Strain and Golden Splendor Strain. Each strain produces trumpet flowers of about the same height but confined to one part of the color spectrum. All things considered, buying lilies by strains is the best investment for the ordinary gardener. This gains uniformity of flower but does not lose the disease-free characteristic since these lilies too are usually raised from seed. The astute breeder knows which lilies to use as parents, raises them in quantity and culls out those that do not conform to the strain's standards.

In any large planting of lilies from seed, a few will stand out from the others because of unusual color, shape, height or vigor. Such a lily becomes a named *clone*, representing the breeder's idea of the best of a class. Each is propagated vegetatively from scales of the original, and every lily so offered should be exactly like the first. It will have a capitalized name such as Harmony, and usually, although not always, it will cost more than either strains or hybrids of comparable

Harlequin Hybrids

Connecticut Yankee

Paisley Strain

Afterglow

parentage. Clones are the best choice for a spot where you want a clump of lilies all exactly the same height and color. A clone that has been around for some years such as Enchantment, one of the first De Graaff hybrids, has proved itself over the long test and is an excellent investment. But it is possible for clones to carry disease. One of the reasons lilies gained a reputation as being difficult a generation ago was that growers raised much of their crop vegetatively and stocks carried disease. This is being guarded against by today's more informed growers.

SPECIES OR HYBRIDS?

All of this may leave you wondering where to begin. A current bulb catalog is the best guide, for it tells you what is available at what price. Most catalogs also give colors, heights and blooming times as well. Not every catalog will have all of the species mentioned here, and there are dozens of others I do not have space to list. But some of the finest presently available are given as examples. Only the easiest species are listed. Should you become enamored of the genus, the lily specialists carry dozens of species from all parts of the world with which to experiment.

In addition to the fact that species lilies are more demanding in their requirements and lack the vigor of hybrids, disease can be a real drawback. Some suppliers offer species lilies that are collected in the wild or grown vegetatively. Either way, they could introduce disease into your garden. At best, this will only result in the species failing to prosper; at worst, it can start an epidemic in your garden. Try, if you can, to buy species lilies from a bulb specialist who has grown the stock from seeds.

Failing a source that certifies that the species lilies are disease-free, you can grow your own from seeds. For some pointers on this consult page 136. Many of the species are not easily propagated this way, and seeds may be hard to locate. Your best bet, if the clan has your devotion, is to join the

North American Lily Society or one of its local affiliates. The meetings and publications are most worthwhile, and you will learn much from other fanciers.

One of the reasons that the lily specialist is enamored of the species lies in the sheer beauty of many of the wildlings. These have a grace and daintiness that are lacking in many hybrids. I have to stress, however, that the hybrids are by far the better choice for most gardens.

The gorgeous color pictures in most catalogs will help you to find lilies of the hues you prefer. There are, moreover, many that bloom in July and August, and a majority of the new hybrids range from four to six feet in height when well grown. A few are listed below that lie outside these boundaries.

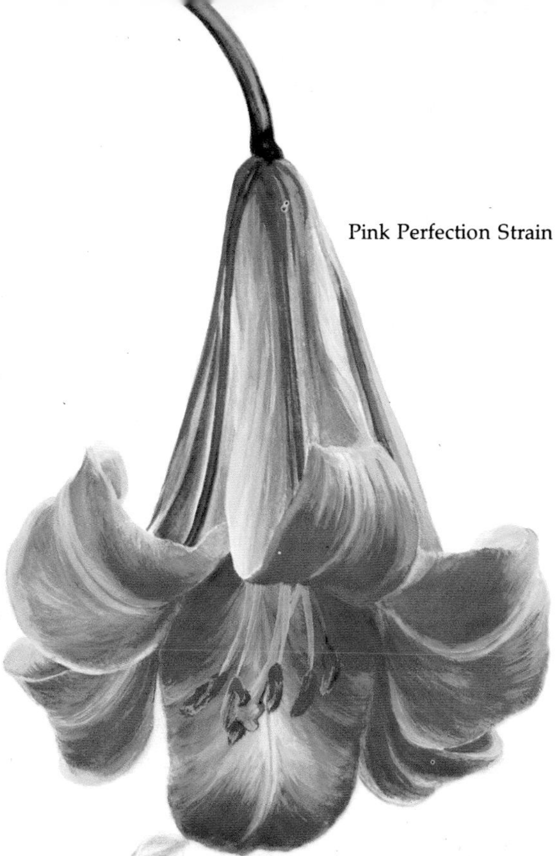

Pink Perfection Strain

SHORTER LILIES

The shortest lilies, seldom exceeding two feet, include Little Rascal, forms of *L. pumilum* and *L. concolor*, *L. rubellum*, *L. cernuum*, Pastel Hybrids, Gold Coast, Love, Sunrise and Firebright.

In the range of two to three feet are Cinnebar, Enchantment, Fireflame, Golden Chalice, Harmony, Paprika, Prosperity, Sundrop, Magic Pink, the Rainbow Hybrids, Autumn Sun, Crown Jewel Strain, Golden Goblet Hybrids, Cream Wax and Ruby.

Lilies from three to four feet tall include Corsage, Destiny, Challenger, *L. martagon album*, Joan Evans, Hallmark, Discovery, Pepper, Pirate, Scout, *Speciosum* Red Champion, Achievement, Tabasco, Peacock Strain, Fuga, Gold Brocade, Rosette Strain, Connecticut King, Cohoe, Rose Dawn and White Gold.

Olympic Hybrid Strain

EARLIER LILIES

The earliest lilies start in late May and include forms of *L. pumilum*, the Golden Chalice Hybrids, Rainbow Hybrids and Golden Goblet Hybrids.

89

Royal Gold Strain

Heart's Desire Strain

By June you can expect color from Cinnebar, *L. concolor,* Gold Coast, Fireflame, Harmony, Achievement, forms of *L. martagon,* Paprika, Red Flare, Enchantment, *L. rubellum,* Sundrop, Tabasco, Paisley Hybrids, Mid-Century Hybrids, Pastel Hybrids, Crown Jewel and Fairy Jewel Hybrids, Sunrise and Apricot Glow.

OUTSTANDING HYBRIDS

If height or season make no difference, your choices are varied. Using De Graaff's proposed classification, here are some outstanding lilies to look for. Enchantment is the best known of the early upright Asiatic Hybrids; all come in bright yellows, reds and oranges (June–July). Also try Cinnebar, Destiny, Challenger, Harmony, Tabasco, Ruby, Rosebelle and the Mid-Century, Crown Jewel and Rainbow Hybrids.

Outward-facing early Asiatics include Corsage, Firebright, Redbird, Prosperity, Fireflame, Rapture Strains and Pastel Hybrids.

Pendant hybrids in this section feature large candelabras of flowers: Amber Gold, Connecticut Yankee, Nutmegger, Discovery, Burgundy Strain, Hallmark Strain, Harlequin Hybrids, Ball Strains, Bronze Queen and other Patterson Hybrids.

The Martagon Hybrids (June) are offered mostly in mixtures such as the Paisley, Fairy Jewel (Bemis) and Painted Lady Hybrids, but Achievement is a uniform waxy pale yellow. All have pendant flowers and accept light shade.

Hybrids of western United States lilies

90

(July) are the bright Bellingham Hybrids and the San Gabriel Strain. Good clones are Afterglow, Robin, Buttercup, Shuksan, Sunset and Nightingale.

The Aurelian Hybrids (July) contain the best trumpet lilies any garden can sport. They are found in strains of nearly every shade imaginable: Pink Perfection, Golden Splendor, Copper King, Apricot Reflections, Topaz Temple, Shellrose, Green Royal Trumpets and Seagold, for example.

There are also Aurelians with bowl-shaped flowers: Milky Way, Heart's Desire and Moonstone. Golden Showers is one of the few pendant Aurelians.

Still others have starry, flat flowers: the various Sunburst and Corona Strains.

Finally come the gorgeous Oriental Hybrids (August and September). Many are quite fragrant. Some have wide bands of gold or red, others contrasting spots; a few are self-colored.

Bowl-shaped ones include American Eagle, Crimson Beauty, Empress of India, Fairy Pink, Dutchman's Gold, Red Baron and such strains as Magic Pink, Pink Glory, Red Band and Coral Mist. Flat-faced are the various Imperial Strains: Sunday Best, Cover Girl, Harbor Star, Bonanza Red and White Frills. Recurved flowers include Allegra, Acclaim, Black Beauty, Jamboree, Cinderella, Journey's End and Garnet Fire. There are also very good variations of *L. speciosum*.

Orange Sunburst Strain

Magic Pink Strain

Imperial Gold
Strain

Red Band Strain

LILIES FOR FORCING

Some dealers offer precooled bulbs for forcing, but you can do this yourself (see page 133). Enchantment, Harmony and Tabasco are very easy, but almost any Mid-Century Hybrid is a possibility. Allow about six weeks in the refrigerator if you are cooling your own bulbs (put them inside a plastic bag with some damp peat moss). When you pot up the bulbs, for best results grow them in a cool room where the temperature does not rise over 60°F. Use only the biggest bulbs for forcing. It will take close to three months from potting to flowering.

Forms of Easter lilies (usually *L. longiflorum*) are also available for home forcing, but they are not as easy to bring into good bloom without a greenhouse. They require a cool rooting period in darkness the same as daffodils and take more than four months to come into bloom after planting. Never start to force them until a good mass of roots has been formed. You may find them listed as Croft, Ace or Estate lilies. You can also pot up lilies in the fall, winter them over in a cold frame and then have them for spring and summer bloom (depending on the variety). This is a nice way to have some unusual container plants for the porch or patio, but make sure you choose hybrids that do not grow too tall.

Imperial Silver Strain

LILIES FOR CUTTING

Lilies make lovely cut flowers, but do not remove long stems or many leaves. Snap off spent blooms before seed forms. With very tall lilies it is possible to remove the top two feet of stem without too much damage to the bulbs. This means you could use the whole candelabra of bloom in a bouquet if you wished. Blossoming the next year after this treatment may not be as prolific, however, which is why it is wiser to remove only shorter stems if you do not have lots of lilies. Most of the new hybrids increase well, so that after a few years of growth you might well feel you could be more cavalier with a few.

The individual blossoms are quite lovely in bud vases or floating in a bowl or brandy snifter. For the gardener with limited garden space, this sort of display makes more sense.

Lilies are also perfect in corsages, particularly those that have flattish flowers. Remove the pollen-laden anthers before you do any work of this sort to prevent staining the petals. The glass vials often used for orchid corsages work equally well to keep the lily flowers fresh as long as possible. To fashion a makeshift corsage, wrap a little wet cotton around the end of the lily stem and then waterproof it with a piece of aluminum foil to protect your clothing.

In these few pages I have been able only to touch lightly on hundreds of hybrid lilies, and I have not even begun to enumerate the many species. The brief classification outline here summarizes the hybrids. Use it as a quick reference to check against your current catalogs and against the descriptions in the previous pages. Hopefully it will make it easier to find what your garden needs.

PLANT: *L. candidum* one inch deep in limey (alkaline) soil; others three to four inches for small bulbs, four to six inches for larger ones, six to 12 inches apart, in well-drained loam with mulch; sun, but afternoon shade in hot weather is advisable. Autumn planting preferred.

Jamboree Strain

PROPOSED LILY CLASSIFICATION

Division I. Asiatic Hybrids: wide color range, many early-flowering
    A. Upright flowers
    B. Outward-facing flowers
    C. Pendant flowers

Division II. *L. martagon* Hybrids: pendant flowers, mostly June-flowering

Division III. *L. candidum* Hybrids: rare

Division IV. American Hybrids: so far only from western species; June–July-flowering, some fragrant

Division V. *L. longiflorum* Hybrids: rare

Division VI. Aurelian Hybrids: wide color range, some fragrant; mostly July-flowering
    A. Trumpet or funnel-form flowers
    B. Bowl-shaped flowers
    C. Pendant flowers: rare
    D. Sunburst or starry flat flowers

Division VII. Oriental Hybrids: many fragrant; wide color range, July–September-flowering
    A. Trumpet flowers: rare
    B. Bowl-shaped flowers
    C. Flat-faced flowers
    D. Recurved flowers

Division VIII. Any hybrids not provided for above

Division IX. All true species and their botanical forms

Lycoris squamigera

Lycoris
RESURRECTION-LILY

This Japanese relative of the amaryllis has the surprising habit of popping up almost overnight in late August and blooming on bare stems, long after the foliage has disappeared. For this reason it is also called magic-lily and sometimes naked lady. Each two- to three-foot stalk is topped by a cluster of fragrant, pinky-lavender, funnel-form flowers. The full name is *Lycoris squamigera*.

The wide straplike leaves emerge in early spring, then dry up during the summer. Mark the site to prevent disturbance. If the spot is one that gets sun during the spring but is later shaded by trees, the foliage will be able to do its job adequately. A fern that does not require too much moisture is a good overplanting, and the fern fronds will help set off the rather naked-looking stalks of the lycoris when it blooms. This bulb is decorative among shrubs too if the leaves receive enough sunshine during the crucial growing period.

Lycoris also does well as a border plant where its late-summer blooms perk up a garden that may need such a tonic. In such a situation, place the lycoris toward the back. Plants in front will adequately face the naked stalks to the ground. Your only problem will be to remember not to dig up the bulbs during the summer when the foliage is not present to remind you of its home. I have seen this lycoris growing in profusion in Vermont, so it is certainly one of the hardiest amaryllis. *L. sprengeri* is quite similar but a darker color.

Less hardy are the yellow *L. aurea*, red *L. radiata*, white *L. albiflora* and orange *L. sanguinea*. South of Philadelphia try them in a warm, protected spot because flowering is late and foliage appears very early. Lycoris are best planted in the fall and, since they resent disturbance, may sulk for a few years. Some gardeners treat these less hardy species as pot plants.

PLANT: four to six inches deep, six inches apart, in well-drained soil; sun, part shade.

94

Mertensia

BLUEBELLS

There are upward of three dozen different species of mertensia, many of them native to North America, but the most popular is *M. virginica*, Virginia bluebells. It grows wild all over the eastern United States on rich flood plains, but it is equally at home in the garden. In late April and May it produces graceful clusters of nodding bluebells two to three feet high. Rarer forms with flowers of pure white, pink and lavender also exist.

Since mertensia blooms much better if the quick-developing foliage gets plenty of sun, it is a good choice for the edges of a copse of deciduous trees. Ferns make good companions because the mertensia foliage turns yellow and disappears by the end of June. Most ferns revel in the same rich, damp bottomland that the mertensia fancies and will like the shade as the trees leaf out. The tubers are best moved in fall and are offered in bulb catalogs.

In the wild, *M. virginica* is of course found growing in sites particularly adapted to its wants. On bottomland near a stream it may make lush fountains as much as three feet high and nearly that across. Plants farther from the water will be only half that height and width, and this is the size to expect in the average garden. During a dry spring the plants definitely benefit from some extra hosing during and immediately after flowering. Over many years and in several gardens I have found this species to be very adaptable to many situations, with the reservation that it does not flourish and increase as well in drier spots.

There is a western United States species, *M. ciliata*, that is reputedly also a good garden subject. *M. sibirica* is native to eastern Siberia, and references say its foliage lasts through the summer. I have not seen either species offered commercially. If there is a mertensia native to your own section, such might be better suited to your own garden conditions. *M. virginica*, however, is one of the loveliest native plants of spring. In garden situations it is especially charming, with white or lemon-colored daffodils.

PLANT: two inches deep, eight inches apart, in rich, humusy soil; likes spring dampness.

Mertensia virginica

M. armeniacum
and perennial alyssum

Muscari

GRAPE-HYACINTH

Some of the members of the genus *Muscari* do indeed resemble tiny bunches of grapes, but there are others that have different characteristics. Several could be described safely as eccentric. Native to lands of the Mediterranean and Asia Minor, they are nearly all very hardy. Bloom is mostly in April and May, on stems that seldom exceed eight inches. Many muscari produce the grassy foliage in the fall. The most common sorts spread quickly, so even a few bulbs make a respectable patch in no time. The rugged constitutions of the various blue forms of *M. armeniacum* suggest they be used en masse in shrub borders and even in rougher parts of a property rather than in special niches. They are also effective when used as foils for bright tulips and daffodils.

For a long time, Heavenly Blue was the most popular form of the typical blue grape-hyacinth, but it has been superseded by Early Giant and Cantab. Blue Spike is a double form of *M. armeniacum*, which is a bit heavy-looking but very splashy in mass plantings. *M. tubergenianum* is a Persian species, with two shades of blue on its spikes. One of the earliest to bloom is *M. botryoides album*, a dainty white-flowered species. While perfectly hardy, it does not increase prodigiously and so may be used anywhere. *M. paradoxum* has very dark flowers, almost blackish blue, with yellowish-green interiors, and blooms in May. *M. moschatum* is often called musk hyacinth because of its strong scent. Its flowers mature to a yellowish-olive color, but *M. macrocarpum*, sometimes listed as *M. moschatum flavum*, has good bright-yellow blossoms. *M. ambrosiacum* is closely related. The last five listed are much harder to find in catalogs than the first three—in the United States at least. Those who have smelled the musky ones stress they are very strong.

Paradoxically, two really strange muscari are widely offered in American catalogs. The tassel-hyacinth *(M. comosum)* has loosely placed olive-green flowers along the stem and a tuft of small purple ones at the top of the spike. The best that can be said of it is that it is a fascinating oddity for the collector. It blooms later than the others.

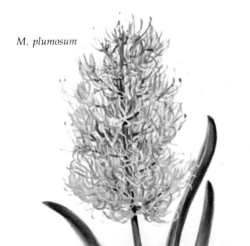

M. plumosum

M. comosum

M. Blue Spike

Also late is the feather-hyacinth, which may be cataloged as *M. comosum monstrosum* or *M. plumosum*. Its strange flowers bloom into June here, and I rather like them. All the blooms are sterile, and they have been converted by a capricious nature into long, mauve, curled streamers that do look rather like a plume. Planted in a close grouping, it makes a good patch of color at a time when there are not many bulbs in flower. Give it a clean mulch of some sort, however, for the heads are heavy when wet, and dirt seems to adhere tenaciously to the long filaments. This is one muscari that seems to require full sun for decent blooming.

Rare muscari include the pink *M. massayanum*; the very late *M. argaei album*, which is white and dainty; and *M. neglectum*, with fragrant dark-blue flowers, edged with white. Europeans will be surprised to hear that Americans can seldom obtain *M. racemosum*, which is closely related to *M. neglectum* but larger in every way. Both are sometimes called the starch-hyacinth and have notable fragrance. *M. racemosum* has spread so rampantly in Europe and England that it is there considered a bit of a weed. Perhaps this is why it is not popular for export. Since it is the earliest of the grape-hyacinths, it would be nice to try it, keeping it for hard-to-plant places just the way we do *M. armeniacum*. No experienced gardener would put the latter in a special rock garden or a niche next to a delicate plant because of its spreading tendencies. But it is sometimes very satisfying to have handy a plant that can take care of itself in harsher areas.

If I had room for only one muscari, I would vote hands down for the white form of *M. botryoides*, which is sometimes called pearls of Spain. It will increase slowly but is hardly rampant. This muscari makes a perfect foil for other plants that bloom at the same time—violas and forms of *Anemone blanda* being two favorite combinations of mine. (Bulbs cataloged as *M. azureum* are *Hyacinthus azureus*, and that is the way you will find them listed in this book.)
PLANT: three inches deep, four to five inches apart, in almost any soil; mostly full sun.

M. *botryoides album* and pansies

Music Hall

Trumpet Daffodils

Broughshane

Unsurpassable

Narcissus

DAFFODIL

Spring without daffodils would be less joyous. Their cheerful gold and silver decorate cottage gardens and great estates with equal abandon. Almost all are hardy in the coldest climates; the few exceptions are widely used for winter flowers indoors (see page 173). Before I start their evaluation, you should know that the words *Narcissus* and *daffodil* are completely synonymous, the first being the botanical term for the second.

There are probably 25 to 30 wild species, native mostly to central Europe and the Mediterranean region, with a few from China and Japan. A majority of those in the trade today are named hybrids, with all the health and vigor this implies. Unlike the lilies, where there are still new break-throughs occurring, the daffodils have been hybridized long enough so that certain formal divisions have been adopted. They are based on family strains and on certain common characteristics. In accredited daffodil shows the flowers are always staged by the

98

official divisions, and specialists' catalogs also use these as a handy way to organize their offerings. For the ordinary gardener, picking bulbs by divisions is an easy way to make sure your garden displays all that the genus has to offer. There is much more to spring than the trumpet daffodils, although these biggest members of the genus are outstanding for garden decoration. By adding clumps from other divisions you gain much more in color and form. And more important, you also add weeks of daffodil bloom, because *Narcissus* from other divisions bloom both earlier and later.

Whichever daffodils you plant, there are certain cultural rules to consider. While many will live in almost any soil, they do best in deep, well-drained loam with humus content. To get decent bloom they require at least half a day of sunshine, and their foliage needs to flourish until it has accomplished its yearly duty of replenishing the bulbs. Braiding daffodil leaves to make the garden neater is self-defeating. It may look tidy, but it is not graceful, and it definitely discourages the leaves from their important manufacturing task. Better to put some later-flowering plant in front of your daffodils so they can go through the food-storage period without calling attention to the flopping leaves. If spring is very dry, extra watering will help them. Where they are naturalized, do not mow the grass until after the daffodil leaves are turning yellow.

Early-autumn planting is advised for all daffodils so that good roots are formed before frost. The leaves and bulbs, which have a narcotic property, are not attractive to either rabbits or deer. Early daffodils do well under the high shade of late-leafing deciduous trees, but they sulk in deep shadow. Oftentimes daffodils are planted while trees and shrubs are small and competition for light and soil is minimal. As the trees grow larger, however, the bulbs gradually refuse to flower and eventually die out. Daffodils also tend to increase prodigiously, especially if planted shallowly. To save work, plant them initially as far apart as possible for the display wanted. Every three or four years those in the garden (where they grow closer than when naturalized) will require lifting and separating after foliage matures. Otherwise, size and number of flowers will fall off simply because too many bulbs are competing for the available space. After separating, allow to dry for a week in a cool, airy spot, then replant.

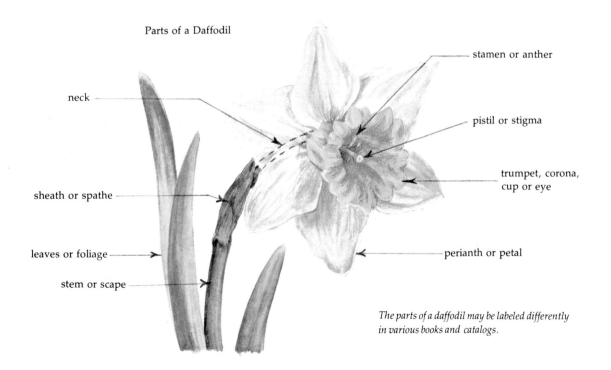

Parts of a Daffodil

stamen or anther

pistil or stigma

trumpet, corona, cup or eye

perianth or petal

neck

sheath or spathe

leaves or foliage

stem or scape

The parts of a daffodil may be labeled differently in various books and catalogs.

Large-cup Fleurimont

LARGE-CUPS

Division II is formally known as Large-cupped, but often its members are cataloged as Weatherproofs. Many compare in size with the trumpets, and the most varied colors of all daffodils are found here. Far more daffodils are officially listed in this class than any other, and some belong in practically every garden.

All daffodils look best and give the greatest effect if planted in groups of a single variety. This is especially true of this divi-

Large-cup Louise de Coligny

THE TRUMPETS

Trumpet daffodils (Division I), such as those pictured on page 98, are a good way to start your daffodil collection. There are many dark yellows from which to choose. Unsurpassable, Kingscourt, Dutch Master and Rembrandt are easy to find. King Alfred is scorned by fanciers because it lacks giant size, but it has been delighting gardeners since the turn of the century. Lighter yellow trumpets include Grapefruit, Hunter's Moon and Luna Moth. Good bicolors include Spellbinder, Music Hall, Preamble, Straight and Trousseau.

Many white trumpets open first as yellow, then pale with age. Good garden ones are Mount Hood, Beersheba, Rashee, Broughshane and Prestige.

sion, which has many with cups of orange, pink or red. Their colors fight with each other but are marvelous when separated by clumps of other plants or by pure white or yellow daffodils.

Outstanding large-cups, with both the outside perianth petals and the cups yellow, include Galway, Carlton, Fortune and Yellow Sun. Even brighter are those with yellow perianths and red or orange cups. Try Red Goblet, Carbineer, Scarlet Elegance or Ceylon.

Large-cups with white perianths and colored cups are even more varied. Kilworth is a great red-cupped one, Flower Record has an orange cup, Green Island a lemony-

Large-cup Binkie

green crown. Binkie reverses the combination with a yellow perianth and a white cup. Some other favorites: Duke of Windsor, Alicante, Eddy Canzony and Orange Bride.

Most of the "pink" daffodils are in this class. There are new ones constantly, but for garden use the very old Mrs. R. O. Backhouse and Louise de Coligny, which dates to 1948, are still hard to beat. Newer ones include Salmon Trout, Toscanini, Pink Rim, Azalea and Allurement.

All-white large-cups are most striking against evergreens. Try Ice Follies, Eastern

Large-cup Kilworth

Large-cup Bergen

Morn, Castle of Mey and White Plume. Some of these open with the cups definitely yellowish, but they turn paler as they age.

Many daffodils in this division have wide flaring cups; often they are prettily ruffled. Royal Orange and Lemon Cup are two outstanding examples. There are even some daffodils in this class that have cups of two colors. Florissant has a white perianth and a yellow cup edged with white. Roulette has a yellow cup edged with orange against a white perianth.

Not only are the flowers in this division nearly as large as trumpet daffodils, but the stems are sturdy and tall too, so they may be used in exactly the same way in the garden

as the true trumpets. The only real difference to the gardener is the dazzling color range they provide.

SMALL-CUPS

Division III includes the small-cupped daffodils, and here the difference between these and the trumpets is noticeable. Again there are wide color variations. Of those with a yellow perianth and colored cup, the most novel is Apricot Distinction. Jezebel, Edward Buxton and Chunking are very splashy, with reddish cups. Those with white perianths and colored cups are a bit easier to work into the garden. They vary from Fairy Tale, with a pale citron cup-bordered orange, and Blarney, with a yellow and orange cup, to those like Firetail, Mata-

Large-cup Green Island

Small-cup Apricot Distinction

Small-cup La Riante

Small-cup Edward Buxton

pan and Limerick, with red cups. Among many novelties: Johannesburg, with a frilled triple orange crown. Finally, there are all-white ones, many of them late-flowering: Frigid, Dream Castle and Cushendall are some popular examples. Another delightful member of this division is Shantallow, which has green tints in its lemony cup.

Unfortunately the pure white varieties of this division do not always exhibit the vigor we have come to expect from hybrid daffodils. Some varieties dwindle away after a few years.

One explanation for this may be that the genes that account for the white cups brought along with them some undesirable characteristic. The daffodils of this division are the result of crosses between large-cupped varieties from the previous division and forms of *N. poeticus* from Division IX, all of which have red rims on the cups. Indeed that reddish tendency from the *N. poeticus* varieties has been the main source of the red and pink cups now so popular in many other classes. The *N. poeticus* influence is of course evident in the small cups of this division. Many are more literally described as an eye rather than a cup.

You will notice fewer entries from this division in most catalogs. This is because at present it offers the least for garden decoration although the flowers are good cut.

THE DOUBLES

Double narcissus exist in many of the other divisions, but in shows they are all collected in Division IV. Some are somewhat blowsy, but they have the distinction of remaining in bloom a very long time because they are usually sterile. More care in situating them is needed. When wet, their heads are extremely heavy. A good clean mulch like wood chips will protect the petals from splashing soil. This is a good technique for all daffodils but particularly important for these. Some overhead protection helps too. A tree not yet in leaf offers its branches to break the force of the rain. If the doubles are planted on the outer edges of trees where the sun still shines in, they will benefit greatly from this slight umbrella effect in heavy rainstorms.

Two of the best doubles for the garden are Cheerfulness and Yellow Cheerfulness. These are sometimes listed under the Tazettas of Division VIII and bear several small flowers per stem. They are notably fragrant. Erlicheer is another dainty double. Some larger ones are Texas, White Marvel, White Lion, Golden Ducat, Mary Copeland, Snowball, Patricia and Windblown.

There is a wide difference between the flower forms of this division, even though all are loosely called doubles. The old *N. telamonius plenus* (also called Van Scion) was mentioned by Parkinson as far back as 1629. It is a scraggly kind of flower with all the petals in thin strips, some of them greenish. That is a far cry from the neat Cheerfulness, which almost resembles a tiny gardenia. Many of the more recent doubles have a definite outer perianth in the center of which are overlapping petals of varying size. Often two colors are present.

The doubles are actually mutations of other daffodils. Golden Ducat appeared in a planting of King Alfred and White Marvel in one of Tresamble. White Marvel has several flowers per stem, and its cup is literally crammed with ruffled petals.

TRIANDRUS HYBRIDS

The Triandrus Hybrids of Division V are probably the daintiest of all daffodils. They are sometimes nicknamed orchid daffodils because of a fancied resemblance. There are both yellow and white representatives, and all bear several more or less pendant flowers per stem. In most the perianth is somewhat reflexed, and the cups are fairly small. As a class they are late-blooming so that the addition of some of these prolongs the daffodil season in the garden. Foliage is much more slender than for the trumpets, making it less noticeable when maturing. They take well to lean soil and spots that bake dry in summer.

Double Golden Ducat

Double White Lion

Double Texas

N. triandrus Liberty Bells

These are worth a little extra effort because they give the garden an ethereal effect. If you have considered the daffodil a somewhat stiff flower, these members of the clan will change your mind immediately. A group of them in bloom gently dancing in the breeze often makes me think of butterflies.

CYCLAMINEUS HYBRIDS

Division VI, the Cyclamineus Hybrids, has some of the first daffodils of the season. Planted in a warm spot facing south and protected from the cold winds by a rock or evergreen, these will open several weeks before the trumpets. Of them all February Gold is one of the most dependable. Its perianth is not as reflexed as many of the others. Try Charity May and Little Witch if you favor this tendency. Peeping Tom has one of the longest trumpets you will ever see, a characteristic transmitted from its species parent.

There are some wonderful diminutive daffodils in this section, ideal for rock gardens. Beryl is yellow with a small orange cup. Dove Wings and Jack Snipe are bicolors. Jenny is nearly pure white. It is

Combined with their smaller sizes, this makes them adapt well to rock gardening, or where space is limited.

There are not nearly as many varieties offered in this and the next few divisions, which are organized strictly along family lines. All are charmers, however.

The pure white *triandrus* are especially delightful with bright tulips. Other favorites are Rippling Waters, Tresamble, Thalia and Moonshine.

Yellow *triandrus* include Liberty Bells and Forty-niner, plus the miniatures: April Tears, Hawera and Stoke. These last three are under ten inches tall. Dawn, with a white perianth and lemon cup, is one of the very few bicolors.

Not all gardeners have as good luck with the *triandrus* varieties as they do with the more common trumpets and large-cups. Perhaps they kill them with kindness, for this class definitely does not want rich garden loam. Try rather poor, thin soil with absolutely perfect drainage.

N. triandrus Thalia

hard not to love any daffodil from this division because they come early enough so that we have not yet stopped longing for the color of sunshine after the gray winter. Foliage is not quite as wide as most of the trumpets and ripens more quickly than many other types, so you can make these the feature of the forefront of the garden to get the most from their gaiety.

Every hybrid in this division has as one of its ancestors the tiny *N. cyclamineus*, which grows wild in Portugal and Spain. Although it had been described in the seventeenth century, it had been lost to cultivation for some 250 years until its rediscovery in 1885. Its botanical name is based on the resemblance of its very recurved perianth to that of the cyclamen.

Most of the breeding has been with trumpet daffodils. This explains how the diminutive *N. cyclamineus* could parent plants with flowers the size of February Gold, February Silver and March Breeze. There are also a host of miniatures that bring fine early color to the rock garden or any small niche. One of the oddities of plant breeding is that three of these tiny beauties (Jumblie, Quince and Tête-à-Tête) came from a single seed pod.

JONQUIL HYBRIDS

Division VII, which is based on hybrid daffodils with *N. jonquilla* parentage, is another late-blooming group. Its most famous characteristic, however, is the fragrance of its flowers, of which there may be two to six per stem. Foliage is rushlike and never objectionably obtrusive, so this is another type of narcissus that is easy to position.

Yellow is the predominant color, but Cherie has an ivory perianth and a shell-pink cup. The all-white Alpine is rare. Trevithian, Sweetness, Tittle-tattle, Golden Perfection and Orange Queen are all good. Dainty miniatures include Bebop, Lintie and Bobbysoxer.

Grant Mitsch of Oregon has been very active in breeding this division and has some beauties, all named for birds, but they are not widely offered. The campernelles are also in this division. *N. odorus plenus* and *odorus* Orange Queen are the easiest to find. Both have deliciously scented flowers.

N. cyclamineus Beryl

N. jonquilla Trevithian

One of the brightest Jonquil Hybrids is Suzy, which contrasts an orange-red crown against a clear yellow perianth. It bears several flowers per stem and ranges from 15 to 20 inches tall. It is the easiest to locate with this color combination, but there are some others available from daffodil specialists.

As a class these daffodils are hardy, disease-free and long-lived. They take heat much better than some of the earlier varieties, which wilt quickly on a hot day.

TAZETTA HYBRIDS

Division VIII covers the cluster-flowered Tazetta Hybrids. In some catalogs these are still called Poetaz. If one hedges about the hardiness of daffodils, it is in this section. They are not all hardy in the coldest climates, but they are so colorful that it is well worth experimenting with some.

Generally these are later-flowering, and Silver Chimes, a hybrid between a *tazetta* and a *triandrus*, is one of the very latest daffodils. Fragrance is good in this whole group. Many are recommended for forcing indoors for winter bloom.

Some favorites: Matador, Hiawassee, Geranium, Cragford, Laurens Koster, St. Agnes and Innocence. Several are listed in the double class. Almost all tazettas will take

a little shade. A clump makes a noble spot of color in full bloom. Because there are so many flowers per stem, only a few bulbs are needed to create a focal point, and I like to use these daffodils for this purpose.

POETICUS HYBRIDS

The Poeticus Hybrids of Division IX are among some of the oldest daffodils in gardens. Many of them are among the last daffodils to flower in the season. As a group they have a white perianth and a small cup rimmed with red, and they naturalize well. Only a few are available: Mega, Actaea, Cantabile, Recurvus (the old Pheasant's Eye), Red Rim and Queen of Narcissi. White Sail is a double.

Very little work has been done on this class of late. Mega was introduced in 1950, and it is the newest in general commerce. Mostly the *poeticus* daffodils have been used in breeding to bring new color to other divi-

N. tazetta Yellow Cheerfulness

N. tazetta Geranium

sions rather than to improve themselves. There is very little difference between them, and their main importance is to stretch the daffodil season for a few days longer. They are also nice for cutting.

MISCELLANEOUS DAFFODILS

In addition to these sections and to Division X, which covers the true wild or species daffodils, there is the miscellany of Division XI. It contains various odd daffodils that do not fit into any of the other categories, but the main denizens are the so-called split coronas. They are also called Butterfly and Collar daffodils. While not new, they are just entering many American bulb catalogs. In all of them there is no longer any trumpet or cup; this part of the flower has split into petaloids. In some there are six inner petals that lie flat against the perianth. In others the petals of both parts are interspersed, but the general effect is still rather flat. Daffodil fanciers have mixed opinions about them. Many feel they do not look like a daffodil and are consequently disappointed. Others are intrigued by the novelty. Since botanists feel that split-corona narcissus may have been the ancestors of the cupped ones, it seems high-handed to condemn them without trial. I can say that Mol's Hobby is one of the most fragrant I have ever grown, that Papillon Blanche has been a delight for years and that the very split ones like White Orchid and Gold Collar are certainly different. Try some and make up your own mind.

The split pictured here (Orangery) is perhaps one of the brightest combinations, but there is a wide latitude already in this class. You can find pure white or pure yellow as well as various bicolors. The Dutch firm of Gerritsen and Son has been very active in this area of daffodil breeding.

It stands to reason that as other breeders continue to make crosses, there will be more daffodils that do not fit into the formal classifications. However, the divisions as they stand now will be able to absorb the greatest number of them. The classification system is

N. poeticus
Cantabile

of prime importance in helping to organize a large and very diversified genus. Without such an aid, no one could deal very easily with the multitude of daffodils now in commerce. Use it to find what you need for your garden to stretch season, color and flower form.

THE SPECIES DAFFODILS

True species daffodils are not used as often as they might be except, perhaps, by rock-garden enthusiasts. This is probably because they are not as easy to grow as are the hybrids with their built-in vigor and adaptability. They do not have the flamboyance of the big hybrids, either. Their daintiness has a charm of its own, however. They need lean, sharply drained soil for the most part,

Split Orangery

N. triandrus albus

very reflexed perianth but flowers much later. There are several color variations, but the one usually offered is *N. triandrus albus* or Angel's Tears. It has clusters of creamy white flowers and also accepts spring dampness.

The hoop petticoat daffodils *(N. bulbocodium)* are not recommended for the coldest climates. Offered in several colors, they are appropriately nicknamed. They prefer a damp, gritty soil in sun during the spring but seem to want summer baking.

N. canaliculatus bears several small flowers

should never be fertilized and should be well marked so they are not disturbed during summer dormancy. Many are hard to obtain and are fleeting in the garden, possibly because they get too much water during the summer. A few of the most popular are described here.

N. cyclamineus is a darling—bright yellow, very early, with a long trumpet and a perianth so reflexed it looks like a rocket. It will take some shade and seems to like a damper soil than most. Its physical shape is aptly illustrated by the flower on the right here. Its various hybrids are more nearly like the larger bloom to its left.

N. triandrus is equally beautiful, also has a

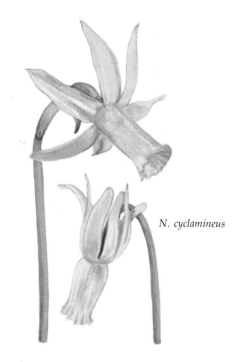

N. cyclamineus

N. bulbocodium conspicuus

with a white perianth and golden cups. Too tender for far northern gardens, it needs a warm, well-drained site.

N. asturiensis (N. minimus) is perhaps the earliest of all daffodils to flower. Hardly three inches tall, it needs lean soil and full sun. Give it a clean mulch to protect the flowers.

Several jonquil species are often available. In a warm, well-drained spot they do very well, particularly in the South. *N. jonquilla (simplex)* has tiny flowers and an almost overpowering scent. It also has a double form. Closely allied is *N. gracilis*, which is

108

thought to be a wild or natural hybrid. Very fragrant. Such species as *N. juncifolius*, *N. rupicola*, *N. scaberulus* and *N. watieri* also belong with this group but are not as easy.

Rock gardeners and those who lean toward daintiness may find the hybrid miniatures are a much better solution than the true species. Many of them are most diminutive, and they have the advantage of their hybrid parentage to make them longer-lived. Show schedules are strict about what is admitted as a miniature, but the gardener is concerned only with health and size. Al-

N. asturiensis

N. jonquilla simplex

SUMMARY OF DAFFODILS
Official Divisions

Division I. Trumpets: large flowers
Division II. Large-cups: wide color range
Division III. Small-cups: graceful
Division IV. Doubles: long-lasting flowers
Division V. *Triandrus:* dainty, multiflowered
Division VI. *Cyclamineus:* early, vigorous
Division VII. *Jonquilla:* late, very fragrant
Division VIII. *Tazetta:* cluster-flowered, fragrant
Division IX. *Poeticus:* late, fragrant
Division X. Species: quite varied
Division XI. Miscellaneous: mostly splits

ready I have cited some of the smaller daffodils in each division. Here are some others worth trying where daintiness is wanted: W. P. Milner, Lady Bee, Bambi, Sun Disc, April Tears, Wee Bee, Sneezy, Tanagra, Xit, Pencrebar, Baby Moon, Tête-à-Tête, Taffeta, Jumblie, Quince, Shrimp and Suzy.
PLANT: hybrid daffodils five to six inches deep, four to 12 inches apart (depending on usage), in well-drained loam; full to half sun. Species go two to four inches deep, depending on size, two to three inches apart, in sharply drained soil; full to half sun.

Miniature
W. P. Milner

Ornithogalum umbellatum

Ornithogalum
STAR-OF-BETHLEHEM

This immigrant from Europe, *Ornithogalum umbellatum,* is nearly a weed where I live, but its loose clusters of white stars six inches tall can be depended on as a bright note in almost any soil or situation in late spring. Keep it from the rock garden or a special niche where it might overwhelm the other inhabitants. Rather, let it naturalize in spots where nothing else will prosper. *O. nutans* is nearly as indestructible but more interesting. Its starry flowers are borne on stems 12 inches tall. The outsides of the flower are a soft jade green, much prized by flower arrangers. *O. balansae* is earlier-flowering, a tiny dwarf, only a few inches high. *O. arabicum* is a handsome species with clusters of white flowers, each with a black "bee" in the center, on 18-inch stems. It cuts well but is not reliably hardy in very cold sections. North of Philadelphia it should have some winter protection.

Some authorities consider that *O. umbellatum* may be the "manna from Heaven" of the Bible. We do know that the bulbs are eaten by peasants in both Europe and the Middle East. The little white stars have the curious habit of opening during late morning and closing before the end of the afternoon. Because the outsides of the petals are greenish, it is difficult to locate the flowers except when they are open. Their opening might well have seemed like a miracle to a hungry people.

PLANT: three to four inches deep, four inches apart, in any soil; sun or semishade.

Puschkinia
LEBANON-SQUILL

Perhaps to escape the sneezy sound of its name, gardeners sometimes also term this striped-squill. It is a diminutive charmer that increases quickly by both seeds and offsets. Clusters of small fragrant starry bells bloom in early spring. Blooms are milky white, with a pale-blue stripe on each petal. At maturity the slender stems are hardly eight inches high and the foliage is never obtrusive, making it a nice choice for the foreground. A dainty, rare white form exists, and it is an exquisite jewel for a special niche.

Most bulbs sold nowadays are listed as *P. libanotica,* which is an improved form of the species *P. scilloides.* Named after a Russian count, it is native to Asia Minor, where it is found in damp places. It is undemanding, however, making it an excellent bulb for naturalizing.

The noticeably strong fragrance reminds me of wild grapes. The first honey bees of the season go mad over it.

PLANT: three inches deep, five inches apart, in any soil; full sun.

Puschkinia libanotica

110

Polygonatum

Smilacina

Polygonatum
SOLOMON-SEAL

Smilacina
SOLOMON-PLUME

These closely related plants are members of the lily family, and they should be in every shady garden. Both bloom in spring, but they are even more useful to give an interesting note to such a spot in summer. Their arching stems create a graceful line to accompany the vertical fountains of ferns. Both plants will flower in fairly deep shade, but they do best in filtered shadow from high trees and require a deep humusy soil and a cool mulch from leaves or wood chips.

They grow from thick, creeping rootstocks. Smilacina is the showier plant, with large heads of tiny, starry white flowers and a cluster of bright-red fall berries. Polygonatum bears pairs of small pendant white bells followed by dark-blue berries. The various species differ mainly in height, but soil richness has to do considerably with this. All species commonly offered (except *P. multiflorum* from Asia and Europe) are native to North America.

PLANT: one to two inches deep, one foot apart, in deep, humusy soil; shade; mark well, as plants may sulk a season.

Scilla sibirica

Scilla

SQUILL

Native to the mountains of southern Europe, the squills usually offered, with one exception, are flowers of spring, and a happy lot they are. Earliest to blossom is *S. bifolia*, which often produces its first gentian-blue stars while snow is still around. There are also pink and white forms of this. The clusters of flowers are seldom higher than six inches. They are a lovely accompaniment to snowdrops and winter-aconites. A delicate light blue, *S. tubergeniana*, also is very early.

Slightly later flowering are the various forms of *S. sibirica*. All of them bear several small flowers on stems about six inches high. Both a blue and a white form are widely offered. For the greatest effect, plant scillas in colonies of a single color rather than a mixture. Or surround a group of one color with a colony of another.

S. sibirica taurica is a clearer, brighter blue than the parent, and Spring Beauty is a named selection that bears bigger flowers on longer stems. Both of these are somewhat earlier to bloom than the ordinary *sibirica*.

All of these early squills do best in full sun,

but they also will bloom well in half shade, particularly if it is filtered. The foliage of all is never obtrusive and matures quickly, so you can plant good-sized colonies of them in the foreground of any garden without worrying about the effect of the foliage as it dries. The later-flowering types are often placed in front of early daffodils.

One of the prettiest groupings of bulbs I ever made was a combination of blue squills and white *Anemone blanda* in a half-shaded spot. *S. sibirica* is also excellent to naturalize under shrubs or deciduous trees. Mulch well and do not disturb a planting for quick increase.

There are several other European squills seldom offered in America. Among them are *S. verna, S. amoena, S. autumnalis, S. pratensis amethystina* and *S. monophylla*. South African species such as *S. violacea* are much less hardy. Their mottled foliage makes them interesting as dwarf house plants.

Another group of bulbs was for a long time considered as late-blooming squills, but it has now been changed to *Endymion*, the name by which you will find it listed in this book.

Closely related to the chionodoxa, the squills have been crossbred with it. The results are called *Chionoscilla* and are reputedly quite handsome but still rare.

PLANT: two to three inches deep, three inches apart, in well-drained soil; sun.

S. peruviana is a fairly hardy relative that blooms in summer. Although native to the central Mediterranean area, it is often called the Cuban or Peruvian-lily. It bears large, roundish heads of many blue stars on a stout stem about ten inches tall above rather wide basal leaves. Not reliably hardy in very cold climates but worth trying in a warm spot elsewhere. There is also a white form. Both are widely used as potted plants for winter bloom indoors. There are several other species that are considered wild flowers in Europe but are seldom offered in the United States.

PLANT: four to six inches deep, eight inches apart, in well-drained loam; sun.

112

Sternbergia

I have often wondered whether this beauty, if it had a fanciful popular name, would be planted more widely? It ought to be, for sternbergia brings to the autumn garden the bright yellow lacking in the fall-flowering crocus. The various species are native to Palestine, Greece and parts of Asia Minor. Flowering occurs toward the end of September and into October. If your climate experiences hard frost early, you cannot expect it to do much. It wants a south-facing site where the snow melts quickly in winter and summer baking is the rule. The leaves of the most common species, *S. lutea*, appear with the flowers and provide a nice green note in the garden all winter long. They disappear in May, hence the need for a spot where they get winter sunshine to do their work. *S. clusiana* has even larger flowers, but the leaves do not emerge until later, so it needs a small underplanting to set it off. Because its stems are only a few inches high, it is less graceful than *S. lutea*, which averages eight inches in height.

Bulbs should be ordered as early as possible and planted immediately on arrival in late summer. Often it takes a year or two before they settle in and begin to bloom well, particularly if they have been planted after September 1. Do not disturb a clump until it becomes very crowded; then dig up, separate and replant the bulbs as soon as the foliage browns off in late spring. The rare *S. fischeriana* blooms in spring. I have never seen it, but its leaves are supposed to appear with the flowers. With all the fine yellows available in spring from the daffodils, I cannot get too excited about this sternbergia.

The fall species, however, are really worth any extra trouble they may take. At one time they were even called winter or autumn daffodils as well as *Amaryllis lutea*. Like their narcissus relatives, the sternbergias apparently have foliage unappetizing to hungry rabbits, so they can be grown in gardens where fall crocus never have a chance.

Several other gardening authors have commented on a phenomenon I discovered in my own garden, so I pass it along: Sternbergias always seem to do best with a boulder or a rock wall immediately to their north. I suppose that the rock not only protects the winter foliage from the worst of the cold winds but also generates extra warmth. PLANT: four inches deep, four inches apart, in well-drained soil; sun.

Sternbergia lutea

113

T. grandiflorum

Trillium
WAKE-ROBIN

Not many bulb catalogs list these lovely Americans, but every wildflower specialist and many other plantsmen offer them. The thickened rootstocks are best treated as bulbs and planted in the fall when dormant, although very early spring planting is possible. They require a soil that is high in humus and well drained but not too dry. They are plants of the open woodland, so filtered shade is what they want rather than deep shadow. The east side of a tree is perfect. Flowers should never be picked, because it is almost impossible to do so without removing the all-important leaves. Such an accident will kill or at least set back the plant. The scanty foliage is the only source of nourishment, and it will not produce another set in that season.

Often called wake-robins, the trilliums need a coolish site; most do best in soil on the acid side. Peat moss added during planting will help them. Use leaf mold or wood chips as a mulch.

Of the more than 20 species, the best for garden use is the large eastern _T. grandiflorum_, which can reach 18 inches. Its white flowers age pink. Much like it is _T. ovatum_ from the West Coast. A miniature copy of these is the snow trillium, _T. nivale_, which often opens in late March. It needs a drier site and neutral soil—a good choice for

114

a sloping rock garden with some shade. It has white flowers.

Nicknamed stinking Benjamin and wet-dog trillium, *T. erectum* has white, yellow and red-purple forms. It resembles *T. grandiflorum* but on a slightly smaller scale.

Quite different are the various toad trilliums *(T. sessile)*. There are forms with purple, green, yellow or white flowers, but the main attraction is their curiously mottled leaves. Planted in a group on the edge of the shady garden, they are interesting even when the rather insignificant blooms are gone. *T. luteum*, with yellow blooms, is a favorite.

Although graceful, the nodding trilliums are not as decorative because their blossoms are half hidden by the leaves. *T. cernuum* may have white or pink flowers; *T. nervosum*, often listed as *T. stylosum*, is a rose pink.

T. undulatum, the painted trillium, is a beautiful white with pink markings, but it requires a cold, damp, very acid soil not usually found in gardens. If you do not have these conditions, please do not buy it. Many of the plants in commerce are collected from the wild, and this beauty is rare enough without encouraging such depredations.

If spring is very dry, it is wise to give your trillium planting extra water to prolong the life of the all-important leaves as long as possible. Wind protection is also a good idea, for the stems are brittle. If snapped off early, the plant will be badly weakened.

Wild ginger is a good choice as a ground cover for trilliums, and ferns that are not too invasive are also ideal companions. The foliage of both will take over during the summer months when the trilliums have disappeared. This not only makes for prettier gardens but also reminds you not to dig in the area. Dormant trilliums do not take kindly to disturbance.

Very rare double trilliums also exist; they are unbelievably beautiful.

PLANT: two to four inches deep, depending on size of tuber, six inches apart, in deep, humusy soil; filtered shade.

T. erectum

T. luteum

T. cernuum

Cottage Mrs. John T. Scheepers

viridiflora Angel

Darwin Reliance

Cottage Balalaika

Mid-season
Apricot Beauty

Darwin
Paradise

Single Early
Princess Irene

Tulipa

TULIP

These springtime favorites perform many duties in the garden, but their greatest contribution is to bring bright color to winter-weary eyes. From the earliest species to the last Darwin, tulips offer the gardener-artist every shade imaginable except true blue. Moreover, they come in varied sizes and many different shapes. Truly, there is a tulip for every garden. Most of the species are made to order for the rock garden or the intimate niche, while blocks of stately Cottage or Darwin tulips can be used to create great sweeps of color in the largest park.

Lists of currently popular hybrids are not nearly as important as a working knowledge of the types of tulips available. Each year bulb catalogs reflect the trends (and the prices). What you need to know is that by choosing from among the various classes you can stretch the tulip season from the earliest thaws of March to the warm days of late May. And also that tulips vary from some a few inches high to those that reach 30 inches.

Tulips are native to a wide area that includes much of the Mediterranean lands, Asia Minor and the Caucasus. Generally they want a cold winter, enough water in spring to mature the leaves, then a good baking in summer. Most of the United States offers just what they want. In areas where spring rains are scant, some irrigation should be provided so the leaves do not brown off too quickly. In the far South where winters do not provide the necessary cold, precooled bulbs often can be obtained or opened packages of bulbs can be left in the home refrigerator (not the freezer part) for six to eight weeks before planting in January.

Obviously, tulips have to be treated as annuals where there is no winter, but outside the frost-free belt this is a waste. Given a decent loam, adequate drainage for fairly deep planting and plenty of sunshine, a planting of tulips should last for years in the garden. Granted that in subsequent years the flowers may not be as large as during the first season in your garden, they can still give a good show.

The idea that tulip bulbs should be discarded after one year of bloom is a hangover from the days when great estates could hire a squad of gardeners and afford the cost of new stock every year. This technique is still followed in exhibition gardens, where it is important that every flower be of exactly the same size and height. For the ordinary garden, however, leave tulips in place for as many years as they continue to give bloom. As the bulbs split, you will find you have tulips of several different sizes and heights; and this effect is often more graceful in the small garden, particularly if the tulips are planted in round groupings. Avoid lining up single bulbs in thin rows; no tulip looks its best that way. If you want a long line of color from your tulips, plant them in rows at least four to five bulbs wide and as many feet long as wanted. In most garden situations a clump of ten to 12 bulbs makes a good show of itself. If you plan carefully in the selection of your varieties, you can achieve a garden where tulips and daffodils bloom together for a gorgeous spring show; use the earlier-blooming tulips for this.

Tulips have been a favorite flower in Turkey for many centuries, but they did not reach western Europe until 1554, when an Austrian diplomat brought them back. From that small beginning they have spread over the temperate world. New varieties are always being produced, but it is worth noting that today's catalogs still list some venerable ones. Zomerschoon dates to 1620, Royal Standard and Keizerskroon (Grand Duc) to 1760, the Prince of Austria to 1860.

The old Turkish sultans preferred the lily-flowered tulips; but the Dutch and English, who have done the bulk of the breeding, concentrated for a long time on producing egg- and goblet-shaped flowers as well as doubles. In the past generation the breeders have followed still another path by crossing many of the more spectacular species with each other and with other classes of tulips. The most famous of these has been the Red Emperor (Mme. Lefeber), which took its first prize in 1931 but did not really come into its own until after World War II. It has been followed by a host of others with its *T. fosteriana* ancestry as well as the *T. greigi* and *T. kaufmanniana* hybrids. These are especially valuable for their earliness. That same characteristic, plus great size and vibrant color, have made the Darwin Hybrids another popular innovation. Holland's Glory and Lefeber's Favorite, introduced in 1942, were among the first of these great tulips. A decade later the Dutch came out with General Eisenhower and Gudoshnik; others of this class continue to be introduced. Judging by past performance, there will continue to be new hybrids based on fresh genes brought in from the various species tulips. As with lilies, new techniques are making possible additional crossings of hitherto rare species.

A formal tulip classification exists, but it is not closely followed in any of the current catalogs. Some bulb specialists list their offerings partly by season, partly by ancestry and partly by flower form. All of these fac-

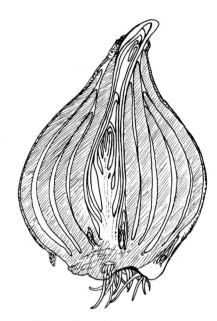

A mature tulip actually contains an embryo flower in its center as this cross section shows.

tors can be important in determining which tulips you want. Your main concern may be fringed, parrot and viridiflora tulips because they adapt so well to interesting flower arrangements. Or you could want the massed color of bouquet tulips, the long-lasting characteristics of the doubles or the majestic effect of large sweeps of stately Darwins. More likely you just want some tulips to brighten your garden as much as possible. So, in describing the various kinds available, I will start with the hybrids, which flower first, and advance through the season. Most of the true species are grouped at the end, as are some particularly prized by arrangers, because these are more specialized. If you plant some of several different types, you will have flowers over a much longer period. Not all colors are available in all classes, and generalities about heights are only that. Most catalogs list the heights of individual tulips and may use the letters E, M and L to indicate relative bloom times within a class. All these aid you in finding just what you want. Bloom may be earlier or later, depending on where you live in relation to Philadelphia, but the sequence will be roughly the same. If you are forcing tulips for early bloom inside, always choose from among those types that naturally flower earliest.

Early Single Keizerskroon

Always buy top-size bulbs when ordering tulips. They are essentially bulbs for sunny places, but a touch of high shade in the afternoon will not hurt. They do better on a lean diet than heavy applications of fertilizer. For garden sites where tulips are wanted as more or less permanent residents, plant them deeply—up to about ten inches of soil above the bulb if it is a large one, about five inches for some of those with smaller bulbs. They require sharp drainage, so where the water table is high, you will have to plant less deeply, and they will not be as long-lived.

Of all the important hardy bulbs, tulips are the least amenable to variations of moisture. They will not take any standing water or even soil on the moist side that easily supports daffodils. If you cannot guarantee good drainage for them, you will have no recourse except to fashion some raised beds, explained in the introductory section of this book.

Except for the species *T. sylvestris*, tulips are seldom suggested for naturalizing. Perhaps this is because the tall Cottage and Darwin types (the most popular) are too stately to blend in appropriately with the informal types of plants found under such situations. It is also a fact that adequate sunshine is very important for tulips, and the later they are to flower the more this point needs to be stressed. Unlike earlier bulbous flowers, the tulips do not begin serious leaf production until later in the spring when the trees are already casting shade. They also accomplish this important task in a much shorter length of time than the daffodils, for example. So they simply must have good sunny spots to prosper.

It is also a factor that the tulip bulb does not keep growing larger. When it reaches maturity, it splits into smaller bulbs, which again have to grow before they reach peak flowering size. So you do not plant a few tulips with the thought that in a short time you will have a large clump of them as you do with daffodils. It is this characteristic of splitting that prompts the exhibition gar-

Darwin Hybrid Gudoshnik

dener to dig up all the tulips and start fresh with new ones each fall.

Where you are gardening on a less formal basis, however, you can adapt them to a more or less naturalistic style in the bays of shrubs or in the rock garden. They are particularly effective on hillsides where there are large outcroppings of rock. There you will find that a planting of tulips several years old may have a special charm. (This is

Lily West Point

119

T. kaufmanniana Heart's Delight

really a form of naturalizing.) There will be flowers of many different sizes and heights, and these blend into the landscape more gracefully. Especially useful for such purposes are the early hybrids such as the *Kaufmannianas*, *Greigis* and *Fosterianas*. Since most of these bloom at the same time as the daffodils, you can make some very effective companion plantings. In such less formal beds it is much less important that all the tulips be of uniform height and size.

Conversely, the rather stiff habit of taller tulips, such as the Darwins, lends itself well to narrow beds next to buildings. They are made to order too for small parks and beds in cities where a certain neatness is essential. Jumbled beds that would merely be friendly gardens in the country tend to look unkempt in the more stratified confines of the city.

Think too of using tulips in any garden as a focal point either because of vibrant color or as a way of utilizing the very stiffness that in some other position might be a disadvantage. For such purposes it is probably better to put in new bulbs each year. The old can go into a cutting bed somewhere else.

KAUFMANNIANA HYBRIDS

Except for some special species, the first tulips in my garden are always Kaufmanniana Hybrids. In some winters they may open even in March, otherwise very early in April. The species itself or its variety The First are the earliest. Both show creamy white interiors and pink or red exteriors. On warm sunny days the flowers open wide, illustrating why they are often popularly termed water-lily tulips. At nightfall or on cloudy days they are shut, and the long tapering shape is quite different. Because the weather is still cool, these tulips last a long time in bloom. As the years pass, a clump becomes increasingly graceful, with flowers of various sizes facing each other.

Heights range from the salmon-orange Cimarosa at four inches to the yellow and crimson Vivaldi at 12 inches. Exteriors of all are a darker color than the insides, and some have interesting center markings. Cesar Franck, Stresa and Goudstuk are yellow inside and have red exteriors. Shakespeare is a combination of orange, apricot and salmon.

Magnificent and Heart's Delight are rose. Scarlet Elegance, Alfred Cortot and Brilliant are dazzling reds.

Personally, I never saw a Kaufmanniana Hybrid I did not love. They combine well with daffodils, especially pure white and yellow varieties. As an underplanting with these early tulips the lovely blues of both chionodoxas and squills contrast well.

FOSTERIANA HYBRIDS

The Fosteriana Hybrids, to which the Red Emperor belongs, begin opening a few days after the Kaufmannianas. Often they overlap by a week or two. It is well to remember, if you live where a sudden few hot days may occur in early April, that the darker red and orange shades of both types of tulips do not last as well as do the lighter-hued ones. Perhaps this is because the darker colors absorb the sun's heat.

As a class the Fosterianas are larger-flowered, and many have taller stems than the Kaufmannianas. The orange-red Rockery Beauty is barely eight inches tall, but Purissima (White Emperor) and Pink Emperor can reach 20 inches. The latter, incidentally, may be found sometimes listed under Greigi Hybrids, but it blooms with the other Emperors. Many of this class show vivid markings inside their cups. Dance is one such, with a red exterior and the creamy-white interior oddly marked. Golden Eagle, Yellow Empress and Easter Parade have added yellow to the spectrum available in this class.

All in all the Fosterianas are harder to work into the total garden picture because they are so bright and exclamatory, but, where such an effect is wanted early in the year, they can be depended on to give it. Pure white trumpet daffodils are good companions for most of them.

Don't be surprised if some of the tulips you buy as either Fosterianas or Kaufmannianas show some of the striped foliage that is the mark of the Greigi Hybrids, which will be discussed a bit later. These newer hybrids

T. kaufmanniana Shakespeare

T. kaufmanniana The First

T. kaufmanniana Stresa

often show some characteristics of both parents. Classification is made on several bases. Generally, however, you can figure that if a tulip is listed as a Fosteriana, it will be taller and usually have a larger, fatter flower than the Kaufmannianas. The Greigis tend to have rounder flowers and are rather short. It really doesn't matter that much to the ordinary gardener who wants just some colorful early tulips, which these classes will definitely give.

Which brings up a cautionary phrase that occurs often in this book: Try to plant your tulips of all three of these classes in groups of a single named variety. So many are so bright and excitingly colored that in mixture they fight each other or lose some of their effectiveness.

OTHER EARLY TULIPS

Following on the heels of these early birds are the single early tulips. The red and yellow Keizerskroon and the orange Prince of Austria are but two of the oldest; many others have proven themselves over many years. Because they seldom have stems much taller than 14 inches, they are great for making pools of color and can be planted in front of where later, taller Darwins will bloom. They come in nearly every color, and some have a faint scent. Try Bellona and Mon Tresor, yellow; Diana and White Hawk, white; Gen. de Wet, orange; Ibis and Pink Beauty, rose pink; Van der Neer, violet purple; Doctor Plesman, scarlet.

Unrivaled for bedding purposes are the early doubles. With their late counterparts, they are often called peony-flowered tulips, and blooms do resemble these flowers. Plant the earlies only a few inches apart where you want to achieve a ribbon-of-color effect. Many of these in commerce are sports of the famous tulip Murillo, which dates back to 1860. Today's gardeners have the improved Murillo Maximus, a white flushed rose; Electra, carmine pink; Mr. Van der Hoef, pure yellow; Schoonoord, pure white; David Teniers, violet purple; Wilhelm

Kordes, an orange-and-yellow blend; Orange Nassau, scarlet orange; and Peach Blossom, rosy pink. All are descendants of the one famous early double.

Generally the early doubles are just a shade later than the early singles and are a few inches shorter. They should be well mulched so no mud can splash on their full-petaled flowers. They are fairly weather-proof, but heavy rain is hard on them.

MIDSEASON TULIPS

Midseason sees a wealth of tulips. Among them are the aforementioned Darwin Hybrids. Often their big flowers are borne on stems 26 inches high. So far, this class is limited in color. Jewel of Spring is pure yellow; President Kennedy is yellow with red flecking; Apeldoorn, orange scarlet. Most of the others are shades of orange and red.

T. fosteriana Mme. Lefeber (Red Emperor)

122

T. fosteriana Purissima
(White Emperor)

T. fosteriana Summit
(Yellow Emperor)

Old catalogs listed both Mendel and Triumph tulips, but today you may find both types lumped together under midseason. They are most valuable for introducing more subtle shades and average out at about 20 inches high. Some to look for: Apricot Beauty, Sulphur Glory; the white-edged pink Her Grace; Dutch Princess, a blend of orange and gold; First Lady, violet-flushed purple; Elmus, cherry red, edged white; and Orange Wonder (Tulip of Albany), a dark orange red.

For a moment, now, let's digress in our story of the tulip season and talk about fragrance. It is not a word one hears often in connection with tulips. Back in 1797 the name *Tulipa suaveolens* was advanced for a group of European tulips distinguished by fragrance and earliness. They are now believed to be wild descendants of the first tulips brought from Turkey. They were much used to breed a group of tulips known as the Duc van Thol class. It no longer appears in most catalogs, but there are some tulips among the early singles and among the midseason tulips too that trace their ancestry to this source. The fragance of any tulip is hardly overwhelming, not to be compared with some of the sweetest daffodils, for example. But there are still a few tulips in the trade that do have some per-

fume. The easiest to find are Bellona, a golden yellow; De Wet or Gen. De Wet, golden orange; Doctor Plesman, orange red; Prince of Austria; Orange Wonder (Tulip of Albany), orange scarlet; *T. sylvestris*, yellow species.

THE GREIGI HYBRIDS

Some of the newest tulips in gardens are the Greigi Hybrids. They bloom at midseason, too, although there is some variation. One warning: Do not buy one of the so-called peacock mixtures. These are another vibrant class of tulips, and the mixture is simply too much of a kaleidoscope as well as having great variations in height and time of flowering. Rather, plant your Greigis in groups of a single variety. All true members of this class exhibit strange brown-to-maroon mottling on the leaves, a legacy from the parent from which they are named. The stems seldom exceed 12 inches, and they are very sturdy tulips. Some good self-colors are Royal Splendour, a brilliant red; the scarlet Red Riding Hood; and the vermilion Margaret Herbst. Most of the others are bicolored. Plaisir (illustrated) is one of my favorites, but also try Dreamboat, salmon-flushed yellow; Cape Cod; Oriental Splendour; and Zampa, all of which show combinations of yellow and red. Perhaps because of the curious foliage, these tulips look best when planted by themselves with evergreens or with white daffodils. Because they are fairly short-stemmed, these tulips may be planted in front of the taller daffodils to create a really beautiful contrast of color and form. In the beginning the Greigi Hybrids were quite expensive, but prices are now on a par with the others for the most part.

Incidentally, if you have sharp eyes, you may notice a certain percentage of eight-petaled tulips among the Greigis and also hybrids of the Fosteriana and Kaufmanniana classes. This phenomenon does not occur among any particular variety more than others, as far as I can see, and there may be only one flower out of a clump that exhibits the aberration. Nevertheless, I have seen it too often in my garden of late for it to be merely coincidence. The most obvious explanation is that the combining of new chromosomes has had some effect on the petal structure. I suppose it is not too far-fetched to expect that eventually there may be some doubles in these classes. And I wonder whether it will be an improvement because the contrast of colors exhibited in these tulips is definitely part of their charm. If doubled, this effect might be lost.

LATER TULIPS

Just before the Darwins take over, the lily-flowered tulips begin to open. They are extremely graceful with large flowers. As they age, the petals are often beautifully reflexed. Stems range from 20 to 30 inches. They combine well with almost anything else in the garden. Some examples: Mariette and China Pink, pink; White Triumphator; Picotee, white, feathered rose; West Point and Golden Dutchess, yellow; Spitfire and Red Shine, red; Queen of Sheba, reddish brown; Poet, purple; and Maytime, mauve, edged white.

If our tulip story were set to music, the climax would come now with the May-flowering Darwins, Cottage and Breeder types in the illustration on page 116. Botanists and breeders may blanch, but the gardener is wise to consider all of these together as late-flowering single tulips on tall stems. Darwins are supposed to have a rectangular outline to the lower part of the flower, Cottage tulips to be more egg-shaped, Breeders oval or cup-shaped. No matter. The differences are often hard to discern.

The solution is to sit down with your bulb catalog and choose late-flowering tulips by

T. greigi Oriental Beauty

124

T. greigi Plaisir

colors. Between these three classes there is a full range, from the blackish maroon of Queen of Night (Darwin) to the brown tints of Cherbourg (Breeder) through the pure white of a Cottage such as Carrara, with every color between except true blue. Remember, when planting these types of tulips, that many have stems a good 30 inches high the first year. They belong at the middle or even the back of the spring garden. As the bulbs multiply and break, the stems may not be as tall in subsequent years, but they still are not insignificant flowers. Go outside before ordering and look at your garden, visualizing what else was in bloom last May. Then make your selections of tall tulips to go with the rest of the property and the way you live. Yellow or white varieties show up at night and contrast beautifully with evergreens, for example. They are also easy to add to the garden picture because the two shades blend so well with all the other colors.

Where you are using tulips in quantity, some breathtaking combinations are possible. You can plant a drift of tulips that blends from lemon yellow to dark gold to apricot to orange, scarlet and finally red by carefully planning which varieties go where. The same color monochromatics can be done with tulips in the rose-and-pink spectrum or in the lavender-to-purple range.

Or you can juxtapose very different colors to make a study in contrasts. White tulips are effective this way. Pretend you are playing with swirls of paint.

Dark purple or brownish orange tulips show up better against a lighter background. They are striking against buildings or with statuary. One of the vivid memories of my childhood is of a group of dark, almost brown, tulips planted to be seen with a white bench in the background. Companion plants such as arabis and perennial candytuft can give this effect too if their white flowers are positioned thoughtfully.

125

Double Eve

Fringed Swan Wings

Assorted Parrot Tulips

Shrubs and trees also make pleasing companions for tulips, but watch out for too much shade. One of the easiest and still very effective combinations is lilacs and late tulips. Flowering crab apples and dogwoods are two other possibilities.

May also sees the double late tulips in bloom, and these, too, are great for picking. Their stems are much longer than the early doubles. This can be a handicap in a wet spring, because the flowers are so full of petals that the water actually collects in the heads, and they may be broken off or badly bowed. If possible, try to situate these tulips at the edges of a high tree where the branches will break the force of the rain. Put them on the south side of the tree so that sunshine can get to their leaves. There is a full range of hues from which to choose, and most catalogs offer a good selection. In addition to those of a single color, there are some interesting combinations. Most have been grown for a long time and are quite dependable.

Again, avoid ordering a mixture, for the double tulips are most useful for creating a big splash of color in the landscape; you can do that only if you plant them in groups of a single variety. A dozen of one kind makes a spot of color no one can overlook. These double late tulips are also long-lasting in bouquets if you can bear to remove a few from the garden. They usually have lovely long stems, too.

Technically the next group of tulips to consider belongs to the Cottage group, but almost all catalogs now list them separately as Bouquet, Bunch-flowering, Multi-flowered, Branching, Candelabra or Tree tulips. Because their growth habit is so different, this makes sense. They are not new, but they have become popular again. Branching tulips is the most apt description. They send up one stout stem from the bulb, which then branches off at various points into smaller stems with a flower at the end of each. They have a natural grace that many other tall tulips lack, because the effect is more of a fountain. In the garden they are particularly good for making a big splash of color. Unfortunately, they do not always retain the branching habit after a year or two of growing, but for the first season they are great where you want a lot of color. Some of the best are Wallflower, mahogany red; Rose Mist, white, mottled rose; Georgette, yellow, edged red; Mon. S. Mottet, creamy white; Mme. Mottet, rosy carmine, edged white; Keukenhof, scarlet; Emir, red. Some of the species tulips have this branching characteristic too.

TULIPS FOR ARRANGERS

Also blooming in May are some extraordinary tulips that have more merit for the flower arranger than in the garden, although there are those who love them. The Fringed tulips are a fairly recent offering. The edges of their petals are fringed, giving almost a lacy look. I have not found them long-lived. The Parrot tulips, on the other hand, date back before 1700 and are persistent in the garden. Their petals are twisted, sometimes fringed, often of more than one color. Both Parrots and Fringed come in a range of colors. The most sensible course is

to order them with particular attention to what use you intend for them. Many colors will work themselves into the garden, but for indoor use they should merge with the containers and the decor of the rooms in which they will be displayed.

Tulips are lovely in bouquets. As long as you do not remove the basal foliage, there is no reason why you cannot use your tulips for indoor pleasure. It is much better for the bulbs not to go to seed, and picking is the nicest way to ensure against such an event. You will notice, however, that tulips have a way of folding up their petals when not in

Bouquet Summer Love

Broken Tulips

Cordell Hull

Mme. Dubarry

Belle Queen

May Blossom

direct light. If your arrangement requires that your tulips remain open, try placing a few drops of melted candle wax in the center of the bloom. The flowers will then stay more nearly the way your design requires. For mixed bouquets, merely pick and enjoy without the extra trouble. Even the short-stemmed early types can be worked into cheerful small arrangements for the table, but the tall May-flowering types adapt to almost any type of bouquet.

Other favorites for arrangements are "broken" tulips. You may find them listed also as Bizarres, Rembrandts or Bijbloemen. In these the petals are feathered and flamed with a second color. They were once in great fashion and are often used to create bouquets in the old Dutch manner shown in many paintings. Your catalog descriptions will tell you what is available.

One tulip that stands by itself is Picture, officially a Darwin. Its petals are rolled inward to give it a distinct, fascinating shape.

Arrangers also enjoy the Viridiflora tulips, all of which have a certain amount of real green color on their petals. Groenland (Greenland) is the shape of an ordinary Cottage type, but the others are closer to the lily shape. Angel, Artist, Golden Artist, Court Lady, Hollywood, Pimpernel and Viridiflora *praecox* are widely offered. Most of these last extremely well but do not show up much in the garden.

While these last few paragraphs have been devoted to tulips that are likely to have special appeal to flower arrangers, I do not intend to suggest that anyone confine themselves merely to these varieties. Any tulip is a fine subject for a bouquet. If you do much flower arranging or enter many spring shows, however, your regular garden will not be able to provide you with enough raw materials for your designing. For one thing, the border where you envisioned clumps of pink tulips for a special effect will take on a drab look if you gather all the flowers for inside. No matter how many blue ribbons you bring home, your eye is going to miss the outside decoration.

Obviously, the solution is to raise some tulips just for picking and arranging. Even at today's prices, you can choose a tremendous variety of good tulips by the dozen for no more than a few dollars. When compared with the price of buying a dozen cut tulips in the spring from a florist, this is a real saving.

Tulips need not be planted until quite late in the fall (although I personally try to get most of mine in the ground early). So there is no good reason not to plan on a block of them to replace the tomato plants, which you can pull up after the first frost. Simply turn over the soil well first and then make some trenches in which you can put the tulip bulbs a few inches apart. After you have gathered your flowers in the spring (and hopefully won an armful of prizes), pull up the tulips, bulbs and all, and discard them on the compost heap. With such a program you will save money in the long run, and you will be able to have cutting tulips in quantity in the hues and shapes you like best. You will be able also to enjoy your outside garden color scheme—and so will every person who passes by.

PLANT: five to ten inches deep, three to five inches apart, depending on size of bulb, type of soil and your water table; nearly full sun.

SPECIES TULIPS

In previous pages I have discussed the hybrids of three species tulips in particular: the Kaufmannianas, the Fosterianas and the Greigis. All three groups are notable for size and bright color and the hybrids for vigor and adaptability in garden situations. These

Groenland

Artist

T. acuminata

129

T. marjoletti

T. sylvestris

last two characteristics are almost always found among plant hybrids.

When we come to the true species tulips, we are dealing with what are essentially wild flowers. To be successful, you have to pay attention to their idiosyncrasies. Most want well-drained spots and thrive on hot summer baking, so they should not go where you are likely to do extensive summer watering. Many are native to mountainous areas where the soil is lean, so they should not have fertilizer.

Moreover, many of the species tulip bulbs in commerce are collected in the wild rather than being grown to flowering size by bulb firms. The best advice is to mark their sites well after planting and be patient. If the first year they produce just a single leaf from the bulb, chances are the collected bulbs were simply not big enough to flower. If your garden site is to their liking, they may eventually mature and bloom.

With a few exceptions, the true species tulips are smaller in stature and shorter of stem than the garden varieties; many are made to order for rock gardens and little niches along a path or in the foreground of the spring garden. Slopes or raised beds are good, too.

Planting the species extends the tulip season a good month at least. By choosing among the various kinds you can have both earlier and later bloom.

But you will have to exercise more care in selecting habitats. Be careful too that you do not put the smaller species tulips next to overwhelming ground covers or perennials. Perennial candytuft, for example, is too big a companion for most species tulips; it will literally smother them. You will never get bulbs up to size if the foliage does not get plenty of sun. Some of the species tulips are stoloniferous in habit. They keep sending out underground roots and starting new bulbs instead of blooming. Thin, rocky soil may inhibit this characteristic.

Not all species tulips are easily located, and prices are not always low; but if you can give them the right location, they often make themselves permanently at home and increase slowly. I have room for only a brief résumé of some of the best, with heights in parentheses. Blooming times are approximate. Some selected forms are listed as well.

T. chrysantha

T. clusiana

T. turkestanica

T. pulchella violacea

T. acuminata (Horned or Spider tulip, *cornuta, stenopetala*) (18); long, twisted petals in yellow and red (April).

T. batalini (7); creamy yellow (April); Bright Gem is a selection.

T. biflora (6); several small white flowers on each stem (March).

T. chrysantha (*stellata*) (8); small yellow, red exterior (April).

T. clusiana (Lady or Candlestick tulip) (15); white and cherry; quite adaptable to gardens, stoloniferous (April to May).

T. eichleri (15); crimson, center black and yellow (April).

T. hageri (8); red and green flowers (April).

T. kolpakowskiana (10); yellow and red; wavy foliage (April).

T. linifolia (8); scarlet with dark basal blotches (April).

T. marjoletti (22); primrose, exterior tinges of rose (May).

T. persica (*breyniana*) (8); several small starry yellow and bronze flowers; one of the latest tulips (May).

T. praestans (9); several vermilion flowers on each stem (April); Fusilier and Zwanenburg are good selections.

T. pulchella humilis (6); variable but usually pink to magenta with yellow center; thin petals (March).

T. pulchella violacea (5); bright red-purple cups (March).

T. saxatilis (12); several pinky-lilac flowers with yellow centers; foliage appears in late fall (April).

T. sprengeri (12); scarlet; the last to flower; will take a little shade (May to June).

T. sylvestris (*florentina odorata*) (16); nodding yellow; will take a little shade; fragrant (April to May).

T. tarda (*dasystemon*) (6); several medium-sized yellow stars, tipped white, on each stem; great for rock garden (April to May).

T. turkestanica (10); many starry white flowers with yellow centers on each stem (March to April).

T. urumiensis (6); several yellow stars on each stem; similar to T. tarda in effect (April to May).

T. whittali (12); fairly large orange flowers (late April).

PLANT: three to eight inches deep, depending on size of bulb, three to five inches apart, in well-drained, lean soil; full sun.

T. saxatilis

T. tarda

Forcing Hardy Bulbs

"Forcing" is really the wrong word to use about the process of bringing hardy bulbs into flower early in the house. Perhaps "hurrying" is a better choice, for you are not making the bulb accomplish something it is not programmed to do; a mature, healthy bulb wants to flower. What you are doing is cutting short the period of stem development which, when outside, is retarded by winter's cold. What you cannot do is curtail the early development of a healthy, strong root system.

Two rules make forcing easier. First, choose bulb types that naturally flower early in spring, then further select those species or varieties of each bulb that are known for their earlier blooming. Always use the largest and best bulbs for forcing. You are, after all, going to some extra trouble, and you want to stack the cards in your favor as much as possible.

Second, you will have to provide a dark, cool place in which root development can take place. A ventilated cold frame, a cool corner of the cellar, a root cellar, unheated

bedroom or attic—all are possibilities. You can easily put a large box over the pots to keep out light, but if the space is too warm, the flowers will blast. A garage may do, too, but don't let the pots freeze. You want a place where the temperature range is from around 40°F. to no higher than 50°F. I have known gardeners who successfully used a home refrigerator, but space limits how many you can put there. A freezer does not work, incidentally. It is far too cold.

Old-time gardeners used to dig an outside trench deep enough to be below the frost line, then they placed the planted pots there on top of a layer of drainage material, filled the trench with dry leaves and covered the whole with boards. This did give the bulbs a chance to develop good root systems, but it is more work than most busy gardeners seek. And a deep snow often makes it difficult to get the pots out when it is time for the next step in forcing.

Daffodils, particularly the tender kinds, are often forced in pebbles (see page 173). Special hyacinth glasses are sold for forcing single large bulbs in plain water, as are crocus glasses for small bulbs of many kinds. For most gardeners it is just as easy to use a mixture of equal parts of loam, peat moss and vermiculite (or perlite) in ordinary clay bulb pots. These are wider and not as deep as regular pots, allowing space for several bulbs per pot.

Bulbs to be forced should be ordered as early as possible. Some time after September 30, plant as many bulbs per pot as will fit comfortably with about one half inch between bulbs. Place tops of the bulbs just below the soil surface or even slightly above it for large bulbs. Set the pots in a tray filled with water and allow to soak until the top of the soil feels moist. Then remove pots and position where forcing is to take place. A pot of the same diameter inverted over the planted pot is one way to ensure adequate darkness and air circulation over the bulb but discourage mice.

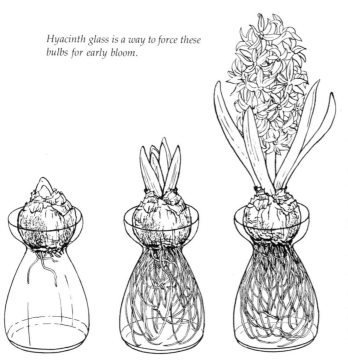

Hyacinth glass is a way to force these bulbs for early bloom.

For most hardy bulbs you should now allow eight to 12 weeks for good rooting. Add some water from time to time if necessary. The soil should not be wet, but never let it become bone-dry. If you plant several pots, you can leave some in the cool spot longer and thus have staggered bloom, but do not start any forcing until roots show in the drain hole at the bottom of the pot. That, plus some top growth, is the signal that the bulb is finally ready for the hurrying process and warmer conditions.

First, remove the cover for a few days so that the shoot can turn green in shade, thus preventing sunburn of tender new growth. When the shoot is green, bring the pot to a sunny window in the coolest room of the house. Too much heat at this point often blasts the flowers. Now treat as for any cool-loving house plant, watering as necessary and turning the pot daily to encourage straight stems.

When the flowers break bud, you then bring the pot to the living room for fullest enjoyment. Placing it on a table out of the sun for this period extends the life of the flowers. So does extra water and a nightly trip back to the cool room.

After flowering is over, either discard the bulbs or take the pot back to the cool window and encourage the foliage to stay green as long as possible. The bulbs can then be planted in the garden in the spring at the proper depth for the type bulb involved. Often, after a year of catching up with itself, a forced bulb will return to normal and bloom outside at the proper time. If you plan to keep the bulbs, give them a weekly half-strength drink of soluble plant food after flowering. You have nothing to lose by trying this with any hardy bulb forced in soil, but those grown in water become worthless.

Bulb catalogs often indicate which tulips, daffodils and hyacinths are recommended for forcing. These are the varieties to order for this process. Tulips are tricky to force, so for your first attempt with them, confine yourself to one of the early singles or early doubles and never try to hurry them.

Daffodils are one of the most popular hardy bulbs for forcing, and there is a wide choice. Among the highly successful are Dutch Master, Golden Harvest, Rembrandt, Unsurpassable, Celebrity, Cantatrice, Mount Hood, King Alfred, Carlton, Carbineer, Flower Record, Verger, Barrett Browning, Edward Buxton, Texas, Cheerfulness, Cragford, February Gold, March Sunshine, Charity May, Beryl and W. P. Milner.

Early-blooming lilies force well, too, particularly those cataloged as Mid-Century hybrids. The famous Easter lily is not easy without a greenhouse. Give lilies a long period for root development, then force slowly in a cool, sunny spot.

Small bulbs that also respond to slow forcing include the various crocuses (there are special pots on the market), *Iris reticulata*, the early-blooming muscari and scilla, chionodoxa, snowdrop and puschkinia. Also try lily-of-the-valley pips lifted from outside in a thaw, then potted.

Actually, it is possible to lift many other bulbs besides lily-of-the-valley directly from the garden. Some of the little bulbs—such as grape-hyacinths, for example—produce foliage in the fall. Many crocus and other small bulbs show the tips of their leaves in earliest spring. During a thaw, you can find

A homemade hyacinth glass can be produced by bending crossed wires over a drinking glass to hold bulb above water level.

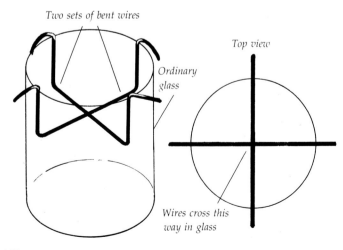

133

Plant bulbs close together when forcing hardy types to ensure a generous display.

Hardy bulbs are not ready for forcing until roots show in the drainage hole of the pot.

these easily by the foliage. Dig them out carefully and pot, disturbing the roots as little as possible. They will need a few days of very cool conditions and sufficient watering to prevent the foliage from wilting during an adjustment period. Then they can be placed in a sunny window in a not too warm room. Flowering is often quite rapid, particularly if you lift them later as spring advances. Such a method would never produce bloom in the earliest part of the winter, but it can give you an advance preview of spring with very little trouble.

The whole realm of forcing bulbs is one in which inventiveness and ingenuity yield amazing results. Instead of buying hyacinth glasses, which are comparatively expensive, you can utilize a hollow-stemmed beer glass; but you will have to watch the water level more carefully because the stem does not hold much liquid. The bulb, of course, sits in the wider top of the glass. You can even convert an ordinary drinking tumbler into a container for water culture. Use baling wire or some other grade that is fairly malleable. Depending on the size of the glass and the bulb, it will take two to four pieces of

wire bent as illustrated on page 133 to fashion a basket for the bulb. The important thing is to keep the bulb itself from sitting in the water. Early-blooming daffodils can be forced this way, too. This water culture is most recommended for apartment dwellers who do not have soil readily available. Persons with a garden just outside the door usually prefer using soil because bulbs so treated can be tucked into the garden afterward with much better hope of success.

One ingenious gardener I know has window wells off her basement laundry. They have several inches of stone in the bottom so that drainage is no problem. She puts her pots of bulbs to be forced atop the stones in the well, then covers them up to the top of the well with leaves she has raked up. Her husband made a cover of hardware mesh that fits tightly over the edges of the well. He put in a couple of cup hooks along the house side to hold the wire in place along that edge. This effectively keeps out rodents. Her forced bulbs are watered naturally by the rain and snow, kept at an optimum temperature for root growth by the outside weather, and the leaves prevent the pene-

Roots of paper-white daffodils may force bulbs out of pebbles; gently press back into medium.

one for dark cold, the other warmer and sunlit.

The outside cellar entrance to old houses is another useful gardening annex. The temperature on the lower steps nearest the cellar door itself is well nigh perfect for hardy bulbs to root well. The folding doors keep out the light, and access is easy via the cellar door. In such a place you can check almost daily on development without any trouble at all. Protected as they are from the rain, such pots will need regular watering, however. Slug bait again may be indicated, and rodents may be present. You can keep them out with an inverted pot over the planted pot if its hole is small or stuffed with a crumpled piece of chicken wire. The main thing to remember, whatever spot you choose, is to force bulbs slowly.

tration of any light. When she wants to take some pots in, it is easy to get at them. She is even foresighted enough to put tall labels in each pot so that she can find just the one she wants without rummaging around too much. Aside from the wire mesh, her only precaution is to spread slug bait liberally in the wells several days before she plans to put the pots in.

Another gardener, incidentally, uses her window well as a makeshift cold frame and reports that it works well. Hers is covered with clear heavy plastic, and she gains access by opening the window from the inside. Pots of bulbs for forcing in such a situation will need to be covered to prevent light from reaching the shoots too soon in the forcing process.

It takes practice to utilize a cold frame fully. In moderate climates the glass may allow too great a heat buildup for bulb forcing. You can, of course, keep bulbs easily in a cold frame that is further covered with old rugs to keep out the sun's warmth. The perfect solution is to have two cold frames—

Pot of well-forced daffodils will brighten any room in midwinter.

Bulb Propagation

Although most bulbs can be propagated by seed, this is the least recommended way for the ordinary gardener to increase stock of most bulbous plants. Hybridizing of bulbs, however, is always done through the medium of seed. When you learn that it often takes seven years before the first bloom arrives on a new daffodil hybrid, you may better appreciate the dedication of professional growers, but such specialized work is beyond the scope of this book.

If you have enough patience, however, you can raise almost any bulb from seed. In cases of rare species this may be the only way to obtain them. Very often the bulb seedlings will show no top growth the first year, but the seed may have sprouted and the tiny bulb be developing undergound. For this reason all pots or flats containing such seed should be labeled well and given at least two full growing seasons before you give them up. Hardy bulb seed sometimes needs a cold period before germination will take place, so containers may be left outside over winter but protected from drowning, rodents and curious birds. Never subject the seeds of tender bulbs to freezing.

With holes punched in the bottom and a layer of crockery to ensure good drainage, the bottom half of a large waxed-paper milk carton makes a good small flat for special seeds. It will survive two winters before losing its shape. A mixture of equal parts of loam, peat moss and vermiculite makes a suitable medium.

Remember that seed production weakens any bulb. Except for special reasons, remove all spent flowers before seed begins to form, whether in the garden or on potted bulbs.

Most bulbs, however, increase by vegetative means, often more rapidly than the gardener wishes. Planting a hardy bulb as shallowly as possible in a particular climate encourages it to increase faster by means of offsets, small bulbs that form next to the parent bulb. This is one way to increase more rapidly your stock of something rare or expensive.

Almost all true bulbs increase this way eventually, so you do not really have to do anything to encourage the process unless you're in a hurry. If a clump of bulbs is not separated, in time it may become so crowded that flower production is cut sharply. In such cases the largest bulbs can be put back into the garden and the smaller ones grown on in a nursery area until of flowering size. When you separate them, always be sure that each bulb has a portion of the basal plate and allow them to dry in a cool, shady place for a few days before replanting. Potted bulbs need to be separated, too, when they become too crowded. Repot the largest and discard the babies or give extras away so that you won't have too many for the available space.

A few true bulbs increase also by scales, lilies and fritillarias, for example. You can peel off some of the scales and plant them in a flat, as you would large seeds. In time they will form new bulbs. Some lilies and other bulbs also produce tiny bulblets on the stems, and these too may be planted in the nursery to develop size. During their first winter, baby bulbs need some protection from freezing, such as a dark cold frame.

Corms reproduce quite differently. When you dig up your gladiolus in the fall, the

A cardboard milk carton with one side removed makes a fine small flat that will fit on most windowsills. Peel one side down for easy access to seedlings when transplanting.

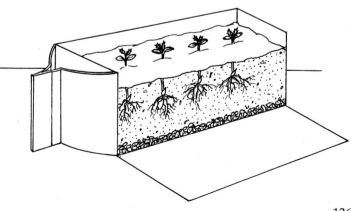

Eucharis bulbs have increased by offsets to crowding point and must be separated. Whole soil mass is first lifted from pot.

Harvest of eucharis bulbs is amazing. Soil mass was thoroughly soaked and bulbs gently pried apart, with as many roots preserved as possible.

shriveled-up old corm will be found underneath the new ones. It has depleted itself and should be pried off and thrown away after the corms are cured a bit. Crocuses undergo the same process. After some years a planting of them should be dug up after the foliage is brown, then replanted; otherwise, the new corms that form above the previous year's will eventually get too close to the soil surface, where they are prone to frost damage or to the ravages of hungry rodents. There will be corms of several sizes.

Again the tiny cormels can be grown separately if you wish to increase your stock. With hardy types this can take place on the periphery of a planting of larger corms, but with tender plants, the small corms need to be gathered before frost and stored, as with the parent corms. The hard little cormels sprout better if given a 24-hour soaking in water before planting in the spring. They are planted shallower than those of flowering size. Most gardeners discard the smallest offsets or cormels.

It is a strange fact that when a bulb is injured, as when you slice through one with a spade, it sometimes produces bulblets along the scar. This technique is used commercially, especially with hyacinths, but is rather chancy for the home gardener.

Some bulbs also increase by sending out a root that then develops a new bulb at its end. Such types are termed stoloniferous. They spread irregularly through the garden. This habit may not matter with a group of erythroniums in a shady woodland, but it may present difficulties in a formal garden of tulips. Read the small print in the catalog.

Rhizomes increase by sending out new arms, which can be broken off the original and replanted. Usually the ideal time to do this is just after flowering. If you do not care about the current season's flowering, you can perform this operation in early spring. Dust the broken parts with garden disinfectant or allow them to scar over by storing in a well-ventilated cool spot for a few days before replanting.

137

Thickened rootstocks tend to grow longer rather than sending out arms like the rhizome. They can be propagated by division, making sure that each piece has a growing bud. In the garden it is just as easy to let them increase naturally in the ground. If a plant begins to creep beyond where it is wanted, however, it may be dug in earliest spring just as the first shoots show, or, even better, in late or midsummer when the foliage begins to brown off. Cut off the extra lengths of root, each with at least one bud, and replant immediately after disinfecting. Solomon-seal is a good example.

True tubers, such as are found on the cyclamen or the tuberous begonia, are increased somewhat like a potato. The tuber is cut into pieces, each with a budded eye, and these are planted separately after disinfecting. Most gardeners merely let the tubers grow larger slowly; this course is certainly safer. I have never had the courage to try this in my garden, but you may be braver than I.

The tuberous-rooted dahlia cannot be let alone. At the end of the growing season a whole cluster of tubers will be found when the plant is dug. Before planting the next spring, cut these off the old stalk. Each tuber that has a growing eye at the stem end is then planted separately. Well-grown dahlias increase prodigiously. Refer to page 162 for simple directions on separating.

Hard-and-fast rules do not apply in the natural world. With sharp eyes you may well observe some strange behavior among your bulbs. If you have some reason to want to propagate a certain bulb, by all means take advantage of whatever nature offers. One year, for example, I noticed that a rare tulip was producing little bulblets on its stems. Questioning more experienced gardeners did not bring any logical explanation of why this tulip exhibited such behavior, but I planted the tiny bulbs just to see what would happen. Unfortunately, I must report nothing, but it was interesting.

Many bulbs, especially the smaller ones that we are all inclined to overlook when picking dead flowers from the garden, will happily increase themselves by both offsets and seed until you have an exciting drift of them. I have not noticed that this did any harm to the originals. Chionodoxa is one good example. When my patch begins to show its shoots in early spring, I begin to check for small grasslike foliage on its periphery. These are seedlings, and I mulch carefully around them so that later they will not be weeded out or disturbed. My early snowdrop (*Galanthus elwesi*) produces big ripe seeds just at a time when I am busy in the garden and checking things daily. I try to remember to gather these and plant them near the mother bulbs. In this way I have increased my colony of them quicker than if I had left it all to chance.

One year I inadvertently let a speciosum lily go to seed. By the time I noticed, the pod was greatly swollen, so I let nature take its course and eventually gathered the ripe seed. The lilies that resulted after a few years of maturing were magnificent, quite superior to the parent. Again I have no explanation of why, but it was a most satisfying reward for my being a little careless about removing dead flowers.

Jack-in-the-pulpit increases by berries, which turn scarlet in early fall.

Grassy foliage of chionodoxa seedlings shows colony is increasing; mulching helps prevent their disturbance.

Bulbs like Jack-in-the-pulpit and Sol-omon-plume produce berries rather than seeds, and birds devour them quickly. If I get there first, I often plant the ripe berries near the parent stand, and as a result there are increasing numbers of these plants in my woodland garden.

All sorts of exciting experiences await you in your bulb garden. Some will be true sur-prises, as when an enterprising squirrel re-plants a crocus far from where you put the others. You might even notice a sport of some sort in your own garden. These muta-tions can occur anywhere, any time. It might be a flower that deviates advantageously from the norm in number of petals, brighter color, larger size or even a different shape. If possible, never pick such a treasure until you have taken a photograph. Since it may rob the bulb, it is better not to let it go to seed, but mark the spot well and wait another year to see what comes up from the bulb the second time. If the improved flower occurs again, call in an expert to see if what your garden has produced may be good enough for formal propagation. While the characteristics of the mutation might be present in the heredity makeup of some of the seeds, vegetative propagation is the surest way to increase stock of a new form. Until you have extra bulbs of the improved form, it is not wise to let it develop any seed.

Eventually every garden and every house will have a surplus of some kind of bulb. When you run out of space, your extras will make nice gifts.

CULTURE OF TENDER BULBS

Botanically, the bulbs in this book should not be separated as they are into hardy and tender sections. The daffodil is a hardy member of the same family to which the tender amaryllis belongs, for example. But this is a handbook for gardeners, and whether or not a given bulb is able to withstand a freezing winter in the ground of the garden is of profound importance to determine what bulbs to order and how to treat them.

This section could be divided further into those bulbs that are usually grown in the open ground during the warm months and those that adapt to containers in the house during the winter. However, there is possible a certain amount of interchange. Neither type can be subjected to freezing, and many are harmed by temperatures much below 50°F. In warm climates, of course, all can be grown outside all year.

Whether treated as potted plants in the house or as summer denizens of the garden or patio, tender bulbs require more work by gardeners in northern climates. In contrast, the hardy bulbs can be left to fend for themselves for long periods of time. Tender bulbs for garden use have to be planted every spring, lifted in the fall and correctly stored over the winter if you are to get the greatest return on your investment. You could buy new ones every year and ignore the last two steps, but most gardeners are less extravagant.

If your garden is small, however, and your house not adaptable for storing things, consider a few tender summer-flowering bulbs as an annual expense. Gladiolus and dahlias, to name the two most popular, are readily obtained almost everywhere, and prices are not steep for common hybrids. You can buy a dozen top-size labeled gladiolus corms for very few dollars, and

Pendulous types of tuberous begonias are ideal for hanging baskets.
Photo Courtesy White Flower Farm, Litchfield, Connecticut.

mixtures are even cheaper. It takes little money to purchase three tubers of hybrid miniature dahlias that will give you a fine display and plenty of cut flowers in a small plot. Not much of an investment for a lot of pleasure. Then at the end of the growing year, let the tubers rot in the ground and have a carefree winter yourself. The glads may even surprise you by coming up again after a winter in the ground if you live in a moderate climate like mine. (Little bonuses like that are what make gardening fun.)

Most of us want to try to save our bulb stock for another year, however, so we need to think ahead a bit more when dealing with the tender types than we do with their hardier relatives.

Even those tender subjects that are grown in pots inside usually need a rest period of some sort, and they require sunny windows for good growth. The average gardener with limited space and time is well advised to buy tender bulbs for outside use, with careful thought both to the work involved and the space required for storage. How many and what bulbs are chosen for inside is even more severely circumscribed by the available windows, what direction these face toward the sun and how warm the room in which the bulbs will be placed is kept.

Vacation habits are important, too. There is little point in a garden full of tigridias and dahlias if you are away all summer, and a reliable plant-sitter will be required for indoor bulbs if you winter away from home.

Although there are short directions included in the descriptions of the various bulb flowers in the following pages, certain general rules are worth reviewing.

When to plant tender bulbs outside is always a question for the northern gardener. For half-hardy bulbs like gladiolus, any time after the last frost date in the spring to about two months before the first frost date in autumn should work. The bulbs cannot be too cold in the spring, but they require sufficient time to grow and flower before fall frost. For most of the others it is wiser to wait until the soil itself has begun to warm up and the nights are no longer cold. If it is safe to plant tomatoes, you can plant most tender bulbs.

At the other end of the growing season, you as the gardener have to make certain again that the bulbs do not chill too much. The half-hardy ones may have their foliage blackened by the first frost without damage, but the jungle inhabitants may not fare as well with such treatment. Ismene, for example, will refuse to blossom the following spring if it has been subjected to real cold, even though it has not been frozen.

Try to plant the tropicals several weeks after the last frost and to bring truly tender things into the house as soon as the nights begin to drop below 50°F. If your growing season is short, you are limited in what tender bulbs you may use outside, but you can cheat nature by starting some things early inside to get the jump on the season. In the far North it is often much easier to treat most tender bulbs as potted plants.

Garden soil that already supports perennials or vegetables well will usually be excellent for summer bulbs. Those being grown in pots should have peat moss added to the soil mixture to help retain moisture. Coarse sand or vermiculite will aid drainage if the soil is clayey.

One warning for gardeners with limited space: Do not plant tender bulbs too close to patches of hardy ones. It is not possible to dig even those like gladiolus that do not take up a lot of space without disturbing the surrounding area somewhat. The time of year when you are bringing in the tender bulbs is exactly the season when the hardy ones are working hardest at their important root development. It would not do to uproot them then.

Bugs are more of a problem with tender bulbs than with hardy ones simply because summertime is the peak season for insect activity. Japanese beetles can do a lot of damage to cannas, and thrips threaten many of the gladiolus relatives—to name two common pests. Dahlias too are attractive to many chewing insects. Keeping the weeds down around tender bulb plantings is beneficial, since it makes it less easy for the insects to establish breeding populations. Frequent inspections pay dividends because you may hand-kill a few early bugs before they build up to a real invasion. All-purpose garden sprays such as are used for roses may be useful from time to time. If you grow just a few tender bulbs here and there among the rest of the garden's inhabitants, you should have little real trouble. Where you are concentrating on one genus in a big way—as, for example, if you have a large section of the garden devoted to rows of gladiolus for cutting or an extensive planting of dahlias—be prepared to do some spraying. By and large, members of the amaryllis family seem the least prone to insect damage, but I have grown a very large variety of tender bulbs without ever having a rigorous spray program.

Slugs can be a terrible problem in the summer garden that is well mulched, especially during years when rainfall is protracted. These damnable bits of slime are drawn to the dampness beneath pots, too. If you have containers on the ground, buy some slug bait and from time to time sprinkle some under the pots. This will take care of the slugs but hide the poisonous bait from pets and small children. Sow bugs can be a nuisance with potted plants also. They gather underneath the containers and also are found in large numbers in the lower part of the pot. Spray the bottoms of the containers with malathion or Sevin. Both these are fairly safe insecticides, but take time to read the labels carefully and follow directions to the letter both for your own protection and the health of your plants.

Gloriosa-lily nods a cheery welcome at entrance to front porch. (OPPOSITE, UPPER LEFT)

Cannas provide flamboyant touch for summer gardens. (OPPOSITE, UPPER RIGHT)

Pot of caladiums set into old stump behind birdbath stone adds color to shady summer garden. (OPPOSITE, BELOW)

Peruvian daffodil flowers are intensely fragrant.

Perhaps because their growing season is shorter, most tender bulbs benefit much more than hardy ones from additional fertilizing. This is particularly true of those grown in containers, whether inside or outside. You can make a liquid manure by following the directions on a package of dehydrated cow manure. Never apply this to the foliage, however, nor allow the dry powder to touch the plant.

A water-soluble general-purpose fertilizer for house plants is even easier to mix and apply. For plants in the open ground, this type may be administered at the recommended strength several times after growth is well along. Should the season be rainy, use the fertilizer more frequently. Pot-grown bulbs do better if fertilizer is used at half strength and applied every week during active growth. Do not give any food to potted plants at inside windows during the winter period of low light and consequent slow growth, which lasts from the end of November to the end of January in the northern hemisphere.

When watering pot-grown bulbs, give them a good drink, then wait until the soil on the top of the pot is dry again. This deep watering helps leach out harmful chemical salts that otherwise might build up in the pots. Plants in clay pots, which lose some moisture to the air, always need more water than those in plastic containers. Hanging baskets in hot summer will need water at least once daily. Bulbs in the open ground need attention in times of drought, particularly after rapid growth begins and before they flower. Like all bulbs, most should be planted where drainage is good, but in dry times water deeply enough to reach all roots. Except for those with hairy leaves, bulbs seem to like their foliage washed, too. With inside plants this helps keep the leaves clean of dust. A good strong shower at the sink every few weeks also discourages many insects. During the winter, humidity can be very low in a heated house. Setting bulb pans on a waterproof tray full of pebbles and partially filled with water helps increase the humidity. Misting is beneficial, too.

Storing tender bulbs is a real problem in a small house. Generally, those grown in pots may be left in the soil and the pots stacked in an out-of-the-way place where the temperature is above freezing and ventilation adequate. During the winter sprinkle some water on them several times to avoid complete desiccation, but don't get them really wet. When it comes time to break their dormancy, it is usually wiser to replant in fresh soil, although I have ignored this advice quite successfully for one season. At least change to fresh soil every other year.

Summer-flowering bulbs and corms that have a protective papery husk need the least attention of those taken directly from the garden for storage. They are dug up in the fall and the soil shaken off. If the foliage is already brown, it may be cut off immediately; otherwise leave them in a box upright in the garage for a week or two (it should still be warm enough there) until the foliage dries. If they are corms, the old ones may then be pried off and discarded. The corms or bulbs being saved now need a short period to ripen their husks and may be kept where it is fairly warm for a few weeks. Then they can be put into ventilated bags (old nylon stockings are ideal for this), labeled and hung up in a room where the temperature is cool but not freezing until time to replant in the spring.

Tubers and roots cannot be treated so casually. After digging, shake off as much dirt as possible and spread them out in a shaded spot (as in a garage) for a few days until the outside of the tuber is dry to the touch. Then put them in shallow boxes, label, cover with dry peat moss, sawdust or vermiculite and store above freezing. Every month check to make sure they are not drying and shriveling. You want them to remain plump until spring planting. You may have to sprinkle the boxes lightly with water to maintain the proper moisture, but do it carefully because mold from excess moisture is just as injurious. (Specific storage tips for each of the different bulbs are included with their descriptions.)

The problems of storing tender bulbs are compounded if you live in a house without a basement. I used to be able to store successfully all manner of tender bulbs and tubers in corners of the basement away from the furnace. When we moved to a house built on a concrete slab, I had to devise a whole new set of rules for successful storage.

Dormant bulbs in pots of soil I have been able to store on the floor of the laundry room, which is fairly cool. Others like gladiolus-family members that grow from corms also do all right there in bags on the floor, where it is cooler than if I hung them from the rafters. But my space is limited. Cannas and dahlias relegated to the crawl space where the heater is situated either dry out or rot because I cannot give them frequent enough inspection. I am now experimenting with keeping these along the warmest wall of the garage in the hope I can control things better. You will have to try out your own conditions to see what works. Incidentally, the ismene, which dislikes cold, stores beautifully in the warm crawl space if I leave some dirt on the bulbs when I dig them. I am beginning to choose what tender bulbs I use on the basis of whether I can store them or not.

When potting bulbs for any purpose, make sure drainage is adequate by placing crockery in the bottom of the pot. Water well

Foliage of Peruvian daffodil adds interest to summer garden.

once, then only infrequently until top growth appears. Rotate pots at windows a quarter turn every day to keep stems straight. This turning of the pots is a good idea even with plants being grown outside. It makes them grow more uniformly instead of reaching for the light to one side or getting too leggy altogether.

Tender bulbs, incidentally, fit in very well with the increased interest in container gardening. Tuberous begonias, caladiums, dwarf cannas and achimenes are some of the best to try. You can shift the pots around so that those in best flower decorate your outdoor living quarters from time to time. I have pots of gloriosa-lily, cyclamen, eucharis and agapanthus on my front porch every summer. They go indoors before frost, either to storage or to their winter quarters, depending on their habits, and I find it much easier to handle them this way. Some of the tuberous begonias as well as achimenes are fine for hanging baskets, too. Keep in mind that the individual requirements of each plant dictate whether it can go on a sunny patio or needs some protective shade. One thing to remember is that even on a patio shaded in the afternoon, midsummer heat can be decidedly trying for potted plants. The bricks and stones of walls and floors as well as the concrete stay torrid long after the sun has passed. When days are hot and cloudless, potted plants wilt quickly. Water daily.

Bulbs as House Plants

As has already been suggested, what bulbs you can use as house plants are directly dictated by the conditions of your house. What looks absolutely gorgeous in a controlled greenhouse too often rapidly becomes a candidate for the compost pile when brought into the wrong environment. Before you invest in bulbs for indoor use, take a hard look at what your living quarters offer for plants. Then choose those bulbs that not only are most likely to prosper but also offer the most. Factors such as fragrance, floriferousness, long bloom times, good foliage, neatness and how much space is needed are all important.

Do you have limited light such as from windows that face north or northeast or are shaded by porches or overhangs? Then confine your bulbous house plants to cyclamen, caladiums, begonias, gloxinias and achimenes, which do not need high light intensities. You can grow these shade-loving plants at south windows by using thin curtains or by placing the pots a few feet back from the glass. A photo light meter will show you immediately how the degree of light varies.

If your windowsills are too narrow to accommodate the large containers needed by clivia, calla-lily or eucharis, you can grow these as floor plants where sufficient sunlight reaches, or boost them into more sun by placing the pots on some kind of pedestal. As the popularity of indoor gardening increases, there are more and more plant staging devices available.

Are your rooms very hot all winter? Then do not even consider housing cyclamen, freesias or paper-whites. You cannot succeed, for these are plants that require cool temperatures and moist, airy atmosphere.

Indeed, a house that remains from 75° to 80°F. consistently is not a good home for any bulbous plant that I can think of. It isn't even too healthy for people. In these days of fuel shortages it might be wise to see if you couldn't get along in a somewhat cooler environment. But maybe in a warm household there is a room that is cooler than others. This is the one in which to try house plants.

Is your house atmosphere dry in winter? Here is one condition you can do something about. Cool-vapor humidifiers are not prohibitively expensive and make it possible for

When planting a bulb in a pot, put at least an inch of crockery in the bottom to ensure good drainage for soil. Placing pot on pebbles in a waterproof tray helps increase humidity in air around pot; water can be poured into tray without wetting bulb.

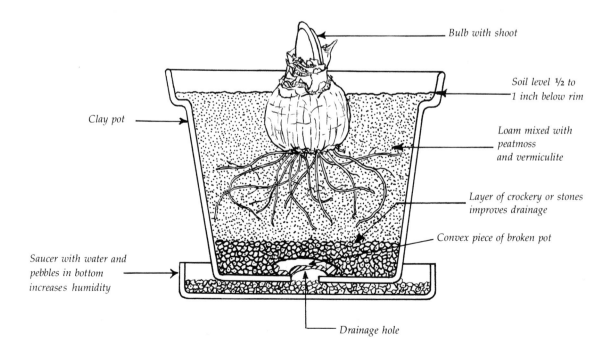

Bulb with shoot

Soil level ½ to 1 inch below rim

Clay pot

Loam mixed with peatmoss and vermiculite

Layer of crockery or stones improves drainage

Convex piece of broken pot

Saucer with water and pebbles in bottom increases humidity

Drainage hole

people to be comfortable at lower temperatures, thus saving fuel. Moreover, the moisture a humidifier puts into the air creates a healthier atmosphere for both plants and people. Because most plants do not thrive on dryness, it is still a good idea to set the pots on a pebble-and-water base, as already suggested in the previous section. This precaution is wise for almost any plants growing indoors except cacti. The miniclimate of more humid air around the tray of pebbles is a real plus. In very cold weather when the heat is constantly on, you can give the plants extra aid by pouring a little boiling water into the pebble trays. You'll see the steam rising. Just don't let such hot water touch the pot or leaves.

Overwatering of bulb flowers indoors can be as dangerous as poor drainage outside. One way to prevent it is to use a porous soil mixture rather than one that is stiff with clay. Always make sure bulbs are potted in containers that have a drainage hole. If looks are a problem, put some pebbles in the bottom of a pretty cachepot, then hide your utilitarian flowerpot with its drainage hole inside. Wait until the surface has a dryish feel before adding more water for all but those that like lots of moisture, such as cyclamen and caladium. Even for these latter two, it pays to set them on a deep base of pebbles or atop an inverted pot so that any excess of water drains out quickly. Two other suggestions to help guarantee good drainage: Put an inch or so of broken crockery in the bottom of the planting pot before you add any soil mixture and place the bulbs so that their shoulders are partly above the soil level at the top.

If you have one sunny room in your house that is consistently cool in winter, you can have real success raising bulbous plants indoors. The minimum temperature should be about 40°F. and the maximum around 60°F. Here cyclamen will thrive, and you can have your cake, too, because they make wonderfully long-lasting cut flowers to decorate other warmer rooms. Paper-white narcissus, ornithogalum, freesia and the many

Indoor light stands for most bulbous subjects must be fairly tall to allow for height. Courtesy W. Atlee Burpee Co.

South African bulbs closely related to them—as well as hardy bulbs being forced for early bloom—all do well under these conditions. Many of these bulbs do not produce plants that are outstandingly decorative, but the cut flowers of all are lovely. This is a much more sensible way to use them, for the ungainliness of the plants can be unimportant in an out-of-the-way room but a real drawback in the living room.

The question of temperature deserves more discussion because it is such a critical factor. You can do things about changing humidity and light, but many bulbs do not have the same needs for warmth as people. Nor is the modern heating system as adaptable as some of the old monsters I have known. We had an ancient coal furnace I grew to hate for many reasons, but it did allow us to cut the heat off from selected rooms. Even when zoned, such highly touted devices as baseboard heating do not give me nearly the latitude of that old heater with its sets of huge air ducts and dampers

for each room. The baseboard pipes do distribute the heat more evenly, however. If you have radiators or forced hot air in ducts, do not put plants too near the source of heat. Conversely, try to keep them out of severely cold drafts also.

Even if you can keep the temperature in your plant room between 60° and 70°F., you still have a wide latitude of bulbs to play with, particularly if your house does not get too dry. From personal experience the following will do fairly well in such an environment: agapanthus, amaryllis and hippeastrum relatives, eucharis, caladium, calla, clivia, gloriosa-lily, gloxinia, ornithogalum, veltheimia, vallota and zephyranthes. Not all will bloom consistently under indoor conditions, but the foliage will at least be a healthy green note most of the time.

If your windows are not sunny enough for growing bulbs indoors in winter, consider investing in a flourescent-light garden that you can place in any convenient space in a house or apartment. Temperatures need to be compatible with the plants you want to grow, but otherwise you can position a light garden wherever you like, even in a basement. Friends in a cramped apartment found space for a little light garden under a draped round library table. Two 20-watt tubes in a reflector that stands on metal legs provide a growing area approximately 12 by 24 inches. The standard arrangement for growing plants under lights is to install a reflector with two 40-watt flourescent tubes approximately 18 inches above a table, shelf or other surface on which flowerpots can be placed. Burn the lights 14 to 16 hours out of every 24. Invest in an automatic timer to assure days and nights of uniform length whether or not you are at home. Growers report success by using a combination of one Warm White with one Cool White tube, or one Cool White in combination with any of the broad-spectrum horticultural tubes, such as Gro-Lux Wide Spectrum. The main

limitation of such a garden is plant height; low-growing gloxinias are better than amaryllis, for example.

Another way to provide better conditions for growing bulb flowers indoors is to install a prefabricated window greenhouse, especially one sized to cover an entire window and fitted with two or three shelves that can be adjusted in height to accommodate different sizes of plants. Use a maximum-minimum thermometer to determine the temperature range in your greenhouse, and then you will be able to adjust accordingly to satisfy the needs of the plants you want to grow. Thermostatically controlled ventilators can make it possible to maintain cool temperatures in winter for bulbs that require coolness; or a soil-heating cable installed in a pebble tray may be used to boost along warmth-loving tropicals. Probably the window greenhouse gives more pleasure for dollars spent than any other way to extend your indoor gardening possibilities.

Whatever techniques and facilities you use for your indoor gardening, remember that this is an artificial environment for growing plants. If you fail at first, try to analyze what went wrong, then try again. Whether you are gardening indoors with natural or artificial light, the space has its own climate just as surely as does a garden outdoors. If you first realistically evaluate the amount of sun or artificial light your garden space receives, the temperature range, amount of humidity during the winter heating season and the availability of fresh air, then you will be able to select plants most likely to succeed without special fussing in your indoor garden. If the plants you want to grow do not seem to fit the conditions you have at present, then you'll have to decide if the necessary environmental changes are feasible. By this approach, the plants you select can be friends, not demanding tyrants. For the home gardener, indoor plant growing that isn't a pleasure has little merit. Life has enough problems without creating a whole new set. Gardening is meant to be fun, not frenzy.

Hyacinths, amaryllis and tulips are easy-to-grow and rewarding additions to any winter garden room or windowsill. Select bulbs that are suitable for the humidity, light and space of your home.

Courtesy of House Beautiful. *Photo by Feliciano.*

Typical achimenes plant

THE TENDER BULBS

Achimenes

WIDOW'S TEARS

Popular as bedding plants for shady spots in the South, these tropical Americans require an early start indoors in the North. They are fine for hanging baskets (particularly strains labeled as cascades) as well as shaded window boxes. Well grown, they provide a profusion of velvety green leaves and showy flowers in many different shades. Because they have long tubes, the blossoms are well displayed.

The scaly rhizomes remind me of little pine cones. Start them in a loam, sand and peat mixture in a pot or flat, covering them no more than one inch. Keep barely moist in a warm spot until growth starts. Grow on in the pot or transplant carefully. The plants must never lack for water during growth, and they cannot take any cold. Dig before frost and store at 50° to 60°F. in the pots or with some soil around them. Check periodically to be sure they are not bone-dry. Increase is prodigious, so that a single healthy plant may give you a dozen new rhizomes for another year. Various forms range from eight to 24 inches high.

Some of the newer hybrids are reputedly quicker to flower, but in the North an early start is always advisable. A spot with afternoon shade is ideal for good flowering. With proper humidity, they can also be grown as house plants in spring and summer.
PLANT: one inch deep, three inches apart, in good loam; shade.

Rhizome (enlarged)

Dulcis

Crimson Glory

Yellow Beauty

Fancy

Purple King

Acidanthera murielae

Anemone

TENDER WINDFLOWER

These large-flowered hybrids are often known as poppy anemones and they are not reliably hardy in the North. Their ancestors came mostly from southern Europe. They make ten-inch mounds in a wide range of colors, and the ferny leaves hug the ground. Before planting tubers, soak for 24 hours in water. In mild climates plant in late fall for early-spring bloom. In the North, plant in early spring, then dig tubers in fall and store just above freezing in peat moss. *A. fulgens* is a scarlet hybrid that is hardier and wants a drier, sunnier site than the others. Good strains: De Caen, single; St. Brigid, semidouble; St. Bravo, double. (These latter types are often cataloged as *A. coronaria*.)

Often described as resembling big buttercups (to which they are related), these anemones are notable for the brilliancy of the petal colors. For this reason it makes for more harmonious gardens if they are planted in groups of a single hue. There are good reds and pinks, purples, violets and pure whites. Many of the colorful hybrids have white eyes in the center. They are frequently grown under glass for use as cut flowers.

The only way to discover if poppy anemones can be treated as hardy plants in your climate is to try them in a protected spot. Plant late and mulch well. Tubers are reasonable enough to allow experiment.
PLANT: three inches deep, four inches apart, in cool humusy soil; semishade.

Acidanthera

These Africans are treated exactly as gladiolus, to which they are related. Plant them all at once rather than staggering the process, however, since the acidanthera tends to keep on flowering once it begins. Corms can go in the ground as soon as frost is definitely out of the soil in spring.

Plants range from two to four feet high, with the same swordlike foliage as glads. Acidanthera's flowers, however, are borne on long tubes, so you can pick them individually. They have a faint fragrance.

A. murielae is the best species, but *A. tubergeni* Zwanenburg is an earlier-flowering hybrid with larger blooms. Dig before frost and store as for glads.
PLANT: four to six inches deep, six inches apart, in good loam; full sun.

Forms of *Anemone coronaria*

Hanging basket begonia

Begonia

TENDER TUBEROUS TYPES

What a great range of color and flower forms is found among these tuberous members of the begonia family! Those available for our gardens today are highly hybridized and bear little resemblance to the original species that came from lands as diverse as Bolivia, Mexico and South Africa. Double flower forms may resemble a rose, carnation, camellia or daffodil, and there are singles with crested centers or ruffled edges.

They do best where summers are not hot and muggy, but if you have the proper site, you can grow them anywhere. It should be a

B. multiflora

spot out of real wind but with good air circulation and with shade and good light. The hotter your summer, the more shade they need. Never let them lack for water.

Start the tubers a month early in the house by pressing them concave side up into damp peat moss. When growth is four inches high, transplant carefully to pots, using a porous, humusy soil mixture and setting tubers a bit deeper. They do not want the sunniest window spot. Do not put outside until all frost danger is over. Grow on in pots or set in open ground. Fertilize during first half of summer only. When frost threatens, bring pots indoors and reduce water, then dry off for a few weeks. When stems wither, knock tubers out of pots and store cool in dry peat moss until time to restart.

For hanging baskets, use one of the pendulous types and water frequently. For bedding, the single hybrids often make a better display. Multiflora types with somewhat smaller flowers but floriferous habits are also popular where lots of color is wanted. Set them one foot apart. Good drainage is essential for all types. Those with large flowers may need staking for best effect.

Except where the climate is very hot and dry, tuberous begonias are not really difficult to grow, but they do not have the tolerance of many other plants. If they get too much heat or if you forget to water them, they will definitely sulk. Nor can they stand swampy conditions, so the soil needs to be

Carnation form

Camellia form

Single form

Picotee form

Narcissus form

well drained but with enough humus content to hold moisture.

Wind damage can be disastrous because the stems are brittle and snap easily, as do the individual flowers and leaves. One way to protect them in the open garden is to set them in front of shrubs or a wall or building with a northern exposure but some barrier against the worst winds.

Many gardeners have success with a lath house built as an adjunct to a house or patio. The filtered light is just what the plants want, and there is usually adequate shelter there from the wind. Begonias definitely do best where summer nights are cool and damp. Northern gardeners thus have a definite advantage in their cultivation.

PLANT: one inch deep, 12 inches apart after previously starting growth indoors, in porous, humusy soil; shade.

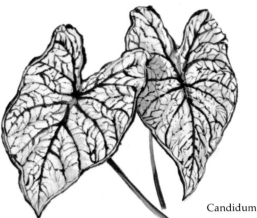

Candidum

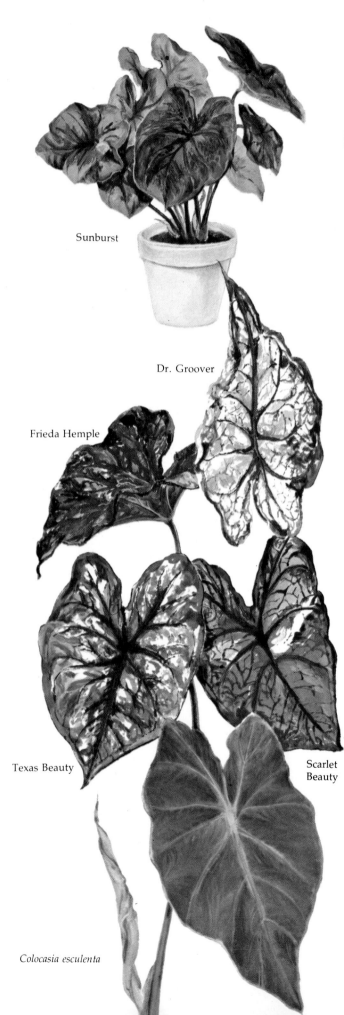

Sunburst

Dr. Groover

Frieda Hemple

Texas Beauty

Scarlet Beauty

Colocasia esculenta

Caladium

These tropical Americans provide striking accents for shady summer gardens. Each tuber produces a profusion of brightly colored leaves. Many varieties feature red or pinkish foliage, but some of the most popular exhibit combinations of white and green. Often the ribs of leaves are a contrasting color. The greenish flower resembles a calla-lily, but remove as soon as it appears to avoid robbing tuber of nourishment at expense of leaves.

Caladiums thrive in warm, moist conditions and benefit from frequent feeding. In the North they are best grown in pots that can be placed to best advantage. Bring in before frost and store at 50°F. in the pots or keep growing at a window all winter. Give plenty of water during growth. Treat elephant's ear *Colocasia esculenta* the same way.

You can buy caladiums either as named varieties or simply by color. The named varieties give more uniform effects. If you are using caladiums as garden accents, plant them in groups of a single kind.

If you are faithful at feeding and watering a potted caladium, you can keep one growing continually for many years. It will winter on a shady windowsill and summer in a similar spot outside. The trick is not to put it outside until late spring when there is no chance of a cold night. Conversely, you will have to bring it into winter quarters early before there is any chance of the heat going on. This prevents shock.

PLANT: one to two inches deep, one inch apart, in rich, humusy soil; half to full shade. Start early inside in the North.

154

Canna

For focal points in the summer garden few plants can compete with these stately decoratives. Most of the botanically important species hail from the American tropics. Modern offerings are highly hybridized, with bigger flowers in a greater range of colors. The blossoms are borne on large trusses well above the bold green or reddish foliage.

Those labeled "giant" in catalogs may grow as tall as four feet. Pfizer's dwarf strain ranges from 30 to 36 inches high. Colors available are red, pink, coral, scarlet, yellow, orange and cream. All have dramatic foliage, but some varieties bear leaves with reddish tints. When thoughtfully placed, these can have a stunning effect without flowers.

Planted in groups of the same color, cannas make excellent accents for the back of the border or among shrubs in full sun. Plant larger types one and one half to two feet apart; dwarf varieties may grow closer and also look handsome in large containers.

Cannas produce successive trusses of bloom. Always remove old flowers before seed can form. During dry periods water well and deeply; apply a soluble fertilizer liberally about once a month throughout the active growth period.

In the North, start cannas early (and inside) six weeks before last expected frost. Use large pots or disposable peat containers in a warm, sunny window. Press root into a mixture of loam and peat until it is just covered. Water sparingly until growth starts. After nights are warm, transplant to garden so several inches of soil cover root. Dig after frost blackens foliage, cut stalk to six inches, shake off excess soil and store frost-free in vermiculite or peat. In spring, large roots

Canna Eureka

Pfitzer's Dwarf Cannas

may be cut into sections, each with at least one bud. Let cut surface dry for a few days before planting. During storage, check your cannas against excessive drying.

In some sections of the United States the Japanese beetle has developed a rapacious appetite for cannas, especially the flowers. While this does spoil your midsummer display, it does not seem to have any adverse effect on later blossoming. Continue to feed the plants, and by later summer they will be lovely again. Cannas flower until hard frost and make a fine vertical line in beds of chrysanthemums.

I still see round beds of cannas, similar to one beside the railroad crossing that impressed me as a child. The cannas stand tall in the center with bedding annuals filling in the rest of the ground. Far too often there is too great a contrast between the height of the cannas and the other flowers in the bed. The dwarfer cannas are a much better choice for this type of use. I personally prefer to have cannas used as colorful accents toward the back of a large border or interspersed among shrubs. In the tropics cannas tower to six feet and taller.
PLANT: three to four inches deep, in rich, humusy soil; full sun.

Chlidanthus
PERFUMED FAIRY-LILY

Scapes of fragrant yellow flowers are borne ten inches above the long narrow leaves of *Chlidanthus fragrans* in summer. Pot indoors in early spring, sink pots where desired for summer. Bring in before frost, dry off and store frost-free in pots. From the Andes, this plant can be shy to bloom. Most gardeners feed it very heavily as soon as the shoots are well up and continue this regimen all summer. I have never been able to flower it in the house. It is good for Southern rock gardens.
PLANT: crowded in pot with tips half protruding, in rich, humusy soil; sun.

Chlidanthus fragrans

156

Clivia

KAFFIR-LILY

Clivias never go completely dormant, so theoretically this native of South Africa should make a good house plant, with its luxuriant fountains of broad evergreen, straplike leaves. Unfortunately, most clivias are just too big for the average house. The plant itself can exceed two feet in height, but it is also nearly that wide. In the South it may be planted out in rich soil, but in the North it is better selected for conservatory or greenhouse unless you have big bay windows. Use a large pot and allow it to fill with roots.

The two-inch tubular flowers in shades of orange and red are carried in clusters on tall, sturdy stems. Most often offered is *C. miniata* or its hybrids.

While in active growth, clivias should be fed often. In late fall stop feeding and reduce water to only enough to keep the leaves from wilting. The signal to resume regular watering is when a new leaf shows in the center of each group of leaves after its period of semi-rest.

PLANT: in rich, humusy soil, in a pot; allow to get crowded before moving; shade, warmth.

Crocosmia

MONTBRETIA

Also listed as tritonia, the crocosmias or montbretias are a crazy mixed-up group. Those offered for sale are usually hybrids that bloom in late summer. Most are in the spectrum from yellow to red, often two-toned. They are closely related to the gladiolus, and the leaves, while shorter, are quite similar. The flowers are on branched, arching wiry stems, farther apart and more graceful than a glad. They are admirable plants for cutting but not always easy to get into bloom. In cold areas treat as for gladiolus; where winters are fairly mild, leave them in the ground. I have had them survive here in Philadelphia. Since they seldom exceed two feet in height, they need no staking and are easier to blend into the smaller garden than are gladiolus.

Most American catalogs offer them only in mixture, but they are much more effective planted by a single variety since the colors are so vibrant. Feed at least once after the shoots are up and never let them lack for water during active growth.

PLANT: three inches deep, two inches apart, in well-drained loam; sun.

Clivia miniata

Crocosmia masonorum

Florists' Cyclamen

Cyclamen

FLORISTS' CYCLAMEN

If given the right growing conditions, no indoor bulb yields flowers over a longer period of time than does the graceful florists' cyclamen, derived from the species *C. persicum*. Often this may exceed six months, during which the butterflylike flowers are displayed above heart-shaped leaves daintily mottled with silvery-white markings. The blossoms come in shades of white, pink, rose and red. Double, fringed and ruffled varieties exist, but the singles are most common and preferred by many.

Cool growing temperatures and adequate humidity are the secrets to growing cyclamen in the house. A north or east window gives enough light, and an unheated room is ideal, but one where the temperature is 60° to 69°F. can be used. To increase humidity, set pots on a deep pan of pebbles in which water is always present. In midwinter a shot of boiling water on the pebbles gives a therapeutic steam bath every few days. During growth fertilize every two weeks and water every day. To ensure perfect drainage, set the pot in which they are growing atop another pot inverted over the pebbles.

Cyclamen make wonderful long-lasting

cut flowers. In this way you can enjoy them in regular house temperatures. When purchasing a plant from the florist, pick one with lots of buds showing. Grow it in the coolest spot you have, and cut the flowers as needed. Freshly opened ones often last two weeks in a bouquet. If you want to show off a plant for a few hours in a warmer room, give it the steam-bath treatment first and again after returning it to cooler quarters.

It is sad how many beautiful cyclamen are killed by kindness. The most perfectly grown plant in full bloom can be ruined over a single weekend. The leaves begin to droop and quickly turn yellow when the plant is left in a warm, dry room or in too strong sunlight. Put in a cool, shaded spot, it may recover, but all is not lost even if every leaf dies. Water it sparingly until new leaves begin to form. I have one such just coming into bud. It was brought to me on the verge of expiring about eight months ago but is now recovered.

When frost is over, transfer the pots and pebble containers to a shady spot outside and continue to fertilize and water faithfully. Cyclamen often begin to bloom again or continue to do so all summer. Bring in before heat is necessary in the house to acclimatize them to the drier conditions they will have to endure there. This procedure is much more satisfactory than the old system of letting them dry off and rest during the summer. Plants often continue in growth for years at a stretch. Actually, it is wiser to buy a nicely grown pot of cyclamen from the florist and treat it so than to try other ways of starting tubers.

My cyclamen sit on a shady porch all summer and are hosed daily in hot weather. Both leaves and tubers get wet, but it does not seem to bother them. When indoors I mist the leaves periodically with water but try to keep the tuber itself dry.

I have cyclamen that have been so grown for more than five years, and they are doing beautifully. Gradually the tubers grow larger, and eventually you will notice that new growth occurs from several different spots on the tuber. Leaf spread of such a plant may measure nearly 18 inches across, and literally dozens of flowers will be produced over many months. These plants do not really have a rest period, although I do not feed them from about mid-November to mid-January. This is because the amount of sunshine is so abbreviated during this season in my part of the country.

In time your cyclamen tuber may outgrow its pot. Put off repotting as long as you can because it does set the plants back, and some never recover. Late spring is the best time to transplant. Let the plant rest a few weeks by withholding all fertilizer. Remove the tuber from the old pot as gently as possible, trying not to break off any leaves. Transfer it to a larger clay pot with plenty of crocking in the bottom to ensure drainage. Many cyclamen are sold in plastic pots, but clay ones work better in my experience. Choose a pot at least two inches wider in diameter than that of the tuber. Remove some soil from around the top of the tuber, but disturb the lower roots as little as possible. Replant so that the tuber protrudes well above the soil level in the new pot, using enough porous, humusy soil to fill the pot. Place plant in good shade and water faithfully until it seems to have recovered.

Today's hybrids are much improved over the species *C. persicum*, which grows wild from Greece to Syria. Seed is offered from several small hybrids between this and the hardier types, too. Sow seed in late summer, grow cool in winter. As tubers grow larger, keep transplanting carefully, each time raising them a bit more above soil surface. A mature tuber should sit on the soil. Depending on the variety, it may take from six to 18 months for bloom from seed. The seed is erratic in germinating but seems to sprout better if placed in total darkness. Cover it with spilled sphagnum moss in a small flat or in individual small pots; transplant to small pots after leaves form above the developing corm.

PLANT: pot, with tuber protruding, in porous, humusy soil; shade, cool, humid.

Pompon

Colarette

Decorative

Dahlia

Long before the white man discovered America the Aztecs of Mexico were growing dahlias in their gardens. They had selected forms and colors to such an extent that botanists are not certain which are the true species. Today's gardener has a wide range of sizes, shapes and colors from which to choose. For a while dahlias suffered a "bad press" because enthusiasts were concentrating on huge exhibition types. With the stakes these needed for support, they looked ugly in the garden and needed floor vases for display indoors. Nowadays, however, there are dozens of smaller varieties that star both as part of the landscape and as sources of cut flowers. No other summer-flowering bulb gives so many flowers over as long a period.

Botanically, dahlias grow from tuberous roots—a point to remember. They dry out much faster than the other types of bulbs and tubers. Once they are growing, never allow your dahlias to suffer from lack of water, although they also need good drainage.

Anemone

Singles

Cactus

A mulch helps retain surface moisture for the tiny feeder roots. Winter storage should be cool, with the tubers completely covered by peat moss and checked periodically to make sure they are not drying out.

An official classification for dahlias exists and is used at all formal shows. What this means to the home gardener is that there are many different flower forms and sizes and that the plants themselves vary considerably in height and spread. A current catalog will detail the names of cultivars available in the various classes, with the expected heights of the bushes and diameter of the flowers. Most of those offered will be either decoratives or cactus types. Flowers in both classes are fully double. The main difference between them is that those in the decorative class have petals that are more or less flat, while those in the cactus classes have petals that are curved so that they appear almost to be tubular. There are further subdivisions within both classes that have to do with the degree of petal curling either from side to side or from front to back.

A dahlia specialist's catalog will usually

have definitions to aid you in finding your way. For the gardener who wants just a few colorful dahlias, the photographs in most catalogs are as good a way as any to pick an order from these two classes.

There are also a number of other flower forms. Orchid-flowering dahlias are singles with more or less tubular petals. Mignons are singles whose plants do not top 18 inches. Anemone dahlias have elongated center florets that look like a pincushion. Collarette dahlias are open-centered, with a row of petaloids forming a collar around the central disk. Ball dahlias have fully double round flowers more than four inches in diameter.

For picking and garden use you should also consider the miniatures, which produce flowers of many different forms but always less than four inches in diameter, and the dwarfs, which have flowers of varying size but bushes seldom more than two feet in height. Many catalogs will list these two classes separately; with others, read the descriptions to find varieties such as Rochencourt, Park Princess, Park Beauty, Cheerio, Fred Springer and Bride. Pompons that have small, round blossoms on neat, short bushes are another great class for garden effect; many catalogs have good color selections of them.

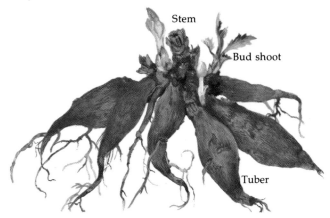

When separating dahlia tubers in spring, each tuber must have a growing bud shoot at the stem end. Blind tubers will not grow.

It is also possible to grow dahlias as annuals, starting with seed early in the house in spring. They will give fine summer flowers and by fall will have formed tubers, which can be saved for another year.

When frost blackens your dahlias, leave them in the ground a few days, then choose a sunny day and carefully pry up each clump with a fork. Shake off excess dirt, tag by color, cut off stalk to a few inches and leave undivided. Let clumps dry off a few days in garage or cellar before storing. A week before your latest spring-frost date, remove from storage, spread out in garage and cover with an inch of damp peat moss to encourage budding. In ten days you should be able to see where buds are forming on the stem end of each tuber. Divide them carefully, making sure that each has a bud before planting one tuber to a hole.

Large dahlias go at least four feet apart; dwarfs may go as close as 18 inches. Dig soil deeply and put tubers flat in holes five inches deep, but initially cover only with three inches of soil. Fill in later. Place any needed stakes before covering tubers. Feed with fertilizer low in nitrogen during summer if soil is poor.

Pinching off the growing tip after there are four pairs of leaves makes for bushier plants. To get larger blooms, remove both side buds on shoots, allowing only the central one to flower. With bedding types this is not necessary. When cutting, place stems immediately in hot water and leave to harden for at least an hour before making an arrangement. Cut off spent blooms to keep your dahlias blooming all summer.

Removing auxiliary buds and shoots (in gray) helps produce larger dahlia flowers.

Since gardens are smaller these days and houses are similarly sized, it really makes more sense to concentrate on the daintier forms of dahlias. These do not need disbudding, so the whole task becomes much simpler. If I were a beginning gardener, I would definitely limit my first dahlias to those advertised as miniature, anemone-flowered or pompon.

Storage can be difficult too for the small householder. If you cannot provide a cool spot for this, treat dahlias as annuals and buy plump, healthly new tubers each year. The cost is minimal.

Eucharis

AMAZON-LILY

If you have the space for it, this native of the Colombian Andes is most rewarding as a potted plant. The big, shiny leaves make a good permanent green mass, and the fragrant flowers appear several times a year on stems two feet tall. Pot the bulbs in a rich loam with the top third above soil level. They like to be pot-bound. Water well once, then sparingly until growth starts. Once the leaves begin to unfold, water well regularly and feed every few weeks. During the winter, eucharis needs a warm, sunny window; in summer, put outdoors in half shade. Never allow the bulb to be subjected to cold.

The bulb never really goes dormant. After bloom is over, refrain from watering until the leaves almost wilt. Keep up this treatment for about five weeks, then resume regular watering and feeding; it will bloom again after a few months.

Do not repot until the pot is literally crowded with bulbs and offsets. A good way to do this is to take the soil mass out of the pot and wash away the old soil with a hose, disturbing the roots no more than is necessary. Do this toward the end of one of its rest periods. Carefully remove offsets at this time, too. An eight-inch pot will take four to six bulbs. Eucharis does well in ordinary house or apartment situations but needs extra humidity. Only the large-sized bulbs flower, and they often sulk a year or two after transplanting. In the far South eucharis can be planted permanently in the garden, but in all but tropical areas it is wiser to grow it in pots that can be taken inside in an emergency.

PLANT: with bulbs crowded, the tips protruding, in rich loam; sun, semishade.

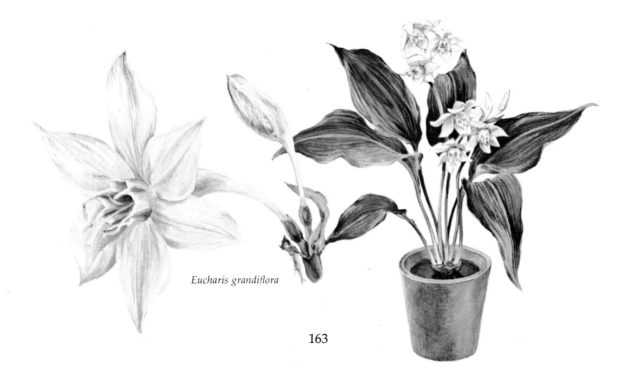

Eucharis grandiflora

163

Eucomis

PINEAPPLE-LILY

Also called the pineapple flower, this South African bears large heads of flowers in white and green shades, sometimes marked in purple. Stems of most species are one to two feet high above a basal rosette of leaves. The flower raceme is topped by a tuft of foliage, pineapple-fashion. In mild climates it may be planted outside in the fall, a few inches deep in a protected spot for late-summer bloom. In the North, pot or plant in May, bring in before frost and store cool in peat moss. It can also be used as an indoor potted plant; start it into growth in the fall at a sunny window in a cool room. After flowering, gradually reduce water and allow to go dormant for a rest each year. The flower truss lasts a long time.

E. bicolor is the most readily available species. Planted an inch deep in a four-inch pot, eucomis will not need repotting for several years; just let it rest in the pot. It makes a most interesting plant for a patio container. Since the flowers last so long, it is excellent for such use.

Freesia

One of the most fragrant of all flowers, the freesia may be planted outside in the fall in the South, or specially treated bulbs can be ordered for planting toward the end of April in the North. Set them two inches deep and two to three inches apart in full sun. Where the climate dictates, these tender South Africans should be dug before the soil freezes and stored in the manner used for gladiolus.

Culture indoors as winter-flowering plants is not easy unless you have a very sunny window in a room where the temperature remains in the 45° to 55°F. range. A sun porch is ideal. In such cases plant the bulbs one inch apart in a large pot, water well once, then place in cold frame or sheltered spot outdoors until hard frost is due; bring in

and keep in cool, dark spot until good roots show in the drainage hole and the shoots are beginning to lengthen. Water sparingly at first. Freesias straggle even in the sunniest window and need some support. Never allow them to lack for water. Fertilize when in active growth and be on the lookout for aphids. Use the flowers for cutting. Keep foliage growing as long as possible; store cool when dormant.

Treated much the same way are several other bulbs from South Africa. Some of the babianas (baboon root) that resemble freesias also are fragrant. Ixia (corn-lily) bears spikes of flowers on wiry stems, while sparaxis (harlequin or wand flower) has only a few flowers per stem. Corms of all four of these are usually offered as hybrids in many different colors.

Lapeirousia cruenta (Anomatheca) takes slightly higher temperatures. While there are several species of this African in various colors, this is the one most readily available. It bears bright-scarlet flowers usually less than a foot tall.

Tritonia crocata (the flame-freesia) is still another South African bulb that is treated as the freesia. The most often offered species is a fine orange, but cream, white, pink and yellow hybrids are also in commerce.

Bessera elegans (coral drops or lady's eardrops) is a Mexican with umbels of small orange-red flowers marked with white. It too requires freesia culture and similarly requires staking because the stems are often three feet high.

All these bulbs could be termed half-hardy. If given a cool, dark place to root first, they are ideal for the cool greenhouse. With heating bills the way they are, many gardeners are taking a second look at tropical plants and deciding to convert their greenhouses into homes for plants that do well at much lower temperatures. Any of the bulbs on this page are good subjects for a cool oasis in cold weather. The cool rooting period is a must, however; darkness during that time inhibits the shoots from emerging until after a good root system has been formed.

Freesia

Sparaxis

Eucomis bicolor

Ixia

165

Gladiolus

No summer-flowering bulb offers a greater range of color than the gladiolus. Every shade in the rainbow is available, even some tinted green. Originally native to Africa and Mediterranean lands, they are not hardy in northern areas. Botanically, they grow from a corm. Even in the South glads require replanting every few years because new corms form on top of the old ones and thus soon work to the soil surface.

Modern hybrids include many with ruffled, waved and frilled petals, plus the tendency to open numerous flowers at one time. Throats or edges may be marked with a second hue. There are still many stately tall glads, but the miniatures are gaining in popularity because they never require staking and are daintier and more useful for today's homes and gardens.

The North American Gladiolus Council is active in encouraging development of good new gladiolus. In addition, many catalogs feature All-America gladiolus, so it is not hard to locate some of the best and newest varieties. It is noticeable of late that some miniature varieties are always included. Official classifications used in formal shows concern themselves with color and size of the individual florets along the stalk. These range from Miniatures with florets under two and one half inches to Giants of five and one half inches and up.

To stretch the gladiolus season, plant some corms as soon as the ground warms

166

Representative Gladiolus

up, then a series every two weeks until the end of June. Or choose early, midseason and late varieties when ordering.

Except where exhibition glads are the goal, you can avoid staking by planting about six inches apart in a trench six inches deep. Space rows at least 18 inches apart. Cover with about two inches of soil at first, then gradually fill in the trench as the shoots lengthen. Apply a mulch to keep down the weeds all summer.

With their swordlike foliage and impressive flower spikes, gladiolus make fine accents in the border. Or set a row for cutting in the vegetable patch. You get the most for your money by planting groups of a single color. Select shades to harmonize with your indoors, because this is a splendid flower for bouquets. Individual flowers can be cut and floated in water. When cutting, leave four leaves on the plant to help the new corms develop.

Gladiolus require a plentiful supply of water during growth, but they also need good drainage. If soil is of reasonable fertility, they need no extra feeding, but a little superphosphate may be sprinkled on top of the soil on either side of the row immediately after planting. Avoid high-nitrogen fertilizers.

In early fall, after foliage turns brown, dig corms, cut off tops and cure in warm, dry, airy spot for a few weeks. Then separate the biggest new corms from used-up old ones at bottom. Hang up for winter in cool (but not freezing) site in old nylon-stocking bags.

Tiny cormels may be discarded or grown separately until of flowering size. Soak these in water for several days in spring, then plant in rows two inches deep.

Thrips are the major insect enemy. New corms will be treated by the grower, but your own harvest may contain eggs. Just prior to spring planting, soak corms for three hours in a dip of one and one half tablespoons of Lysol to one gallon of water.

Unless you have a huge garden or are dealing with a special expensive new hybrid you are anxious to propagate, there is little sense in saving small-size corms. You will have enough increase without them. If you get to the point where you have more corms than you can handle, do some experimenting with their hardiness in your climate. Leave some in the ground at fall clean-up time, but make sure that old stalks are removed as soon as they are dry to get rid of any hibernating insects or eggs. Such a trial should take place only in well-drained soil with high humus content. You may be surprised, for some hybrids are really astonishingly hardy. A mulch is a good idea.

Gladiolus are a good choice to plant in the sunny bays of a shrub border. Do this in groups of no less than six corms to gain a decent effect. The greenery provides a fine background, often gives the glads just enough support to make staking unnecessary, and the tall spikes are quite in scale with the shrubs.

PLANT: six inches deep, six inches apart, in well-drained loam; full sun.

Gloriosa rothschildiana

Gloriosa
GLORY OR CLIMBING-LILY

Barbed tendrils on the leaf tips enable *Gloriosa rothschildiana* to cling to a light support such as netting or string. It may grow to six feet, especially indoors. The most popular species has red and yellow, reflexed and waved lilylike flowers prized for cutting. Handle the brittle tubers carefully. It is best treated as a potted plant and often blooms twice a year: once at a sunny warm window inside in winter or spring, again during the summer outside. Each time after bloom, gradually withhold water and let plant go dormant. Store tuber dry in the pot of soil for rest period of several months. Repot in new soil annually; water well once, then sparingly until growth appears.

You can tell when it is time to start gloriosa into growth again by the strange pink buds that appear on the tubers. Dig carefully into the soil to check. Increase is good, but only fairly long tubers will bloom.

Littonia modesta is a similar plant but rarely offered. Gloriosa is native to tropical Africa. PLANT: in large pot with pink growing tip just under surface, in rich soil; full sun; always keep warm.

Gloxinia

SINNINGIA

This tuberous plant is the exception in our alphabetical listings. True gloxinias are seldom if ever seen, but at least in the United States the common name has become too deeply imbedded in the gardener's lexicon to dislodge. We acknowledge that the gorgeous house plants grown under this name are really hybrids of *Sinningia*, many fairly recently developed in America; species are Brazilian. The huge bells may be self-colored or edged or stippled with a contrasting hue. Some are waved or ruffled. There are doubles, too. Colors are shades of red, purple, pink or white.

Growing conditions should be warm, humid and shaded from the brightest sun. Most successful growers suggest three good hours of morning sun, so an east window is the best bet. Unfortunately, mature gloxinias brought into the ordinary house after developing in the kinder atmosphere of a greenhouse often falter quickly. You can help them by providing a bed of wet pebbles on which to set the potted plant. I have also set back a gloxinia badly by assigning it to too cold a room.

Once in growth, they should never want for moisture, but avoid very cold water and never wet the velvety foliage. Feed regularly when in active growth. Ater flowering is over and growth stops, rest the plant by withholding water gradually. Store in a warm spot, but sprinkle with water from time to time so soil does not dry out completely. Keep an eye on it, because dormancy is often quite short. When a new sprout shows, repot and return to good light. Plants will be more shapely if you allow only one sprout to develop.

If you plant your own tubers instead of buying plants in bloom, the shock of moving can be avoided. Plant them with the knobby or slightly concave side up. Tubers potted in early fall will flower before spring. Those started February to March will give summer bloom. Supplemental flourescent light during the winter months aids good flowering. These and other gesneriads are some of the best subjects for the indoor light gardener.

Propagation is as for African violets. Place a leaf stalk about an inch long in moist vermiculite. It will eventually form a tuber from which a sprout will arise. Keep the original leaf cutting moist and warm; the longer it keeps growing, the larger the tuber formed.

There are also some charming species with slipper-type flowers; they remain in flower for very long periods.

PLANT: one tuber per six-inch pot, in rich, porous loam with no more than one inch of soil on top of tuber; part sun in warmth.

Gloxinia Hybrid

Hippeastrum

AMARYLLIS

There is no reason why these huge trumpet-flowered bulbs can not be grown in the open garden. In warm climates they can be left in the ground indefinitely, but in the North do not plant until after all frost has gone in spring. Choose a spot that is half shady. Lift the bulbs before frost in the fall and store indoors for the winter in damp peat moss and sand, being sure to leave the roots on the bulbs. If you want bulbs for this use, order early because they are not usually shipped after the first of April.

Much more popular usage is to grow them indoors during the winter. Bulbs are offered in a range of beautiful colors. Use a good loam with some peat mixed in.

The bulbs bloom better if pot-bound. Use a pot just an inch wider than the bulb and plant so one third of the bulb is above the soil level. Water well once, then sparingly, and keep in warm spot until growth appears. Often bloom precedes the foliage. After the leaves begin to grow, place pot in a sunny window. When frost is over, transfer to a semishady spot outside. Feed every week after the leaves appear. Before frost, bring the pot in and give less water as the foliage dies down. Turn pots on their sides in a cool spot and allow to rest for two months. Some types are evergreen. With these, water sparingly during the rest period. After resting, bulb can be started again as before. Repot only every three years, but each year replace the upper inch of soil with rich, fresh loam.

The same general treatment is used for nerine (Guernsey-lily), haemanthus (blood-lily), cyrtanthus (Ifafa lily), *Amaryllis bella-*

Representative Amaryllis

170

donna (*Brunsvigia rosea* or *Callicore rosea*) and the various crinums and amarcrinums. All may also be planted outside in spring for late-summer bloom, but in the North it is easiest to grow them in pots, starting them in late winter.

As with so many other bulbs in this section, only experimentation will decide whether some of these amaryllids can be wintered over safely outside in your garden. With the hippeastrum, such treatment is not suggested north of Washington, D. C. We Northerners must either grow them in pots or learn to treat them like any other tender bulb with the consequent spring planting and fall digging.

In a protected spot (close to a south-facing wall is the English choice), some of the others are worth trying at least as far north as New York City. I know of a *Haemanthus coccineus* that has flowered after a winter in the ground 20 miles north of Philadelphia. The hybrid crinums Cecil Houdyshel and *powelli* and *Amarcrinum howardi* (sometimes called *Crinodonna corsi*) are all to be found in the ground in Philadelphia gardens. One of the secrets is deep planting, so that the long neck of the bulbs is not where frost can reach it.

Some of these bulbs are quite expensive. Caution suggests that you wait for experimenting until after you have some increase to play with. Often you may find that the bulb will put forth foliage but never flowers. Picking a spot with winter dryness and putting a light, airy mulch atop the ground are helpful.

The big Dutch and American hybrid hippeastrums, incidentally, are almost always listed as amaryllis in general catalogs. Many are offered prepotted and have been especially prepared so that they bloom five to six weeks after starting. They all take average house or apartment temperatures.

All these bulbs require rich soil, plenty of water and fertilizing during growth, then a rest period when they are kept on the dry side at about 50°F. Haemanthus needs light shade; the others want sun.

Nerine

Haemanthus

Amarcrinum

Hymenocallis calathina

Hymenocallis
PERUVIAN-DAFFODIL

Sometimes called ismene, this South American produces its big, fragrant white flowers only a few weeks after planting. Because the bulbs are harmed by even a hint of cold, do not plant until after it is safe to set out tomatoes in your area. The large, strap-like leaves make a good green note in the summer garden. Dig bulbs carefully before any chance of frost. Shake off most of the soil but leave all the roots on bulbs. Store with foliage attached in an open plastic bag well above freezing. Increase is fast, but only top-sized bulbs flower, so grow babies on in nursery or use as foliage accents.

H. calathina is most commonly offered. *H. festalis* has very narrow outer petals. Sulphur Queen is a light yellow hybrid. *H. harrisiana* is a dwarf species from Mexico that seldom exceeds 10 inches in height. *H. amancaes* is a fairly rare and expensive yellow species from Peru that varies from a foot to 18 inches high. *H. caribaea* and *H. littoralis* are sometimes also offered.

In the far South, of course, the ismene can be left in the ground until increase is too great for good flowering. There are several species native to the Southern states, but they are not often found in commerce. Locally they are called basket flowers or spider-lilies.

Elisena longipetala is a relative from Peru and one of the parents of the hybrid *H. festivalis*. *Pancratium maritimum* is an old-world relative, and *P. zeylanicum* is listed as an Asian species. Bulbs of all these hymenocallis relatives are harder to locate, but the flowers are fairly similar. Horticulturally they are all treated the same way.

From my own experience no bulb comes into flower more quickly after planting than *H. calathina*. If you wait until early summer, it will bloom within a week, which is good to know if you have a new garden.
PLANT: four inches deep, at least 12 inches apart, in rich loam; full sun.

Lachenalia pendula superba

Lachenalia
CAPE-COWSLIP

Plant several bulbs per pot in early fall, just covering bulbs with soil. Keep in cool, dark spot. Water sparingly until roots form well, then bring to cool, sunny window. Known as Cape-cowslip in its native South Africa.

If you can provide these South Africans with a cool growing place, they may well stay in bloom for several months. *L. aurea* is yellow. *L. pendula superba* has coral-red tubular bells tipped green. *L. glaucina* bears pale-blue fragrant flowers, *L. contaminata* waxy white blooms. Few species exceed ten inches. European sources have produced some good hybrids.

Milla
MEXICAN STAR

Native to southwestern America, *Milla biflora* sporadically puts up long stems with several white star flowers during the summer. Plant several to a pot in early spring about one inch deep. Water sparingly until growth starts; grow in full sun. Bring in before hard frost, dry off gradually, store dry in pot above freezing for the winter. In the South, plant in open ground. Unfortunately, bulbs are hard to locate in commerce,

which is a shame, since milla provides flowers over a much longer period than many more popular bulbs. It has never failed to be producing still more buds when I have had to bring it in for the winter.

Narcissus
TENDER TYPES

For winter fragrance the tender narcissus such as paper-white or Soleil d'Or (Chinese sacred lily) are delightful. Pebbles in a bowl or soil in a pot are equally effective mediums. Pot in late fall or early winter, with bulbs only about one third covered. Water well and place in cool, dark spot for several weeks. In pebbles, water level should just touch bottom of bulb. (If the bowl is opaque, stick a finger in to check.) When lots of roots show, bring gradually to light and grow on in cool, sunny spot. Discard bulbs after flowering. They are not hardy, so they cannot survive outside except in the mildest of climates. For this reason, do not root them in the colder spot where you are forcing other daffodils. About 50°F. gives best results. Wash and save the pebbles for another year.

Paper-white Narcissus

Polianthes

TUBEROSE

Incredibly fragrant, the Mexican *Polianthes tuberosa* cannot take any cold, so do not plant outside until soil has warmed up well. Both single- and double-flowered varieties exist. Stems are three to four feet tall. Dig tubers before frost and store with foliage attached in plastic bags at 60°F. Where summers are short, start early inside in pots, transplant to garden later. Even then tubers may not replenish themselves, but they are not expensive to buy yearly. Bloom is in late summer or autumn. Foliage is straggly so place behind some other plant.

The tuberose most widely offered is a double form called The Pearl, but the smaller single form is daintier. Oddly enough, although the tuberose is considered a Mexican native, *P. tuberosa* is unknown in the wild there. The conquistadors destroyed the great gardens they found in Mexico, but we do know they existed. Perhaps the Indians had hybridized the plant, as they did dahlias, or brought it from some other part of South America before the white man arrived.

PLANT: three inches deep, five inches apart; full sun; rich loam.

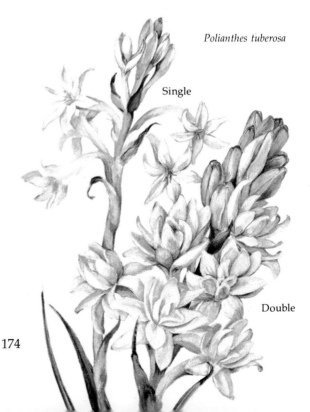

Ornithogalum arabicum

Ornithogalum

CHINCHERINCHEE

One of the longest-lasting cut flowers in the world is *Ornithogalum thyrsoides*, another South African. The bulbs themselves also bloom over a long period because they put up several scapes. Mature bulbs produce a large triangular raceme of starry white blossoms. *O. arabicum*, from the Mediterranean, sports arresting black pistils in the centers of its stars. Both grow about two feet high. Culture is the same as for freesias, but they will take growing temperatures into the sixties. The basal foliage is straggly. To keep flower stems straight, turn plants daily. They require a sunny spot and may be still in bloom when warm weather arrives. Keep growing until the leaves begin to brown. Then withhold water and store dry in the pots until time to repot in autumn. Ornithogalums may be grown also as summer bulbs, as gladiolus.

Polianthes tuberosa

Single

Double

174

Ranunculus

PERSIAN-BUTTERCUPS

Most of these Eurasians are advertised as peony-flowered, but they more closely resemble large double buttercups, to which they are related. The stems of *Ranunculus asiaticus* range from 12 to 18 inches, with blooms up to four inches across. The odd tuberous roots should be planted claw points down. Prized for cut flowers, ranunculus are popular for cool winter greenhouse culture. Start as freesias and grow very cool in a sunny unheated room if you want to try them as house plants. Store dry in peat or the pot. With protection they often survive fall planting quite far north.

Sometimes called turban flowers or Asiatic-roses, ranunculus range in color from pure white through yellow to orange, red and pink. Some of the finest are propagated by California growers and are known as Tecolote Giants.

If you try ranunculus outside, plant four inches deep in a sunny, well-drained spot in late fall and give some winter protection. Or try them in a cold frame.

Representative Ranunculus

Sprekelia formosissima

Sprekelia

AZTEC-LILY

Also known as the Jacobean or St. James's-lily, *Sprekelia formosissima*, a bulb from Mexico, may be grown indoors the same as the hippeastrum, to which it is related. Sprekelia may be grown also in pots or in the the garden for summer bloom. In the North, start inside early in pots and keep foliage growing as long as possible. During growth, feed every week and water heavily. Store dry in the pot at 60°F. for the winter. The flowers appear on 18-inch stems, and they are every bit as bright as the illustration. In fact, some sources call it the Mexican fire-lily. A bloom can measure six inches wide.

Only the largest bulbs will flower, hence the admonition to start the bulbs early in the house and keep them growing as long as possible if you are treating them as a tender, summer-flowering subject. If you use sprekelia as a house plant, you should keep the leaves growing as long as possible by taking the pot outside and sinking it in the garden after the weather warms up. Take inside to rest before frost. It does quite well in fairly warm rooms.

Tigridia
TIGER FLOWER

These brilliant Mexicans, also called shell flowers, were sacred to the Aztecs. Each triangular flower lasts only a day, but each corm produces several in a season. Tigridias are hardy in mild climates but should be treated as gladiolus wherever frost goes deeper than one inch into the ground. Various hybrids may range from 12 to 24 inches high. Leaves are similar to glads but shorter. Try to buy them by color if possible; they are more effective that way than in mixture.

Most of the bulbs in commerce are forms of *T. pavonia*. The colors are brilliant, and the cupped centers are often spotted in contrasting hues. Always plant them in clumps of at least six bulbs.

PLANT: two inches deep, three inches apart, in well-drained loam; full sun.

Vallota speciosa

Vallota
SCARBOROUGH-LILY

A miniature amaryllid from South Africa, *Vallota speciosa* makes a fine house plant but can be planted outside in spring in the South for late-summer bloom. Treat in North much the same as eucharis, watering sparingly until the foliage shows. The brilliant scarlet flowers, 12 to 24 inches high, may appear before the leaves the first time. Foliage is practically evergreen, so once it is growing, merely rest bulb between flowerings by giving less water, but do not let foliage wilt. Bloom is best if bulbs are crowded; repot only when absolutely necessary. A rare white variety exists. Does best in nearly full sun. For pots, plant bulb half exposed above soil. In South, plant two to four inches deep.

Although vallota does not have the color range of the hippeastrums, it is really much better adapted to the ordinary house or apartment windowsill. For one thing, the foliage is smaller and neater. Its flowers too are more in scale with the modern window, and because there is usually foliage present when it blooms, the whole plant is more decorative. Vallota does not seem bothered by living-room temperatures. In South Africa it is known as George-lily.

Tigridia pavonia Hybrids

Veltheimia

Unlike many other bulbs used as house plants, this South African is decorative even when not in bloom because the large glossy basal leaves are delightfully ruffled. Plant the bulbs as for hippeastrum in early fall and grow at a sunny window in a fairly cool room. Usually the flowers can be expected after Christmas, and they last a long time. Fertilize regularly when in growth and keep leaves going as long as possible in spring, even taking pots outside to a half-shady spot, if necessary. When the rosette of leaves finally begins to wilt, withhold water gradually, then place pots on their sides in a warm spot for the balance of the summer. Do not repot until crowded, but replace top inch of soil annually. As summer wanes, take into house and begin cycle again by watering well once, then lightly until leaves appear. This bulb seems to do better indoors if the pot is placed on wet pebbles to increase humidity.

Only one variety is commonly offered, and it may be listed either as *V. viridiflora* or *V. capensis*, with a flower stalk 12 to 24 inches high. A variety advertised as *V. rosalba* with rose and white flowers should be most beautiful. Remember to rotate pot daily when stalk appears so stem will not bend toward the light. In the deep South it may be planted two inches deep in a well-drained, half-shady spot.

Veltheimia does not always die down of itself in the summer. Make a mental note, therefore, to check it around the first of August and summarily order rest by placing the pot on its side where it cannot get water for a full two months. If the bulb produces many offsets, it is wiser to repot, saving only the largest bulbs and starting each in its own container. Set the pot on wet pebbles if you show it off in a warm room while in bloom.

Veltheimia viridiflora

177

Z. elliottiana

Z. aethiopica

Calla Sunrise Hybrids

Zantedeschia
CALLA-LILY

Native to South Africa, the elegant callas may be used either as greenhouse plants or treated as tender bulbs for the summer garden. If high humidity can be maintained, dwarf forms can also be grown at sunny windows. Large arrow-shaped leaves of some forms are attractively spotted white. Calla Crowborough is the hardiest strain.

If they are grown in pots, set the rhizomatous roots so a third is above the soil surface; in the open ground, cover with three to four inches of soil. Water sparingly until growth starts, then never let plants lack for moisture. Feed frequently. Do not plant outside until nights become warm; dig up before any chance of frost. Store frost-free in vermiculite or peat moss. With indoor specimens, allow foliage to mature after flowering, gradually withdrawing water; store until time to repot, and then remove offsets.

For winter bloom callas are potted in late fall. While they revel in the warm temperatures of the house, they require extra humidity. Coupled with their large size, this makes them a difficult subject for house plants. The variety Godfreyana, which is white, and the

Rancho Hybrids, which range through many color shades, are dwarf in habit and thus easier to handle.

If you are growing callas outside, site them to get the benefit of the large tropical leaves, which lend a dramatic note to the summer garden. In the South they seem to do best with half shade. In old books the calla is called Richardia.

Z. aethiopica is sometimes called the white arum or lily-of-the-Nile. It is an interesting plant for the edge of a pond. During growth it is hard to give too much water or fertilizer to a calla, so do not neglect these details. PLANT: in pot or ground, in rich, humusy soil; sun except half shade in far South.

Zephyranthes
ZEPHYR-LILY

Europeans refer to these small members of the amaryllis family as "flowers of the west wind" because all are native to the western hemisphere. The Atamasco-lily (*Z. atamasco*) is native from Virginia south, where it decorates damp meadows in early spring with white funnel-form flowers. Several others occur in Texas, but the most commonly offered are from South America and bloom in summer and fall. *Z. candida* is white and has proved hardy three inches deep in a warm, well-drained spot as far north as Philadelphia. *Z. citrina* and the hybrid Ajax are yellow; *Z. rosea* and *Z. grandiflora* are pink.

They are better grown in pots in a sunny spot, except in the South. Set bulbs one inch deep indoors early or slightly deeper after frost outside. Water sparingly until the foliage appears, then keep well watered until bloom starts, toward the end of summer. Before frost, take pots in and rest by withholding water for several months, after which they may be started into growth again and may give bloom inside at a sunny window. They can be treated also as gladiolus and planted in the open, then stored for the winter in dry peat moss. Foliage of all species is grassy and the flowers no higher than ten inches.

Cooperia (rain-lily), habranthus and cooperanthes respond to the same treatment.

Also known as fairy-lilies, the zephyranthes are understandably popular in the Southern states, where they may be permanently planted and left to spread and flower sporadically after summer and fall rains. Since they are a truly diminutive amaryllid, they are fine to situate on the edge of the garden. They will take half shade, particularly in the South.

In the house they do best in rooms where the temperature stays cool. Plant a number per pot, leaving about an inch between bulbs. If you are clever at manipulating them, you can get intermittent bloom all year. As soon as flowering is surely over, withdraw all water for two months, then resume watering gradually until growth is well up. Feed several times during active growth. Zephyranthes do not need repotting until they become crowded. Do any necessary separating during dormancy just before time to start them into growth.

Z. grandiflora

Z. citrina

Z. candida

No spring garden is complete without bulbs, but trees, shrubs and perennials all have their part to play, too. Courtesy of MALAK, Ottawa, Canada.

THE WHOLE GARDEN PICTURE

When reading a book as specialized as this, there is a tendency to forget that bulbs are only one facet of the garden world. Although they are truly important, a garden in which bulbs are the only occupants would lack a great deal in interest and excitement at all seasons of the growing year. A quick look at how nature does it will show you that bulbs do not exist in a vacuum. Instead, there are trees and shrubs, perennials and annuals of infinite variety as companions for wild bulbs. Such a finished picture should be your goal, too.

In discussing certain bulbs I have already suggested that ground-cover plants can be used adroitly both to mark the bulb planting and to complement the bulb flowers. That is only a fragment of the total garden. Later-flowering perennials can be used to hide ripening early bulb foliage. Their flowers in season fill in the gaps where the bulbs were supreme in preceding months. Spring-flowering perennials such as fringed bleeding-heart (*Dicentra eximia*) or primroses complete a bulb planting, and summer annuals such as petunias and marigolds are easy to set in place above deeper-planted tulips and daffodils.

What you want to create is a garden where bulbs are one part of the total. That garden is surely a joy forever.

Such a garden, however, requires prior planning. There are many ways of doing this, but here are some suggestions that may make it easier for you. Depending on your interest and the size of the garden involved, you can adapt them to your own circumstances.

Unless you are redoing an existing garden, your first step is to look over your property and decide where the garden is to go. Such essentials as ease of access, nearness to toolshed or water outlets and freedom from vandalism are all items to consider. Except when envisioning a bog or swamp planting, choose a spot that is reasonably well drained. Visit it in or immediately after a good rain to check, for appearances can be deceiving. If the site contains long-lasting puddles of water, you will have to improve the drainage if you want to garden with bulbs.

Sometimes deep digging will break up hard pan that has been compressed by heavy machinery and beating rain and sun. Addition of lots of humus will do more to improve any type of soil than anything else you can do. It helps light, sandy soils retain the all-important moisture the plants will need. And it lightens clay soils so that they breathe and drain better. If you don't know how to make compost, start learning immediately. Where a garden is not to be used immediately by plants, you can even bury leaves and garbage shallowly in it and have them turn into rich compost over the months. Peat moss is the easiest soil conditioner to buy. Work it into the soil every time you dig up a new garden, unless you are one of those few lucky enough to have perfect loam. Pine needles, spent mushroom soil, woods duff, even sawdust and coal ashes are all possibilities to work into soil to improve its worth for gardening.

If, however, the topography is such that your projected garden lies in low ground, standing water will be a continual problem in temperate lands with adequate rainfall. Suppose that your projected garden is, for one reason or another, sited in such a low spot. One solution is to buy topsoil and have it dumped on the site (which has been well dug over first). A large garden may require many loads, but eventually you will have a small hill. The bulbs will be planted on its higher reaches to keep their roots drier. Plants such as ferns and forget-me-nots that need damp situations can be used in the lower sections.

Hopefully, you plan to have a bed large enough to hold at least one tree, perhaps more, and a shrub or two. Far too often beginning gardeners start by cutting a hole here and there in the lawn for a tree. Even on the smallest property much more effective gardens are made by making one bed in which several trees will be placed. This cuts down on such maintenance as lawn edging, but even more important, it makes for integrated gardening. A small lawn that is entire looks bigger. By placing the garden to one side of the property you can take advantage of this illusion. At the same time you may be screening out an unwelcome view, creating summer shade for south-facing windows or giving yourself more privacy from a street. All these considerations come into play when deciding where to put a garden. Should your problem be that you have a lawn spotted already with trees here and there, see what you can do about incorporating them into one garden. We bought a front yard like that, and it was only necessary to move two trees to create a garden instead of a haphazard patchwork.

Shape is the next consideration. Sometimes permanent features of a property such as driveways, walks or buildings may determine some or all of the borders of the garden. A bed between house and walk is likely predestined to be rectangular. You can break up this effect by adding some height to the general planting, either with a tree or, in narrow spots, with an espaliered shrub.

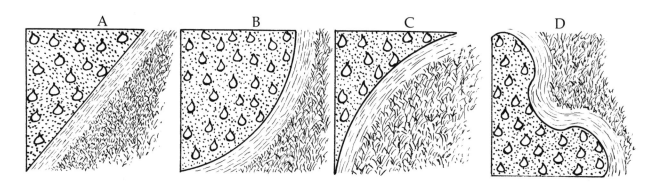

Corner gardens will be larger if the boundary extends outward in a curve (A) rather than curving into the bulb area (B) or cutting across in a straight line (C). A varied edge offers added interest (D).

A garden in the corner of a property is usually triangular. But the free edge of any garden need not be a straight line. A gentle curve is often much more graceful, and it can be fashioned so that it either cuts into the garden or sweeps outward into the lawn. The lay of the land often gives a clue to which treatment will be more pleasing to the eye. A garden is better laid out following a ridge, for example, than crossing it.

If you have trouble, as I do, in visualizing spatial relationships, your garden hose is a great aid. Use however many lengths are necessary to enclose the amount of garden you want. Rearrange the hose until the borders of the garden are satisfactory.

When sod has to be peeled back before the garden can be made, use the hose as a guide for the spade or edger and lift off a few inches all around; this will give you your outline. If there is neither need nor time for this step, pour a generous marker of agricultural lime all along the hose guide to delineate the garden. It is, incidentally, better to peel off the sod and use it either where you need instant lawn or pile it up to make compost than to till it into the soil of the garden—a practice that in effect plants quantities of weed seeds and stoloniferous grass roots into the flower bed. It also tends to allow many insects entry into your garden, because the tilling does not kill their eggs or even sometimes the pupae. Why set up future problems for yourself?

After you have the garden's outlines settled and the sod taken off if necessary, take a good look at the soil and decide what kind of preparation is required. The condition and type may range from the wonder-soft sponge of old woods earth to an impervious hardpan full of debris left by a careless builder. Whatever is called for by your particular conditions, keep in mind that never again will you have such a perfect opportunity to improve the tilth and nourishment of your soil as now before the garden is planted. Dig it deeply if necessary. It's hard to conceive of adding too much humus to a garden, and this is a good time to start. Fertilizer, lime and manure are ideally added now too. Then let the bed settle at least a few weeks before planting.

Meanwhile, you will have been envisioning what is to go into the garden. Before you plant, take time for some real planning. It is far easier to use an eraser on a piece of paper than to move things about after they have been planted.

If you have a precise mind, graph paper is the ideal tool for this stage, preferably one with fairly large squares. You can do almost as well with plain paper. If your bed is to be larger than 20 feet, use shelf paper, which come in rolls, so you have enough space to write in—and later to read what you wrote.

Now go out to the site and take a compass reading. With no compass, dawn and sunset will give you approximate east and west. Possibly you should mark the four cardinal points with four small stakes in the earth of the garden at its center to jog your memory until you have this important orientation firmly in mind. Which direction a garden faces determines the areas of sun and shade, which in turn mandate what can be planted where. Even if no trees and bushes are involved, plants to the north of taller ones will be in shade part of the time.

Measurements are important, too, and the truer they are, the easier your planning will be. At least you need to know the length and width of the proposed bed. A long, flexible wind-up rule is the easiest tool to do this with.

Translating these figures to the paper is easy if the bed is rectangular or perfectly square or round. Many of the most successful gardens, however, are somewhat crescent-shaped. For these you will need to measure the bed at its greatest width, then take several more readings at various points all along its length to get a usable diagram.

On graph paper allow so many squares to the foot, depending on their size. With plain paper plot your garden in the same way by allowing half an inch to equal a foot. Draw in the approximate garden by using your mea-surements. If the site already contains trees, shrubs, large boulders or other features, these too should be accurately located on your plot plan.

Suppose the site was barren of vegetation. The trees and shrubs for the garden are then your first consideration. Everything else being equal, choose at least one flowering tree. Most of these are smaller of stature than stately shade trees and thus will be more in proportion to the total garden. Dogwood, crab apple, stewartia, magnolia, franklinia, hawthorn, sourwood, albizia and styrax are a few favorites in my part of the world. Your local climate will dictate which you choose, but consider the flower, fruit, fall color and winter silhouette when select-ing a garden tree. Where you can fit in more than one, perhaps you will want a tree that blooms in spring, another in summer. You might choose one for the color of its bark. White birches are fast-growing, but many other trees make a surprising amount of growth in a few years too and have equally interesting bark. Check with your county

A few clumps of spring bulbs make a gay note in a small garden along the entrance walk.

agent if you are not sure of trees that do well in your latitude. Try to stay away from species that cast dense shade or that are notoriously shallow-rooted, a habit that interferes with the roots of the garden's other inhabitants. There are some so-called dirty trees that are better avoided for garden use. Horse chestnut, catalpa, an early-dropping crab apple or a thicket-forming locust are some to avoid, too. As the trees grow, keep trimming off their lower branches. This allows light to get into the garden and lessens the amount of ground space that has to be devoted to the tree. If your garden site has some trees already, get busy with the pruners so that the first three feet of trunk are clear of branches.

A projected garden more than ten feet in length may well be able to include a few shrubs as part of its backbone. They help to face the tree down to the rest of the garden rather than having an abrupt transition from tree to little plants. For such purposes I favor evergreen bushes. Such kinds as leucothoe, pieris, dwarf holly, azalea and rhododendron are decorative because they have flowers or fruits. There is no reason either why you cannot use dwarf needled evergreens for such a site.

Even when the garden is quite small you can usually fit in one low-growing tree, and there are some diminutive evergreen shrubs such as gaultheria, *Leiophyllum buxifolium*, daphne, *Paxistima canbyi* and *Andromeda*

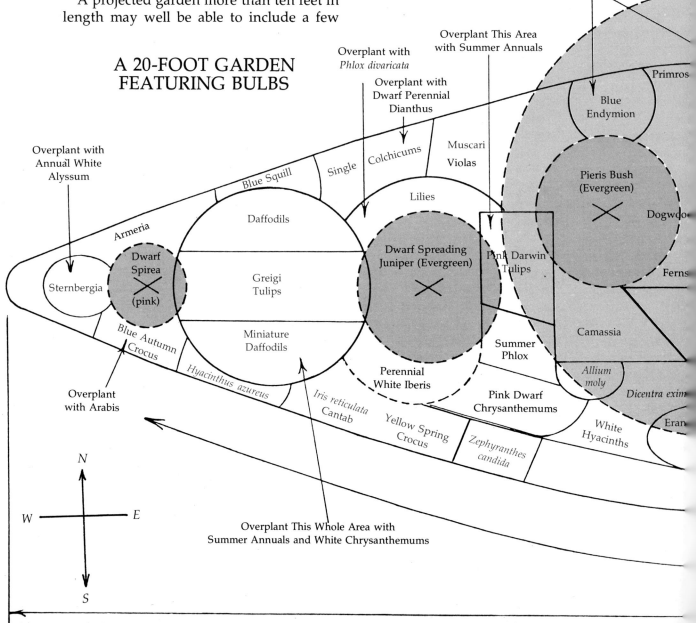

A 20-FOOT GARDEN FEATURING BULBS

185

polifolia that will be very nicely in scale. Some shrubs such as lilac and chionanthus, or certain rhododendrons and viburnums, can actually be pruned to resemble a small tree that will never outgrow the proportions of a small garden.

As you position trees and shrubs on your plot plan, allow for mature size in your thinking. A baby crab apple may look perfect when planted in a small garden, but if its natural proclivity is to reach 25 feet with a spread of 15 to 20 feet, it will soon outgrow where it is planted. You can fill in temporarily with annuals or plants you intend to move later while you are waiting for a little

tree to grow, but there's not much you can do if you choose a tree or shrub that is too rambunctious a grower. Shrubs preferring shade should be planted toward the northern side of any trees where they will get the least sun. All this prior thinking saves you lots of work later on.

Having established the backbone of the garden, you are ready to add the frills that will bring the desired future color. Along the fringes of where the tree casts its shade almost any of the spring bulbs will do well. Be realistic about allowing enough space on your plan for what you intend to plant. You can put a dozen bulbs of a small plant such as puschkinia or crocus in a space six inches by eight inches, but the same number of daffodils requires at least three times that much space in square inches. If you try to

A garden plan that leans heavily on bulbs for color during the growing season. Annuals, perennials, trees and shrubs are necessary to create a whole garden picture.

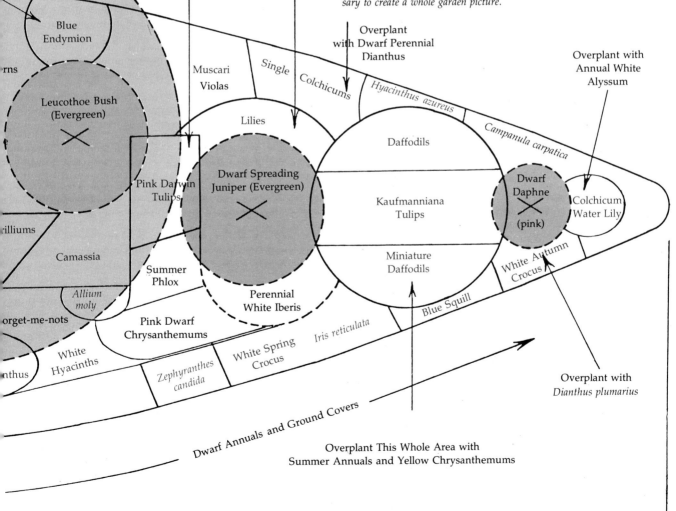

20 feet

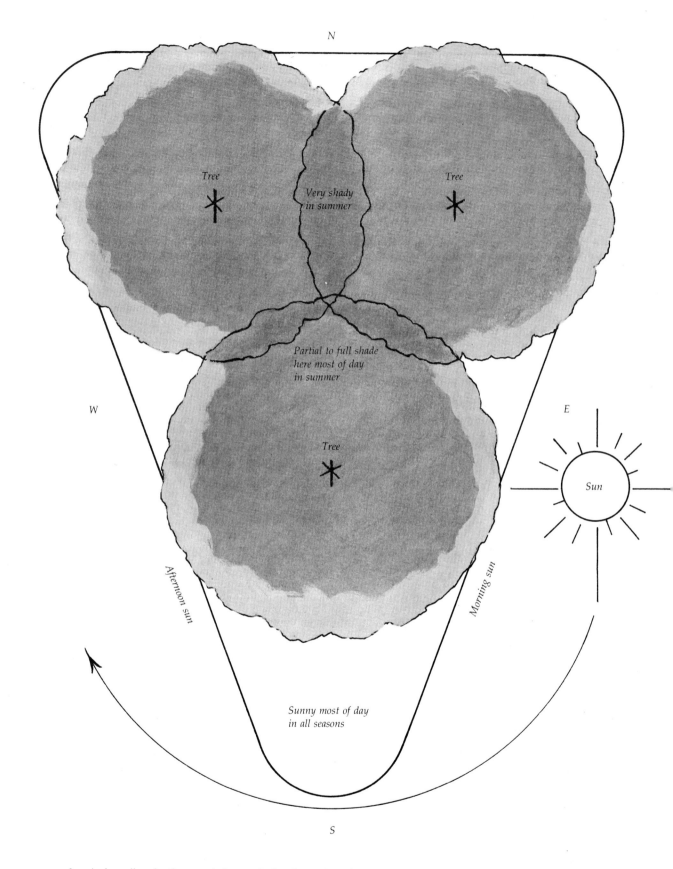

In a single small garden the amount of sun varies from hour to hour during the day, depending on position of trees in relation to path of sun. This garden can accommodate plants that need different amounts of sun or shade.

jam them in tightly, they will need transplanting in no time at all. Unless you are careful about this, you will find that your wishes outstrip your available space before you have hardly begun.

The heights given in catalogs will aid you in positioning your bulbs for the greatest effect. Early tulips such as the *Kaufmannianas* and *Greigis* are usually shorter than the daffodils with which they often bloom, so they belong in front. Most of the later-flowering Darwin tulips, however, are taller. They look better either behind or beside the later daffodils.

Ground covers are ideal for the foreground of the garden, but keep in mind which of the little bulbs are going there too. The lush spring growth of *Arabis alpina*, for example, smothers the daintier species tulips and daffodils as well as many tiny darlings such as squills, spring crocus and *Anemone blanda*. In the fall, on the other hand, the arabis is only a few inches high and so can set off autumn crocus very handily as a foliage plant.

Later-flowering perennials such as May's amsonia, summer's phlox or fall's chrysanthemums can be planted so that their developing leaves hide the maturing bulb foliage of daffodils and tulips. And as each perennial reaches its peak, it will put color back into the garden so you will not even notice the spots where the bulbs have disappeared until next spring.

Should you want summer-flowering bulbs such as dahlias in this projected garden, try to plan so they will not be near patches of spring bulbs. This makes it easier to dig the tender bulbs and roots in the fall without damaging hidden daffodils.

Depending on how knowledgeable you are about things horticultural, this planning of what to put in the new garden may take only a few hours or days of research. Be assured that no lovely garden springs up overnight. The hours of planning will bear worthwhile fruit eventually. And many mistakes can be avoided by making rough drawings and doing some checking about the plants before you order them. It is on such quests through catalogs and books that I first was introduced to plants that later became treasured friends.

Whatever you plan, keep the compass markings in mind. In most of the United States the eastern side of a shrub, tall plant or boulder will receive morning light, the western side hotter afternoon sun. Toward the south there will be the most sunshine and to the north the most shade. Even in a garden without any trees and shrubs, a dwarf plant to the north of a big patch of a summer perennial will be shaded part of the day. Attention to such details allows you to work more kinds of plants into a garden and certainly makes for healthier plants. A sun-loving tigridia just won't do well in shadow, and a trillium from the woods cannot prosper in full, hot summer sun.

Try not to plan or plant in thin rows. This applies to almost everything outside the vegetable garden but particularly to bulbs, which often tend to look stiff. The same number of tulips regimented into a single line will not be half as pretty as when planted in a clump. If you plant your bulbs in clumps, more or less round or oval and at least two rows thick, the effect can be as if nature had done the plan. A dozen tulips in a circular grouping can be spectacular. Strung out in single file, they look like a nursery row. Spotty planting is to be avoided, too. It is much stronger to put three perennials of a single variety in one area to make a forceful statement than to sprinkle them singly in three different places in the garden. Ground covers or perennials that increase quickly by stolons and spread into large clumps are the exception to the rule; but leave room for the increase so they can luxuriate and not become too crowded too quickly. If the garden is large enough, try to repeat a planting at least once. This repetition adds strength to the total picture and helps you avoid too spotty an effect.

Color combinations and comparative heights are usually considered by even the beginning gardener. Texture and growth habit are additional factors that, when handled imaginatively, enhance the effect of a garden. Where you are using a bulb with tall, sharp foliage, such as a gladiolus or acidanthera, a plant that grows in the shape of a mound, such as a dwarf dahlia, many daisy-flowered perennials or a bushy early chrysanthemum contrasts nicely. The dramatic summer foliage of the tender ismene is all the more effective if fronted by lacy dwarf marigolds or the softer shape of bedding petunias.

When it comes time to translate the plot map into a garden, you need not be a slave to your planning, but having the diagram in hand will make it all much easier. Most times it is a good idea, especially if you are fashioning a fairly large garden, to leave some blank spaces on the plan. This allows for last-minute additions or new ideas to be incorporated into the plan as you learn more. Only the imaginary gardens of the painter and the spring flower shows are created in a matter of days.

If at all possible, put in the trees or shrubs first when it comes time for the actual planting. If the season is such that you cannot do this, leave plenty of room both for the tree and for maneuvering while putting it in. Incidentally, a garden so wide that you cannot reach all of it from one edge or the other is much easier to tend if you put some steppingstones here and there. Work always needs doing, even when the soil is wet. These give you a place to put your feet.

When spring is the first season with a new garden, the problem of planting the trees and shrubs is solved. This is the ideal time to put in starts of the perennials as well as annuals too.

But what do you do about leaving room for the bulbs you'll be planting the following fall? There are several ways to help keep the space open easily until fall. One is to cover the spots where the bulbs are to go with several inches of mulch. This will keep weeds out and save the space. If you put a marker in with the name of the intended bulb, your fall planting will be a snap. Or you can place the bulb marker and then plant around it with annuals. You will enjoy their color all summer, then pull them out before placing the bulbs.

When fall planting is the initial step, the bulbs, of course, go in first. Their foliage will be evident during the next spring while you are adding the other parts of your design, so you don't have to worry about disturbing the bulbs. Often at that time you may see where you could improve the garden by adding more bulbs of some sort for another year. Memory can be tricky, so either put in a marker immediately to remind you later or add notes to your plot plan. For anyone who takes gardening seriously, growing and flowering records are important. Such notations can be helpful later when you want to check some detail. I find that index cards are the easiest way to organize a permanent record of my gardening successes—and some failures too.

It is not as easy to do over an existing garden as it is to fashion one from scratch. Even more complicated is the renovation of an inherited garden (either by will or purchase). Go easy about digging up an unknown place until you have lived with it for a full year. Obvious weeds can be removed, but you just can't tell what jewels an old garden may be hiding until spring, summer and fall have all been torn off the calendar. As might be expected, some of the most precious treasures may be the buried bulbs.

Using the hints about transplanting bulbs given in the beginning of this book, you can move bulbs you fall heir to if it suits you. As they bloom, note down what appears and mark the site. It might even be wise in a complicated planting to make a rough diagram of what you have. Oddly enough, if you start plotting the planting, you may even understand why the former owners planted as they did. Just as often their ideas will not fit with yours. Try to leave lily plantings undisturbed if healthy; they are more difficult to transplant than other bulbs. Label the plantings by color and type as you can identify them. Those you want or need

Edged with perennial dianthus, a few dozen bulbs are all that's needed to give a cheery hello for a streetside planting.

to move can then be taken care of, each in its own time. Hopefully you will not dislike the bulbs so much that you want to discard them, but individual tastes do vary widely. One other solution is to gather those you wish to remove and replant in rows somewhere out of the way for a cutting garden.

In these few pages I have covered a tremendous amount of gardening know-how in what can only be described as bare essentials. Please do not be discouraged by dwelling on what you don't know. Every garden and every gardener has to start somewhere.

As I grow older, the more do I realize that gardening is one pursuit where no one ever stops learning. That is part of its great charm and endless fascination. There is always another season in which to rectify your mistakes—and I have learned a lot from them.

A garden should be a reflection of you—your tastes and enthusiasms, not those of any author, neighbor or relative. And it should be a pleasure not only to look at but to take care of. The idea of placing some daffodils as companions to a tree or shrub border is not really a complicated approach to gardening. In the long run it makes for easier upkeep than to tend the tree and the bulbs separately.

White flowers of arabis are a dainty complement to early **kaufmanniana** *tulips.*

Companion Plantings

One of the joys of being a working gardener is falling in love with flowers. Some you will have created almost from scratch by planting from those miracles of life we so casually call seeds. You will have nursed them, fed them, protected them, transplanted, divided and picked them for bouquets. You will learn to plant dormant bulbs on a cold, damp fall day and let your mind dwell on the glories you will be seeing come spring rather than on the creakings of your back and worn skin on your knees.

As your knowledge accumulates, you will automatically begin to think of plants in groups. A tour of whatever garden you have, even in winter, suggests plants that look good together. It may be their colors that complement each other or their form or heights or a whole combination of such factors. Such revelations make for more beautiful gardens. Try consciously to assess your garden in this way, for no growing thing lives in a vacuum, and almost everything looks best with a companion.

190

The growing season, of course, is the best time for noting combinations that work well. Write them down. Keep two factors in mind, however. To make good companions the two plants should require the same sort of growing conditions. You can fudge a little by putting the shade-preferring, plumy bleeding-heart back into the garden a bit from the tulips and daffodils with which it is so perfect. And you can count on developing tree foliage to give it the summer shade it needs. Since the spring bulbs will have pretty much matured their foliage before the tree leaves get thick, you have more latitude on this score than appears at first.

Exposure, however, is something else again, particularly in relation to spring-flowering bulbs. You may notice that the scilla in a cool spot is blooming at the same time as *Anemone blanda* in a warm, protected niche. Unless you are very lucky in choosing a site for them, you may find it impossible ever to get them to bloom together in the same home. No matter; you will have at least created a succession planting, and that is nearly as important a feat.

In a country as large and varied as the United States, the bloom times of a particular plant may differ by several months, depending on the altitude and latitude of your garden. For that reason I have indicated only seasons rather than the exact month of flowering in the lists of suggested combinations.

To get you started, here are a few of my favorite companions for bulbs:

Spring

Blue *Polemonium reptans* with any late tulip.

White endymion with red eastern columbine (*Aquilegia canadensis*).

Early crocus with *Iris reticulata*.

Any *Iris reticulata* form or hybrid with *Erica* Springwood White.

Christmas fern with primroses and endymion.

White forms of **Anemone blanda** *contrast interestingly with blue squill.*

Crocus biflorus *White Lady and* Iris reticulata *are a splendid pair for earliest spring.*

Pretty conceit for a little niche is a combination of violas and Muscari botryoides album. (ABOVE)

Sprightly trio: Narcissus Rembrandt, white form of Anemone pulsatilla *and* kaufmanniana tulips. (RIGHT)

Yellow doronicum with Darwin tulips.

Plumy bleeding-heart (*Dicentra eximia*) with *tazetta* daffodils.

Blue muscari, white *triandrus* hybrid daffodils and Japanese bleeding-heart (*Dicentra spectabilis*).

Midseason daffodils and tulip hybrids from either the *Kaufmanniana* or *Greigi* groups.

Chionodoxa with hybrid *cyclamineus* daffodils.

Puschkinia with midseason daffodils.

Ipheion with *Dicentra eximia*, late daffodils or tulips.

Late daffodils with epimediums.

Allium moly and forget-me-nots.

Early red tulips and white hyacinths.

Blue muscari and *Alyssum saxatile*.

White arabis, yellow daffodils and/or red tulips.

Fritillaria imperialis and white trumpet daffodils.

Primroses and poppy anemones.

Yellow jonquils with dwarf white iberis.

Crocus and chionodoxa.

Snowdrops and eranthis.

Snowflakes and late tulips.

Chionodoxa and *Tulipa turkestanica*.

Tulipa dasystemon in front of late daffodils.

Hyacinthus azureus with early daffodils.

Blue *Phlox divaricata* with late tulips.

Pink *Daphne cneorum* with white lily-flowered tulips.

Mertensia, daffodils and *Fritillaria meleagris*.

Early crocus with snowdrops.

Trilliums and *Polemonium reptans*.

Smilacina and *Uvularia sessilifolia*.

Tulipa sylvestris in shrubbery.

Summer

Caladiums in contrasting colors.

Caladiums and tuberous begonias or impatiens or annual balsam.

Ferns behind caladiums.

Gladiolus as accents in the summer border.

Dahlias or gladiolus with zinnias and marigolds.

White phlox and blue veronica with any of the yellow, red or orange lilies.

Cannas as accents in the summer border.

Orange belamcanda and white galtonia.

Cannas or lilies as accents in a shrub border or against evergreens.

Annual white alyssum provides a fine foil for many fall-flowering bulbs such as these Crocus karduchorum. (LEFT)

No-nonsense knockout for spring is a combination of perennial alyssum and grape-hyacinths. (ABOVE)

Hymenocallis as green accent in annual bed.

Mid-Century lilies with blue flax or white Shasta daisies.

Lilies behind thalictrums.

Orange *Asclepias tuberosa* with lilies.

Late lilies with buddleia.

Madonna lilies and delphiniums.

Tigridias and marigolds.

Achimenes in front of impatiens.

Calla-lilies as accents in summer border.

Pompon dahlias in summer border.

Hyacinthus amethystinum and earliest lilies.

Tuberous begonias or caladiums with dwarf annual lobelias.

Late Summer and Fall

Tuberoses with *Aster frikarti*.

Liatris as accents in border or between shrubs.

Cannas with chrysanthemums.

Tigridias and montbretias with late white liatris.

Acidanthera with zinnias.

Montbretias with yellow marigolds, calendulas, white alyssum.

Lycoris squamigera behind early chrysanthemums or with ferns.

Tuberoses and purple liatris.

Colchicums and thyme.

Pompon dahlias with chrysanthemums.

Dahlias and caryopteris.

Purple liatris with lemon calendulas.

Autumn crocus or sternbergia with annual white alyssum.

Large hybrid colchicums with annual white alyssum.

Late white liatris with gaillardias and calendulas.

Zephyranthes or sternbergia in front of blue plumbago.

Hypoxis hirsuta and fall crocus.

Speciosum lilies with caryopteris

Colchicums in front of shrubbery, *Vinca minor* as ground cover.

Allium stellatum in front of early yellow or white cushion chrysanthemums.

Cyclamen neapolitanum or *C. europaeum* in front of any variety of *Colchicum autumnale* but especially the double forms.

Hardy cyclamen in front of autumn crocus.

Autumn crocus in foliage of *Phlox subulata*, thyme, dianthus or armeria.

Bulbs for Showing

Whether your pleasure is in entering the horticultural classes or those that feature arrangements, showing your bulb flowers can be an interesting adventure.

Handbooks of such organizations as the American Daffodil Society are of some help to the neophyte, and your library may have books on the subject to start you on your way, too. The best course of all is to learn from someone who has been a successful blue-ribbon winner. I do not pose as an expert at either type of exhibiting, but there are some common-sense rules that make such an undertaking more likely to be rewarding.

One of them is to make sure you plant more bulbs than you will need if you are specifically committed to a show. This allows you to choose the best ones. Big-time exhibitors always take more than they will need to the show too, just in case.

It always surprises me that so many flower arrangers do not grow their own raw materials. Even the biggest florist can stock only a limited number of flowers. This is, after all, one of the most perishable of products. Although many show schedules are not put out far enough in advance for you to plan exactly what you will need a whole season ahead, you can do some very close guesswork. You know what colors and forms appeal to your own personality. Unless you live in an apartment or are physically unable, you will have much greater latitude in designing your arrangements if you set aside a small space just for growing show flowers.

Most likely you will begin your show career on a small scale, perhaps at meetings of your own garden club. This way you can learn some of the techniques, and you can also find out gradually what flowers will be in bloom during what month in your particular geographic locality.

The horticultural exhibitor has an easier time meeting show schedules. One does not absolutely have to have pink tulips available for a specific date. In these classes one tulip may do as well as another if it has a straight stem, perfect foliage, unbruised or unbent petals and is correctly labeled. On the other hand, there is the problem of flower size. Where the arranger may need only the effect of pink tulips, the winning horticultural entrant has to make sure that the Aristocrat to be shown is up to size for a Darwin tulip. For that reason serious show gardeners usually plant new stocks of tulips every year (except for the species types). They separate their daffodils frequently too to keep the size of the flowers up to standard. And they keep accurate records because mislabeling can be cause for disqualification.

If you decide to do exhibition work in either the horticultural or the design sections, your first job is to read carefully the show's instructions. Be forewarned that the rules are to be followed, or the entry will be disqualified. Where sizes of entries or numbers of blooms are stated, the requirements have to be met—exactly. Most shows allow only one entry per exhibitor in each class, so plan which flowers can go in which horticultural class if you are anxious to enter as many as possible.

Weather is never normal at any season, but spring can be more capricious than any other part of the year. Many spring shows feature daffodils, and you would be wise to plant a number of different varieties that tend to flower at different weeks of the spring. This way you are sure to have something at its peak at show time. Picked ahead of time when not fully open, daffodils may be kept a few days in a very cool place to slow down their development. Conversely, you can speed up blooming of many spring bulbs by bringing some into the warmer house a few days ahead of time. Try to leave some in the garden too just to cover all contingencies.

An exhibit of spring bulbs at a garden show. Courtesy The Horticultural Society of New York.

The catalogs of gladiolus growers often list the number of days required for a specific variety to come into flower after planting. Knowing your show dates, you can make a fairly good guess on the optimum date for planting. Give yourself some insurance by planting some earlier and some later too. Dahlias for fall exhibiting are better planted later than those for garden decoration, but you will need some experience with your own weather and growing conditions before you do more than guess intelligently. A local gardener who's had some experience can be a great help.

Certain varieties of the more popular bulbs such as daffodils and dahlias take more prizes than others. Which they are changes from year to year and depends on such factors as rarity, form, vigor and health as well as the judges' own preferences. Attend a few shows with pencil in hand to gain insight into these finer points. Some daffodils are not really good garden flowers but are consistent show winners. You will have to decide where to concentrate your own emphasis.

Bruised or dirty flowers can be disastrous for the show gardener. Staking is one aid, especially for tall-growing plants such as lilies, gladiolus and dahlias. You may want to put the stakes in when you plant to prevent spearing a bulb or tuber later. Use soft string or strips of sheeting to avoid bruising the stems. A figure eight with one loop around the stake and another around the stem is one good way to do it. Make several ties at different points along the stem.

A heavy downpour can beat daffodils to the ground too. A clean mulch helps some, but you may have to stake or erect a temporary protective tent to get show-quality blooms. A ring of chicken wire covered at the top with plastic cloth can be moved into the garden on a threatening day to protect something slated for showing.

Conditioning flowers is a necessity for the serious exhibitor. Most authorities agree that flowers should be cut in early morning or late evening with as long a stem as possible, placed immediately in deep, warm water in a container large enough so the flowers will not be crushed together, then put in a cool, dark place for at least 12 hours before the show. Often daffodils and dahlias do better if the water starts out really hot. Do some experimenting to see what works best with various bulb flowers. A small, soft paintbrush is the best tool to remove any specks of dirt from petals. Be careful about washing petals in water; they bruise easily.

Transporting your blooms requires utmost care. If you have only a few miles to go, jars of water can be placed in cardboard carton carriers. Crumpled newspaper around the jars will prevent overturning. Allow plenty of room so the flowers are not squashed. More crumpled paper between the stems will keep them from moving around.

If the flowers have to travel a long way or if the heads are heavy, long boxes such as a florist uses may be better. Carefully place

When staking tall plants, use more than one tie. The figure-eight method (exaggerated here for clarity) works best.

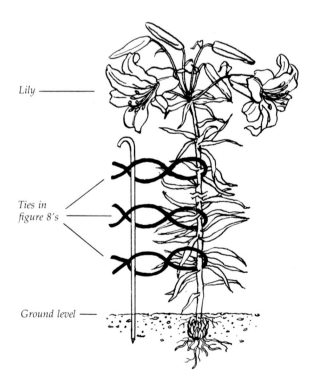

Lily ———————

Ties in
figure 8's ———————

Ground level ———

crumpled tissue or wax paper between the blooms to keep them in prime condition. Make sure that they cannot shift around and that the petals are not bent. Those with heavy heads will need a pillow of paper a few inches below the head to prevent bruising or breaking. If there are anthers with pollen, the petals can get badly smeared. A piece of aluminum foil gently fastened around the anthers will protect them. Always avoid long waits in warm places. It takes only a few minutes for a closed car in the sun to become an oven.

For horticultural classes, check ahead of time on whether containers are supplied by the show. If you are required to bring your own, start a collection of dark-green bottles; these seem to show off specimens better than clear glass. Short stubby ones are fine for many of the little bulbs, but long-stemmed specimens such as most of the lilies require a tall, small-necked container to stand straight and glorious.

Even if you do not plan to do more than show the best of your garden to your own club at an informal show, attention to these basic details will make it easier in the long run. And if you are proud enough of your flowers to want to show them, you certainly want them to be seen at their best.

Preserving and Arranging Bulb Flowers

By all means enjoy your bulbs inside in bouquets. Picking them for this purpose is much more fun than merely snapping off the dead flowers in the garden, a job that has to be done faithfully to lessen the strain on the bulbs themselves. Like most flowers, these are best picked in early morning before they are subjected to much sun. This is especially important for those that come into flower after the weather warms up. Early-spring bloomers can be hastened into flower by picking in the bud. Once inside where it is warmer, they will quickly open to provide a cheery note when you need it most.

The only serious rule about picking for bouquets is to go easy on how much foliage you remove. With tulips, particularly, try not to remove the last leaf on the flowering stem. Most tulips do not last very long after cutting; I usually cut them in bud to get as many days as possible from a bouquet.

Those flowers that have bleeding stems such as daffodils and dahlias need to be put in hot water first to seal the stems for best results. If you are cutting early for later use, store all cut flowers in deep water in a cool place. This conditioning makes the flowers last longer. It is most important for early-spring subjects brought into a warm house and for midsummer flowers cut on hot days.

Perhaps you are more interested in using your flowers in dried arrangements or pressed in flat designs. Because of the body of the petals and the funnel or cup shapes, many bulbs are not too easily used these ways, but a few are excellent.

The alliums as a family are particularly recommended. If the seed heads are left to form, the resulting dried ball lends a fine round note to a dried bouquet. Allow the heads to mature on the plant until the seeds are almost ripe, then pick with as long a stem as possible. Hang in bunches upside down in a cool, darkish spot until the stem dries rigid. They can then be packed carefully in boxes and will last indefinitely. The huge alliums are breathtaking in a large arrangement, but I think the heads of A. karataviense are among the prettiest. You can also cut the smaller alliums while in flower and press with pleasing results. Cut fresh and dried whole in a darkish place, A. moly and A. ostrowskiana retain some color. I separate the stems on a tray for adequate air circulation.

The pinkish flowers of A. schoenoprasum (chives) can be similarly treated but have another more important use. Pick the heads just as they open fully, soak 15 minutes in salted water, then swish to get rid of any insects. Place immediately in a plastic bag or other container and pop into the freezer. Some winter day you can liven your menu in either of two ways. Rub a few flowers together to separate them and add to cottage cheese. Or make a spread by adding a small amount of mayonnaise to cream cheese and mix in some of the frozen chive flowers. The flavor is even milder than that of chive foliage, and the pink color is refreshing.

The small-cupped daffodils, particularly those known as *poeticus* types, press quite nicely. The petals turn a soft shade of cream, and the orange rims remain bright. Cut each flower so that there is no large ovary left at the back and press flat for best results.

Individual tulip and lily petals can be pressed flat and the flower more or less reassembled for a pressed picture. Choose the brightest colors you can find because they always lose some color in the drying.

Flowers from some of the smaller bulbs such as muscari and chionodoxa can also be pressed. Usually it works best to remove some of the individual flowers from the stalk of anything like the true grape-hyacinths, which have many bells on each stalk. That way the head presses more easily, and it will look more interesting when used because the individual flowers can be more easily seen. The single flowers can be pressed for use where you need just a bell or two.

Most bulb flowers have considerable substance to the petals. For this reason they do not dry quickly. It may be necessary to replace the papers between which they are being pressed several times to avoid mildew. Old newspapers work well for this purpose, incidentally. If you do a lot of this work, the best advice I can give is to try lots of different ones to find out which come out best in what colors. Anything that does not have great bulk may press well.

Using silica gel or sand to dry flowers in the round is still another technique. There are many books available outlining the best ways to do this.

The dried seed pods of many bulb flowers provide striking raw material for wreaths as well as other craft projects. The only discouraging word is to reiterate that it takes a lot out of a bulb to produce a mature seed pod. Ordinarily it is best to break off your withered bulb flowers before any seeds can be set. But if you have lots of bulbs, sacrifice a few for this purpose. Tulip and daffodil heads are most interesting. The little species *Tulipa dasystemon* yields lots of small whitish pods. I usually let them develop a bit but pick them while they are still green to save the bulb from using too much of its strength. Lay them flat to dry out of strong light.

It does not seem to harm grape-hyacinths if they go to seed, and their seed heads make fine small, tan-colored fillers for dried

Alliums are favorite bulbs for arrangers. A. karataviense (BELOW) *yields intricate seed heads for dried bouquets. Flowers of chives can be dried for arranging or used as delicate garnish for salads.* (LEFT)

Round seed head of **Allium karataviense** *and seeds of blackberry-lily add interest to dried arrangements. Both are easily grown.*

bouquets. Pick after the seed is completely formed but before the capsules are dry and brittle. Allow to dry well before storing, either by sticking upright in bottles or tying in small bunches that hang upside down. The seed heads of the pasqueflower are lovely and fuzzy; watch them daily as they begin to dry and pick before they blow away. I have let my galtonia and large cammasia go partially to seed, picking the heads after the pods have formed but before they mature. The whole stalk is then inserted into a bottle to dry, after which the pods are removed and kept for craft work.

Blackberry-lily is one of the standbys for dried arrangements. Let the sprays go to seed, but pick them just as the capsules begin to open and insert the stems in bottles for complete drying. The outside pods will peel back to show the shiny black seeds, which do indeed resemble blackberries. Pick this one on long stems since it can be used without any wiring. It lends a dramatic note to dried arrangements, often muted of hue. You can shorten the stems later.

It is worth emphasizing that any dried material may harbor or attract insects. Spraying with insecticide is often a good idea. Mothballs inside the boxes or plastic bags in which such things are stored is another good measure. Never, incidentally, pack anything of this sort for storing until you are sure it is absolutely bone-dry. Mildew can ruin your raw materials quickly.

INTERESTING FLOWERS FOR ARRANGERS

The flower arranger and gardener who has access to unusual flowers has much more latitude than the person who is limited to only those raw materials available from a florist. All the following bulbs are good decoratives either for house or garden but seldom available commercially.

Botanical Name	Color	Season	Remarks
Acidanthera	cream, brown	late summer	graceful arched tubes
Allium	several	spring to summer	umbels of star flowers
Anemone blanda	several	early spring	daisy flowers
Anemone coronaria	several	spring to summer	resemble poppies
Arisaema	green, brown	spring	unusual flowers
Begonia evansiana	pink, white	late summer	foliage especially interesting
Belamcanda chinesis	orange	summer	dried seed pods look like blackberries
Caladium	several	summer, pots	striking foliage
Calochortus	many	late spring	strange flower shapes
Camassia	blue, white	late spring	airy spires of stars
Crocosmia	several	late summer	airy, arching wands of flowers
Dahlia (pompons)	many	summer, fall	dainty flower balls
Cyclamen (florist)	several	pots	leaves, butterfly flowers last well
Cyclamen (hardy)	several	spring, fall	charming miniatures
Eucharis	white	pots	fragrant, unusual flowers, dramatic foliage
Galtonia candicans	white	summer	bold effects
Gladiolus (hardy)	several	late spring	unusual at this season
Gloriosa	several	summer, pots	twisted, recurved petals
Hymenocallis	white	summer	fragrant, unusual flowers
Ixiolirion	blues	spring	arching stems, flowers resemble hyacinths
Lachenalia	several	pots	flowers like tiny kniphofia
Liatris	white, purple	summer, fall	tall spires
Lilium hybrids	many	summer	wonderful for bouquets
Muscari	several	spring	several oddities
Narcissus	several	spring	lots of variety besides the trumpets; try splits
Sprekelia	red	pots	unusual flower shape
Sternbergia lutea	yellow	fall	crocuslike
Tulipa	many	spring	try lily-flowered, doubles, parrots, fringed, green and species
Veltheimia	rose, white	pots	like large kniphofia
Zantedeschia	several	summer, pots	long-lasting flowers, dramatic foliage

Gardeners looking for ideas can find them aplenty at a display garden such as this one at Lenteboden, property of Charles H. Mueller, New Hope, Pennsylvania, bulb dealer. Photo by Derek Fell

Where to Buy Bulbs

Everyone is selling bulbs these days— garden centers, hardware and department stores, discount houses and even some drugstores. I have had excellent results with bulbs from supermarkets where they are handled by the same produce personnel who keep the lettuce fresh. Bulbs stored for long in an overheated general store do not fare as well. Even though they are dormant, they suffer if allowed to dry out. Never buy bulbs displayed in the hot sun, either.

If you want only a few bulbs, any of these sources is a possibility, but if your needs or desires range further, order a few catalogs from the bulb specialists listed on page 203. Not only do they offer a far wider selection of varieties, but they stake their reputations on quality stock in perfect health. From them you should expect bulbs of optimum size, freshness and correct labeling. When they offer a "bargain," it is most likely because of overstocking or for promotion of good customer relations rather than poor bulb quality. And do order early.

BOTANICAL NAMES

Some gardeners are alarmed when confronted by Latin botanical names. They forget that many are already in everyday usage—crocus, gladiolus or cyclamen, for example. If the Latin scares you, think of the botanical name as a way to ensure that you will get exactly what you want when ordering.

Until about 200 years ago plants were identified either by their common names, which varied from place to place, or by long Latin descriptive phrases. International adoption of what is called binomial nomenclature simplified the whole process.

Every plant now belongs to a particular genus—crocus, for example. But all crocuses are not alike, and so each is given a species name to differentiate it from the others. These names are registered to avoid confusion. Today *Crocus medius* (shortened to *C. medius* where no ambiguity exists) is used the world over to identify the same purple-flowered, fall-blooming member of the tribe. Usually the full botanical names are printed in italics.

Nature created the species, but when man began to select and hybridize plants, there were additional complications of identity. There is less confusion on this score for bulbs than for other members of the plant kingdom because growers in the United States and Europe have been faithful about registering their hybrids internationally. A few bulb sellers try to pose as purveyors of something special by giving their own names to a particular hybrid, but there is less and less of this as the public becomes more sophisticated and knowledgeable. Thus, hybrids as identified in the catalogs are usually true to name. A hybrid always starts with a capital letter, as for any proper name—Pickwick crocus, for example. Botanists usually put these hybrid names within single quotation marks, but for the sake of clarity I have dispensed with them. Long lists of hybrids with the quotation marks are confusing to read, and they seldom appear in catalogs, either. Besides, this book is for gardeners, not botanists.

What can be done about the bulb promoter who takes a perfectly good species and gives it a fancy name as a selling gimmick, I do not know. I would not mind if such displays gave the botanical name in parentheses; I consider it dishonest not to do so. With my considerable knowledge at this point, I can guess that "Early Stardrift" is puschkinia, "Buttercup Iris" is *I. danfordiae* or "Sunny Twinkles" is *Allium moly*—to quote a few bad examples. What the beginning gardener is to make of all this I can't conceive. The sources given at the back of this book are not often guilty of this nonsense. Rather than being intimidated by a botanical name, insist on it.

For any reader who is not yet a bulb expert, I have cross-indexed this book with as many of the common names of bulbs as possible. Within both the hardy and tender bulb sections, however, the entries are alphabetized by the scientific names. This arrangement is the only one that obviates confusion, especially since the popular or common names for many plants vary greatly from region to region.

Fashions change in bulbs, and new hybrids are always appearing, especially among the popular groups such as tulips, daffodils and gladiolus. Therefore, this book does not feature long lists of hybrids. What I have tried to do is show the types that exist within any one genus. A current catalog is the best guide to what is available in any bulb division at any given time. What I want to do is enlarge your horizon by acquainting you with the great variety of types and the sequence of bloom. It is possible to have some type of tulip, for example, in bloom for nearly three months of the year if plantings are made of various kinds. What you have to do is decide which classes of tulip will do the most for your garden. Then with catalog in hand you can see what colors are being offered in a particular year.

PLANT SOCIETIES

The nearest horticultural society, garden club or arboretum can supply you with current addresses of the following national plant societies; many of them also have local affiliates. Publications, flower shows and meetings of any of these have much to offer the gardener particularly interested in one type of bulb.

American Begonia Society
American Daffodil Society
American Dahlia Society
American Gloxinia and Gesneriad Society
American Horticultural Society

American Iris Society
Indoor Light Garden Society of America
American Rock Garden Society
North American Gladiolus Council
North American Lily Society

SOURCES OF BULBS

Antonelli Brothers,
 2545 Capitola Rd., Santa Cruz, CA 95060.

Blackthorne Gardens,
 48H Quincy St., Holbrook, MA 02343.

Burnett Bros.,
 92 Chambers St., New York, NY 10007.

W. Atlee Burpee Co., Warminster, PA 18974.

The Daffodil Mart,
 Box 629, Gloucester, VA 23061.

P. de Jager & Sons,
 188 Asbury St., South Hamilton, MA 01982.

J. Howard French,
 Box 87, Center Rutland, VT 05736.

International Growers Exchange,
 Box D, Farmington, MI 48024.

Inter-State Nurseries,
 59 E St., Hamburg, IA 51640.

Kelly Bros. Nurseries,
 Maple St., Dansville, NY 14437.

John Messalaar Bulb Co.,
 Box 269, Ipswich, MA 01938.

Grant E. Mitsch, Daffodil Haven,
 Canby, OR 97013.

Charles E. Mueller,
 River Rd., New Hope, PA 18938.

Noweta Gardens,
 St. Charles, MN 53972 (gladiolus).

George W. Park Seed Co.,
 Cokesbury Rd., Greenwood, SC 29647.

Rex Bulb Farms,
 Box 145, Newburg, OR 97132 (dahlias, lilies).

John Scheepers, Inc.,
 63 Wall St., New York, NY 10005.

R. H. Shumway, Seedsman, Rockford, IL 61101.

Van Bourgondien Bros.,
 Box A, Babylon, NY 11702.

Mary Mattison Van Schaik,
 Rt. 1, Box 181, Cavendish, VT 05142.

Wayside Gardens, Hodges, SC. 29695.

WILDFLOWER SPECIALISTS

Gardens of the Blue Ridge,
 P.O. Box 10, Pineola, NC 28662.

Jamieson Valley Gardens,
 Rt. 3, Spokane, WA 99203.

Lamb Nurseries,
 E. 101 Sharp Ave., Spokane, WA 99202.

Leslie's Wildflower Nursery,
 30 Summer St., Methuen, MA 01844.

Lounsberry Gardens,
 Box 135, Oakford, IL 62673.

Putney Nursery, Putney, VT 05346.

Clyde Robin, Box 2091, Castro Valley, CA 94546.

The Three Laurels,
 Marshall, Madison Co., NC 28753.

Vick's Wildgardens, Inc.,
 Box 115, Gladwyne, PA 19035.

For other sources consult the advertisements in gardening magazines.

SELECTED HARDY BULBS FOR ALL-SEASON COLOR
(In approximate order of appearance)

EARLY SPRING

Galanthus elwesi (snowdrop)
Eranthis hyemalis (winter-aconite)
Cyclamen orbiculatum (hardy cyclamen)
Crocus, winter-flowering species
Iris reticulata (rock-garden iris)
Leucojum vernum (spring snowflake)
Tulipa pulchella (tulip species)
Tulipa kaufmanniana and hybrids
Tulipa turkestanica
Chionodoxa (glory-of-the-snow)
Anemone blanda (hardy windflowers)
Narcissus asturiensis (daffodil species)
Narcissus cyclamineus and hybrids
Trillium nivale (snow trillium)
Hyacinthus azureus
Crocus, Dutch hybrids

MID-SPRING

Tulipa fosteriana and hybrids
Tulipa Darwin Hybrids
Tulipa early singles, doubles
Scilla sibirica (squills)
Hyacinthus orientalis (garden hyacinths)
Narcissus in variety (daffodil peak)
Claytonia (spring-beauty)
Ipheion (spring star flower)
Camassia esculenta (early camas)
Erythronium (trout-lily)
Fritillaria imperialis (crown imperial)
Fritillaria meleagris (guinea flower)
Trillium grandiflorum (wake-robin)
Mertensia virginica (bluebells)
Anemonella thalictroides (rue-anemone)
Muscari (grape-hyacinth)
Leucojum aestivum (summer snowflake)
Endymion (wood-hyacinth)
Camassia leichtlini (camas-lily)
Hypoxis hirsuta (goldeye-grass)
Tulips in variety (tulip peak)
Narcissus jonquilla
Narcissus triandrus Hybrids
Narcissus poeticus
Arisaema triphyllum (Jack-in-the-pulpit)
Ornithogalum umbellatum (star-of-Bethlehem)
Tulips, late doubles
Iris, Dutch hybrids
Convallaria majalis (lily-of-the-valley)

LATE SPRING

Muscari plumosum (feather hyacinth)
Hyacinthus amethystinus
Anemone fulgens
Tulipa sprengeri
Gladiolus, hardy types
Allium karataviense (hardy onions)
Allium moly
Allium azureum
Allium ostrowskiana
Bletilla striata (hardy orchid)
Lilium pumilum (lilies)
Lilium candidum
Lilium Mid-Century Hybrids
Lilium canadense
Lilium superbum
Allium tricoccum (wood leek)

SUMMER

Lilium (lilies—wide variety available)
Galtonia candicans (summer hyacinth)
Belamcanda chinensis (blackberry-lily)
Lycoris squamigera (resurrection lily)
Liatris in variety (gayfeather)
Begonia evansiana (hardy begonia)

FALL

Lilium speciosum selections (show lily)
Cyclamen europaeum (hardy cyclamen)
Liatris, later varieties (September gayfeathers)
Crocosmia (montbretia)
Colchicum autumnale
Crocus speciosus
Crocus zonatus
Colchicum Water lily
Allium stellatum (fall onion)
Crocus kardochorum
Sternbergia
Cyclamen neapolitanum
Crocus medius
Crocus ochroleucus
Colchicum agrippinum

NOTE: Annual fluctuations in climate may alter the dates that the first flowers appear, but the general sequence is the same from year to year.

Glossary

ANTHER: The little sac at the tip of the filament that produces pollen

AXIL: The juncture point of the upper angle of a leaf and the stem

BLAST: Withering of a flower bud

BULB: An underground stem, the main body of which consists of thickened scales

BULBIL, or BULBEL: A small, immature bulb that usually appears in a leaf axil

BULBLET: A small, immature underground bulb

CALYX: The outermost part of a flower, usually consisting of green segments called sepals

CLONE: An asexual derivative of a plant, usually produced by cuttings, graftings, runners or division of a root stock

COLD FRAME: A low outdoor structure with a glass top that is used to protect young plants from the cold

COMPOST: A mixture of decaying organic matter, such as leaves, grass cuttings, vegetable refuse or manure, that is used as soil conditioner

COROLLA: The most conspicuous part of the flower, usually consisting of colorful petals

CORONA: An appendage of a flower (prominent in daffodils) that surrounds the pistil and stamen. A long corona is called a trumpet; a medium-size corona is a crown or cup, and a very small one is called an eye

CORM: A short, fleshy underground stem, similar to a bulb, that lacks outer scales and bears buds on the top surface

CORMEL: A small corm that develops at the base of a mature corm

CROWN, or CUP: A medium-size corona

CULTIVAR: A variety of a plant that is horticulturally or agriculturally derived; a plant variety not found in nature

DIBBLE, or DIBBLER: A pointed gardening tool used to make holes in the soil

EYE: 1) An undeveloped bud that produces a new plant or growth; 2) A very small corona

FORCING: Hastening a plant to maturity or early blooming

HARDY: Frost- or freeze-tolerant plants

HUMUS: Partially decomposed organic matter

HYBRID: Offspring produced by breeding plants of different species

INFLORESCENCE: A flower or the flowering process

MOSAIC: A virus disease of plants resulting in light and dark areas in the leaves or petals

MULCH: A protective layer of various substances, especially organic matter, placed around plants to maintain soil temperatures at a constant level, prevent evaporation of moisture and freezing of roots, and to control weeds

NATURALIZE: To plant bulbs and flowers as they might occur in nature

NODE: Joint on a stem where leaves appear

OFFSET: A shoot or small bulb that develops laterally at the base of a plant that can be detached to start a new plant

OVARY: The hollow portion at the base of the pistil that contains ovules

PERIANTH: Outer two layers of the flower consisting of sepals and petals

PETAL: A portion of the corolla, often colorful

PISTIL: The female or seed-bearing organ of a flower that consists of ovary, style and stigma

PROPAGATION: Breeding or multiplication

RHIZOME: An underground stem that grows horizontally under or along the ground, sending roots down and leaves or shoots up from its top surface; also called rootstock or rootstalk

ROOTSTOCK, or ROOTSTALK: See Rhizome

SCALE: One of the various thin, often overlapping parts of a bulb that protects buds or membranous areas

SCAPE: A leafless flower stem

SEPAL: A portion of the calyx, usually green

SHEATH: The tubular part of a leaf that surrounds or envelops a stem

SPATHE: A prominent bract growing from near the base of the flower, as in the calla-lily and jack-in-the-pulpit

SPORT: A mutation or sudden variation in offspring that often does not reappear in the following generation

STAMEN: The male or fertilizing organ of a flower that usually consists of two parts—the filament, or stalk, and the anther

STIGMA: The part of the pistil that receives the pollen

STOLON: A stem that grows horizontally and takes root at the nodes or apex to form new plants

STOLONIFEROUS: A self-propagating quality in some bulbs that develop a bud and form a root at the tip

STRAIN: A group of plants of the same species that have distinctive mutual characteristics

STYLE: The slender stalk of the pistil above the ovary

TRUMPET: A long corona

TUBER: A thickened end of a rootstock bearing buds, or "eyes," on its sides from which new plant shoots arise

TUBEROUS ROOT: A knobby root resembling a tuber

Index

206

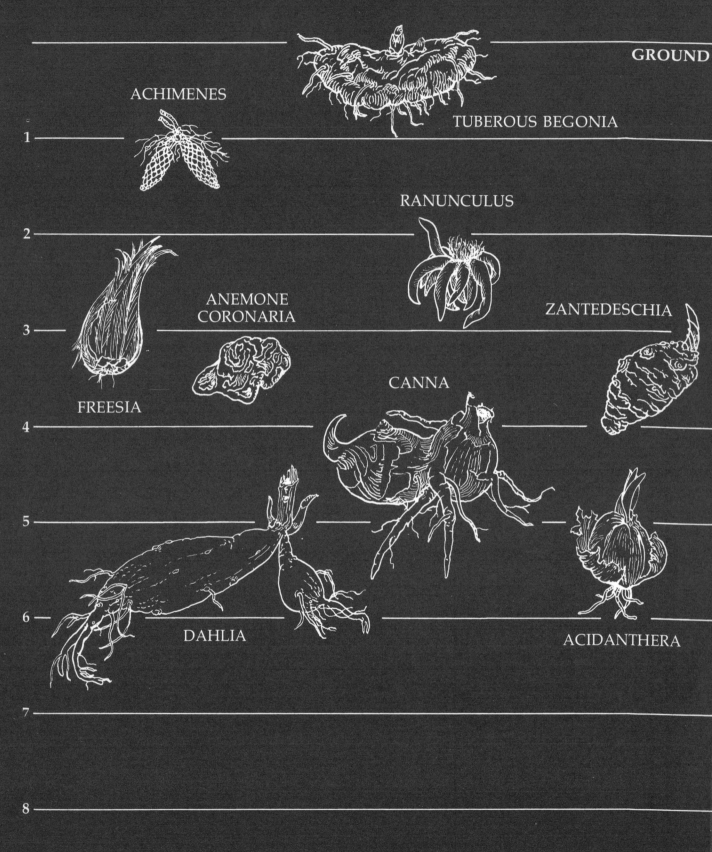

PLANTING DEPTHS

GROUND

ACHIMENES

TUBEROUS BEGONIA

1

RANUNCULUS

2

ANEMONE
CORONARIA

ZANTEDESCHIA

3

FREESIA

CANNA

4

5

DAHLIA

ACIDANTHERA

6

7

8

9